Children Who Survived the Final Solution

To my friend Liz
Thank you for your
interest.

Johanna

Children Who Survived the Final Solution

By Twenty-Six Survivors
Edited by Peter Tarjan

iUniverse, Inc.
New York Lincoln Shanghai

Children Who Survived the Final Solution

iUniverse, Inc.

For information address:
iUniverse, Inc.
2021 Pine Lake Road, Suite 100
Lincoln, NE 68512
www.iuniverse.com

This anthology contains the recollections of twenty-six child survivors from various parts of Europe, who were thirteen years old or younger during the Nazi Holocaust.

ISBN: 0-595-30925-9

Printed in the United States of America

In the Jewish community a young person reaches adulthood at the age of thirteen. Upon reaching this special age, the child provides proof of literacy by being called to the *bima* to say the blessing as an adult, assist in reading the *Torah* and provide a commentary for the week's portion of the *Haftorah*. This event is the *Bar Mitzvah* for a boy and the *Bat Mitzvah* for a girl.

The authors of this anthology are members of Child Survivors of the Holocaust in South Florida. We founded this group thirteen years ago in a living room on Miami Beach. Now that our group has reached the age of adult responsibility, we decided to celebrate by recalling our experiences during the Holocaust and describing our impressions, feelings, joys and fears arising from that terribly dark period, which interrupted the childhood of every one of our members.

One and a half million Jewish children lost their lives during that period in Europe. Against very high odds, each of us miraculously escaped that fate. Each story has some miraculous element. Without miracles none of us would be here to tell about our survival.

Many of us survived because there were some good people who cared and helped. Many of these miracle workers risked their own lives and their families' for someone else's child. There are no words to thank those individuals. Many of our parents also contributed to the miracles by risking the uncertainty of sending their child away rather than waiting together for the "final solution." We dedicate this anthology to four groups:

- to the brave parents who had the courage and foresight to send their children to unknown, but presumed safe havens;

- to our parents, grandparents and relatives who perished in the Holocaust;

- to the brave parents who had the courage to escape and take their children into an uncertain domain that promised hardships as well as possible survival;

- to the gentile miracle workers, doctors, nuns, priests, and ordinary people, whose brave acts contributed to our survival.

Le chaim! and Mazel Tov to our group!

Contents

Foreword

❖

Anthology of Child Survivors of the Holocaust in South Florida

This anthology of the South Florida Child Survivors of the Holocaust group is a reminder of the one and a half million Jewish children who were killed in Nazi occupied Europe, and who comprised 90% of Jewish children at the time. The greatest might of the German war machine was directed to the extermination of this most vulnerable group. Those who survived, like the writers of this anthology, did so through extraordinary luck, pluck and devotion—their own and those of others.

It took forty-five years for child survivors of the Holocaust around the world to start to realise the magnitude of their survivorship, and to own the details of their experiences as real, valid, and able to be talked about. Child survivors started to remember, feel, and understand, and share, in a new vivid way. What helped them enormously was recognition of others like themselves, and sharing their experiences in child survivor groups. They developed a feeling of mishpochah in those groups, because they could speak freely to those who understood them. One such group is the South Florida Child Survivors of the Holocaust group. This is their anthology, on the occasion of their Bar/Bat-Mitzvah.

Bar/Bat-Mitzvah symbolises a coming of age, a declaration of identity. What identity do child survivors in their sixties and seventies declare on their Bar/Bat-Mitzvahs? When most of the child survivors in this anthology were thirteen, their worlds and identities were shattered. What are they declaring now, at their belated coming of age?

The stories in this anthology may seem to be the antithesis of a source of celebration. Instead, the reader will find evidence that children were spared nothing in the Holocaust. The stories will describe children separated from parents to be sent to safe, though not nurturing countries; of children who survived concentration camps; children who were hidden; children who survived starvation, ghettoes, bullets, bombs, murder, separation, everything the Shoah threw at adults.

The children in their vulnerability, if it is possible to imagine, suffered even more. I wanted to highlight individual stories—of older and younger children, of this country, and that, this experience, and the other. But no, they are all equally amazing and sacred stories.

I was struck by the fact that the stories were not bitter, they did not seek revenge. I found the underlying thread in the purpose of the stories to be gifts to the world, given in the hope that the stories and the anthology would contribute to other children not having to suffer such events in the future. The gifts were not easy to produce. The writers had to scrape from the depths of their souls.

The stories provide lessons to the world about childhood suffering, coping with it, its consequences short and long term, and its ripples across the generations. But for me, perhaps the most hidden but powerful underlying message is that of the power of love. The children in this book could not have survived without love-of love given them by parents, relatives and others; but also their own love-of parents, and hopes of future loving. They did everything to fulfill these hopes. They married, and above all, loved that precious commodity—children. Nothing produced more satisfaction than preserving and loving their children. Many now love their children's children too.

A thirteen-year-old child reads a story from the bible that was written thousands of years ago, and fits his or her identity into a prescribed group view. In this case, on their Bar/Bat-mitzvah, the child survivors of South Florida are presenting their own book of stories, with its own lessons and wisdom, to be added to the story of the Jewish people.

This anthology declares the power of life, human aspiration, love, and the creative power of telling the truth in words. It was a hard road to achieve this creation. To have reached it is cause to celebrate. It is for the reader now to become a partner in the purpose of this creation.

Paul Valent, M.D.,
Melbourne, Australia[1]

---

1.   Dr. Paul Valent, an Australian psychiatrist and child survivor, is the author of **Child Survivors of the Holocaust** [Brunner-Routledge, New York & London, 2002], a collection of critically edited interviews with ten members of a survivors' group in Australia.

Acknowledgments

This anthology is the work of the twenty-six authors of their individual stories.

Dena Axelrod proposed our project. Our Book Committee, Dena Axelrod, Frances Cutler, Gunther Karger, Johanna Saper, Peter Tarjan, David Zugman and Jean Zugman coordinated the project. Peter Tarjan edited the text, sequenced the stories, wrote the Dedication and the Introduction, and he assembled the Time Line. Magda Bader and Yosi Lazzar designed the cover. Their stories are in this volume.

We wish to thank individually:

Dr. Paul Valent of Melbourne, Australia, for previewing the manuscript and contributing his insightful Foreword to this collection;

Nancy D. Kersell of Northern Kentucky University for her preview of a sample of the stories and her permission to print some of her comments;

Rabbi Gedalyah Engel, Director Emeritus of Purdue University's Hillel Foundation, and his wife, Mrs. Marilyn Engel of West Lafayette, Indiana, for their careful proofreading of the manuscript and their helpful suggestions.

Introduction

The literature about the Holocaust is vast and includes the stories of survivors. While most such memoirs have dealt with experiences in concentration camps, those in this collection are by survivors—children who overcame the Nazi persecution while they were very young. Our stories, collected in this book, bubbled up spontaneously, without an interviewer's guidance; hence they represent the most permanent memories of their authors' childhood experiences. This book provides a rare vantage point for the reader to look into the diverse lives of children during the Holocaust. Both, professionals and adult survivors have often said, "The children were too young to remember." They could not have been more wrong about that.

Our stories begin in various parts of Europe, from Poland and Romania in the East, to France, Belgium and the Netherlands in the West. A few children were sent alone to safer places in England and Sweden: Johanna, Rita and Ruth S. to England, and Gunther to Sweden. Nellie with her mother and siblings reached England by a rescue ship from France. Anna, born in Holland, survived in a Japanese-run prison camp in Indonesia. Ruth G., at the age of 11, was the sole survivor of her family in a Transnistrian death camp. A few in their early teens, Tova, Magda, George, Jack and Rose survived the concentration camps. Bernard spent 18 months hiding along with more than forty people in a bunker built for sixteen. David and his mother jumped off a train on their way to a death camp. Judy's family escaped to Central Russia. Arnold was able to leave Germany with his parents for the USA at the last minute. Faye walked across the Pyrenees to Spain, holding her younger sister's hand, while their mother was carrying their baby brother. Strangers in the French countryside hid Frances and Louise. Suzanne and her sisters were smuggled into Switzerland by strangers from France. Baby Elzbieta's hair was died blond to make her fit for adoption in Poland. Dena's older brother left her in a church in Warsaw to fend for herself. Bianca fought with the Polish resistance. Eugenia and her mother managed to hide with false identity papers in Holland. Yosi and Peter witnessed the siege of Budapest, one in the ghetto, the other in a house protected by Swiss and Swedish diplomats.—Each story is a testimony to the courage and resourcefulness of the children, their parents and strangers who cared,…and to a fortunate turn of the dice.

It was a matter of luck to escape death. All these children were thrust into chaos at an early age and those memories still haunt many of them even after six decades.

We converged to South Florida along very different and often interesting paths. Inspired by other child survivor groups whose formation was stimulated and inspired by the wonderful work of the late Dr. Judith Kestenberg, a highly respected child psychiatrist, and her husband Milton Kestenberg, a lawyer, founders of "Child Development Research," who also launched the "International Study of Organized Persecution of Children" in New York in 1981. Thirteen years ago we began our own support group on Miami Beach to help each other deal with our loss of childhood and with personal sorrow. We have been successful. We have forged our group into *mishpoche*. We have become siblings who understand each other from our shared experiences and feelings.

Time Line Relevant to the Stories

Jan. 30, 1933	Hitler was appointed Chancellor of Germany
March 20, 1933	The first concentration camp opens in Dachau
April 1, 1933	First anti-Jewish boycott in Germany
Sep. 15, 1935	The Nuremberg Race Laws abolish the citizenships of German Jews
March 1938	Anschluss (Austria is annexed to Germany)
Sep. 28-29, 1938	Munich Conference (Gt. Britain, France, Germany and Italy agreed to transfer certain regions of Czechoslovakia to Germany)
Nov. 9-10, 1938	Kristallnacht in Germany
March 16, 1939	Czechoslovakia is broken up; Bohemia and Moravia are taken over by Germany with the consent of the West
March 1939	The Slovak Republic is created, Transcarpathian Ukraine is annexed to Hungary, Memel is annexed from Lithuania to Germany
Aug. 23, 1939	Nazi-Soviet (non-aggression) Pact is signed in Moscow by Stalin and von Ribbentrop. A secret protocol recognized the Baltic states and Bessarabia to be under Soviet influence, and Poland is to be divided between Germany and the Soviet Union
Sep. 1, 1939	Germany attacks Poland
Sep. 3, 1939	Britain, France, Australia and New Zealand declare war against Germany
Sep. 5, 1939	The United States proclaims neutrality
Sep. 10, 1939	Canada declares war against Germany
Sep. 17, 1939	The Soviet Union invades Poland
Sep. 29, 1939	Germany and the Soviet Union divide up Poland
April 9, 1940	Germany invades Denmark and Norway
May 1940	Germany invades the neutral Netherlands, Belgium and Luxembourg and attacks France

June 14, 1940	Paris is occupied by the German Army
June 16, 1940	Marshal Pétain becomes Prime Minister of Vichy France
June 1940	The Soviet Union occupies Latvia and Lithuania
June 22, 1941	Germany attacks the Soviet Union
June 22, 1940	France falls to the Germans
July 10, 1940	The Battle of Britain begins
Aug. 1940	The Soviet Union annexes Estonia
Oct. 7, 1940	German troops enter Romania
Nov 20, 1940	Hungary joins the Axis Powers
Nov 23, 1940	Romania joins the Axis Powers
April 1941	Germany attacks Yugoslavia and Greece
Dec. 7, 1941	Pearl Harbor is attacked by the Japanese, the USA enters WW II
Dec 8, 1941	The United States and Britain declare war on Japan
Dec. 11, 1941	Germany and Italy declare war against the USA
Jan. 20, 1942	Wannsee Conference plans the "Final Solution"
Sep. 1942	The German army reaches Stalingrad
Nov 11, 1942	Germans and Italians invade unoccupied Vichy France
Jan 10, 1943	The Soviet offensive against the Germans begins in Stalingrad
Jan. 1943	Fighters in the Warsaw Ghetto fire on German troops
Feb 2, 1943	Germans surrender at Stalingrad, Hitler's first defeat
April 19, 1943	German troops reenter the Warsaw Ghetto and the Uprising begins
May 16, 1943	The Warsaw Ghetto Uprising is crushed
March 19, 1944	Germany occupies Hungary, its ally
May 15–July 9 1944	Deportation of 437,402 Jews from Hungarian ghettos by 147 trains to Auschwitz-Birkenau and to Austrian concentration camps
June 6, 1944	D-Day: the Normandy Invasion of France by the Allies
July 24, 1944	Soviet troops liberate the Majdanek concentration camp
Aug 1, 1944	Polish Home Army rises up against the Nazis in Warsaw
Aug. 25, 1944	Paris is liberated

Oct 2, 1944	The Warsaw Uprising ends; the Polish Home Army surrenders
Dec 27, 1944	The siege of Budapest begins
Jan 17, 1945	Soviet troops capture Warsaw
Jan 26, 1945	Soviet troops liberate Auschwitz
April 12, 1945	Buchenwald is liberated
April 15, 1945	British soldiers liberate 60,000 prisoners in Bergen-Belsen
May 7, 1945	Germany surrenders, the war ends in Europe
Aug 6, 1945	First A-bomb strikes Hiroshima
Aug 9, 1945	Second A-bomb is dropped on Nagasaki
Aug 14, 1945	Unconditional surrender of Japan
Sep. 2, 1945	Japan signs the surrender agreement—World War II ends
Oct 24, 1945	The United Nations is inaugurated in San Francisco
May 14, 1948	The State of Israel is born

I Remember

✦

Johanna Franklin Saper (nee Hirschbein)

Our bus has comfortable seats and large windows. Every seat is filled with passengers in their sixties, seventies and even eighties. We are traveling along a very wide boulevard that circles the city of Vienna, the Ringstrasse. We pass beautiful baroque buildings, statues of kings and queens, and palaces of the old Habsburg Empire. There are museums and manicured gardens to view. Our guide tells long stories about the splendor of the city and about the present prosperity enjoyed by all. It is the spring of 1998 and we are all celebrating our survival. We received a "free ride" from the Austrian government to see the city where we were born. Some of us have come from Australia, Holland, England and Canada, and I came from the United States. We arrive at an enormous open space surrounded by parks and ornate buildings. Our guide tells us: "This is the Helden Platz, where Hitler spoke in March 1938 to celebrate his victory of conquering Austria. Forty thousand people came to hear his speech, and now it is impossible to find anyone in Vienna who will admit to having been there. Nobody remembers…"…They don't remember, but I do!

I Remember

It was March 13, 1938; I was home on spring vacation from the gymnasium I started to attend the previous September. My foot was in a cast due to a minor skating accident. My older brothers had been listening to the radio all day. There seemed to be excitement and apprehension as we heard of the Nazis' arrival in Vienna. As a ten-year-old child I had no idea what all this had to do with me, and my family, and how it might affect us. Our apartment had two large windows facing a busy street, and on this day my whole family was looking out of our front windows. Usually we could see horse-drawn lorries delivering ice, and women walking from the grocery store to the butcher, to the milk store, carrying string bags filled with the day's purchases. On this day none of the usual domestic activities were going on. Everybody was rushing into an abandoned building across the street from us, and we watched and listened. I felt happy and secure to be surrounded by my family. My brother Josef, in his twenties, worked during the day and attended lectures and political activities every night. My brother Harry was in his last year at the gymnasium; he had many friends and was active in sports. My father was occupied in his business till late in the evening. Usually when I returned home from school, my mother was there ready with many questions and a pastry with chocolate and whipped cream. I was the youngest and much indulged by everyone: brothers, aunts, uncles, and cousins. They called me "Hannerl," a nickname not easily pronounced by English speakers.

As we waited and watched through the window of our apartment, we noticed an increase of activity in the building across the street. Suddenly hundreds of people streamed out of the building carrying large flags with swastikas and singing victory songs, while our radio announced the triumphant entry of the Fuhrer, Adolf Hitler, into Austria, where the announcer said, "...he belonged, after all." The building across had been transformed into Nazi headquarters. Although we were all very apprehensive and could hardly believe what was happening in front of us, my mother was optimistic. She said, "We will survive this, after all there are Jews living in Germany, and with some hardships, they are surviving."

The invitation to return to Vienna with a companion comes at a time when my husband is unable to travel and my three grown children are occupied with their own families and cannot leave. I invite Rosetta Sherr (nee Glickman) to share the experience with me. Sol and Clara Glickman have passed away and it is in their memory of saving my life that I invite Rosetta.

It is our first day in Vienna. The members of our group, all the "returnees," are anxious to visit the place where they were born. The streets in the 7th district are now very quiet: there are no butcher shops or grocery stores; very few people walk on the streets. Pungent odors of Indian and Pakistani food emanate from restaurants; at one time these were coffee houses. Most of the streets are still cobble stoned. Children no longer play in the little parks of statues and fountains. I notice that some of the people now have a lovely brownish skin tone, not at all Aryan.

I Remember

Overnight, our lives changed. My father's Christian business partner told him not to return. A Jew could no longer work with a gentile. Though their Traffic Manage-

ment enterprise was lucrative, my father received nothing for his share of the business. My brother Harry was imprisoned for "associating with communists." Fortunately, after some weeks, it was determined that he was not actually a communist, and they released him. I could no longer attend the gymnasium and was sent to a Jewish school, where the children, about 80, were cramped into one classroom. There was only one teacher in this crowded room and she spent all her time trying to keep order. There was confusion and disorder all around. On the way to school, children threw stones at me and yelled "Jew, Jew, get out!" I wasn't learning anything, and there was a risk of getting hurt; so my mother said, I didn't have to attend the Jewish school any longer. I don't remember if I attended one week or one month: it is all blurred in my memory.

One spring afternoon in April, two SS troopers intruded into our apartment. I held my mother's hand, watching them open every closet and drawer, and stuffing silverware, jewelry, and embroidered linens into one of our pillowcases. One of them found a small gold watch and my mother pleaded: "This is a birthday present for my little girl here, she'll be eleven next month". The trooper pushed her aside and stuffed the watch in with the other loot.—That SS trooper may be one of the people who "can't remember any of it." Just as the SS were leaving, my brother Harry entered the apartment. "We want him to come with us," they said in unison. My father pleaded that they should take him, instead of his son, but they refused. They wanted someone young, tall and strong, and my brother fit the bill. They put him to work cleaning the newly renovated Nazi headquarters across the street. He scrubbed floors, cleaned toilets. At one point I spotted him on a tall ladder, cleaning windows, while neighborhood boys taunted him: "Red Harry, Jew boy!"

Restrictions and atrocities followed quickly now and my family was making preparations for another type of life. I took English lessons, in case it might prove handy. In June 1938 my parents put an ad in a Jewish paper in England that asked for a family willing to take in an 11 year old girl, preferably a family who had a child of similar age. We received a few answers and narrowed it down to one family living in a suburb of Manchester. Sol and Clara Glickman had a daughter, Rosetta, almost eleven years old. Many years later I learned that on the day our ad appeared in the paper, Mr. Glickman had been in a car accident. The two other passengers were killed, but his life was saved. Being an observant Jew, he felt since God had saved his life, he should save another life, and they answered my parents' ad. My parents sent letters, describing our family. We sent pictures and the Glickman family sent letters and pictures as the arrangements progressed over the months. In the meantime the restrictions were mounting. Only certain stores could sell to Jews and only at certain times. My mother sent me to such a restricted grocery store with a list and I handed the list to the clerk. All who entered raised their arms and declared "Heil Hitler!" I wondered whether anyone noticed that I didn't say anything?

My cousin Inge came to live with us, because they had been living in a house owned by the city, and Jews had to vacate municipal housing. Inge and I had a great time, riding the trolley cars, walking the streets, never realizing our imminent disaster. It was fall and we didn't go to school. In my English lessons I learned a song, "My Bonnie lies over the Ocean…" My brother Harry had a pen pal in the United States. After months of exchanging letters and forms back and forth, the American gentile family kindly sponsored him. Harry left Vienna for North Carolina in November 1938, the day before Kristallnacht. The whole family accompanied him to the railroad station. Suddenly, there was chaos. Old men were beaten in the streets, windows smashed, synagogues pillaged and the activity intensified across the street. We were frightened. My father became very quiet and appeared older. Soon all the papers for my travel to England were completed and by the end of 1938, if all went well, I could be leaving for Manchester. Inge also had found an English family who would take her in while her mother would work as a maid in another household. It all seemed to be working out so well. The three of us would leave together and I was looking forward to it. When we arrived at the Central Railroad Station for our journey on December 31, 1938, about fifteen people had come to say good-bye to us: parents, aunts, uncles, cousins, friends. I never saw any of them again….

Everything seemed to be progressing smoothly on our trip. I was looking forward to an adventure, something like summer camp. A new country, a new language, a new family. I was sure that in a few months I would see my parents and brothers again. I could not imagine even in my wildest dreams that there was no return, and my life would change forever. As we approached the German border, the train stopped and we saw people being ordered off the train. Anticipating problems, Inge's mother told us to lie down on the benches and pretend we were sleeping. Two Nazi soldiers entered our compartment. They looked at our passports and just as they were about to evict us, Inge's mother said in her best Viennese accent: "Please officer, the children are sleeping, I'd hate to wake them up." She flattered and smiled at the young soldiers, and we were allowed to stay on the train. The people who had been taken off, did not return.

On the fourth day of our "return visit" to Vienna, I sign up to visit the Central Friedhof (cemetery). I travel with the group to the cemetery. It is on the outskirts of the city, and the surroundings are not familiar to me.

Upon arrival, we are each given directions to the gravesite we are looking for. With a piece of paper in my hand I start to look for my father's grave. I walk alone among the gravestones and look at the markers; some have been there since the 18th century. His grave seems to be in an area much farther from where the other people are walking, but I follow the directions and finally I am standing in front of my father's grave: **_Moritz Victor Hirschbein_**. The names of my mother and of my brothers, Josef and Harry, are engraved, and my name: Hannerl. Since I left Vienna, no one has ever called me Hannerl. It brings back memories of a childhood filled with love from my parents and two older brothers. I stand alone looking at the gravestone; there are no other people around. It is the first time I have ever seen my father's grave. There are no tears, only memories.

I Remember

My brother Josef, who had also migrated to England and was interned in an enemy alien camp as soon as the war between Germany and Britain broke out, married Berty, a cousin ten years older than him. He met her need for a better quota for getting into the USA and he was able to leave the camp. They adopted me as their "child," and two years after living in Manchester, I left England with them.

I had started to consider the Glickmans as my family. I called them Mum & Dad and considered Rosetta a sister. I acclimated wonderfully to the new school, new language and culture, and corresponded with my parents weekly. After seven months in England, the war began and all communication stopped. Seven neighbors joined with the Glickman family and built an air-raid shelter in a common area adjoining the back of their houses. Most of the men had been in the First World War and were proficient at building trenches. They used their expertise in building our communal air-raid shelter. We spent many frightening nights with our neighbors in the air-raid shelter and wondered if our lives would be spared.

It was a very long trip from Manchester to Scotland, where we boarded a South African ship to Canada and continued by train from Montreal to Grand Central Station in New York. It was early in January 1941 when we arrived at my cousin Friedl's house on Long Island. The three of us were exhausted. I got very excited when I saw my cousin, her husband and four-year-old Susie waiting for us. I had never met them before, but at that time it seemed less traumatic than meeting my English family, the Glickmans at Victoria Station, in 1939. At least I spoke English by now. By the age of thirteen I had met many new people, and traveled a great deal. I had been reshuffled and recultured. I had traveled alone to London several times and had spent two years in an English school. I felt as if the culture shocks were over and I could handle anything. The mood was festive at my cousin's house. There were other cousins and their families, as well as my brother Harry, and my aunt and uncle. Some of them had emigrated *from Vienna before the war and were celebrating our arrival in the United States.*

At one point my cousin Hedy took me into another room and said, " We just heard that your father died a week ago." I was stunned. During the war I was not able to correspond with my parents from England, hence I didn't even know that my father was even sick. How did he die? Where is my mother?—rushed through my mind, but I was not able to speak those words. It was all so overwhelming. My cousin said, "I know this is very sad for you, but you're in a new country now, and you will have a new life.

It would be best if you forget all about this and come and join the party!" During the whole evening and the next day no one mentioned my father. It was years later before I found out how and where he died. Throughout my teens in the US I attended a different school every year and lived with relatives, friends and my brother Josef. The recurrent theme in my life was: Forget the past, be a good student, improve yourself, acclimate!

On another day during my return visit I pass the apartment building where I was born. I look at the two large front windows facing the street. The building is gray, neglected and very quiet. With sadness, I look at the building and the street where I played.

Now, more than 60 years after the Nazi horrors descended on my life and destroyed my family's existence in Vienna, closure comes. But it is anti-climactic and much too late. After several decades of pursuing one reliable lead after another about what happened to my mother, on August 17, 2001, I received the following letter from the American Red Cross:

> **Dear Mrs. Saper,**
> "*Enclosed please find the following information from the Holocaust & War Victims' Tracing and Information Center…. The Austrian Red Cross was able to find the following information about your mother:*
> *Charlotte Hirschbein, born June 22, 1890 (maiden name Frankovits) was deported to Maly Trostinec near Minsk on May 6, 1942…she was probably shot immediately after her arrival. Please note that almost all of the deportees to Maly Trostinec during that time met this fate.*

I will never forget

On the eve before my departure from Vienna, my mother took me into a room, sat me down and said: You are going to live with a family of good Orthodox Jews in

England. If during the religious rituals, they ask whether we observed in the same way, say that we did. I am sorry that we have not been more observant."

Then she took out a bible, made me put my hand on it, put her hand on my head and blessed me: "You are my baby, my only daughter and I love you. Remember everything I taught you and be an observant Jew, my golden child, Hannerl."

Left Behind in Vienna

❖

Rita Bymel

I was born in Vienna to Hungarian parents. As far as I can remember, my childhood was very pleasant, and my parents did everything possible for me to be educated and to participate in the life of Vienna. They sent me to a very good private, co-ed school, the Rudolph Steiner School, where I learned handiwork, classical music, played the flute, went skiing, skating, to the theater, and had very good professors. We had the advantage of also learning French or English—I chose English. My parents did this for me because my uncle, who was head of the family, sent his children there and wanted me to have the advantage of being well rounded. It was very unusual at that time to receive a co-ed education. The school was on the fifth floor of a private house, quite high for Vienna then.

When Hitler came into Vienna in 1938, the Rudolph Steiner School was closed, because it did not agree with Fascist thinking, and I was sent to a Jewish school. All Jewish children had to be together in one school. Even before the Anschluss, it was a disturbing time. You could feel it. There was friction between the Socialists and the Fascists. There was uneasiness, and I was afraid to go on the streets, because the Hitler youth were well established and tried to start fights. I was afraid, but I did not know what the future would bring.

Life suddenly changed from being afraid to being mortified on Kristallnacht, November 9, 1938. We lived in a small apartment. My father was not home when the disturbances started, and we had no way to let him know he should not come home. Although everyone agreed Vienna was a lovely city, few people had telephones, and communication was therefore difficult. My father was on his way home when the Gestapo came into the apartment looking for arms. My mother became hysterical when they threw everything out of the armoire looking for arms. Just then, my father walked in, and the SR (black uniformed storm troopers) took him to the police station for interrogation.

We heard about concentration camps in Germany, and when Hitler entered Austria we received a number of offers from Australia and South America for my father to emigrate. But my father did not want to immigrate and start a new life elsewhere. He felt he was an Austrian and that nothing could happen to him. So Kristallnacht was a rude awakening for him and for all of us. My father, like many others, was sent to the Dachau concentration camp. At that time, only men were sent—no women or children. I must say that my mother was very courageous. She went to the Gestapo every day to see about the possibility of getting my father out of the concentration camp. The first thing she was told was for my father to get out she had to provide a visa to go abroad overseas, as well as a steamship ticket to assure his departure from Vienna. My uncle, his brother and the head of the family, did everything for us, including buying visas to El Salvador in Budapest. He bought it from an honorary El Salvador consul. With this in hand, my mother went to the Gestapo and sure enough at the end of December my father was released from Dachau and was told he had to leave Vienna within two months. To get away from this very nervous tension, I was sent to Budapest to my Aunt who was a Swiss citizen, and I was put on her passport as her daughter.

When I came back, things started moving. My parents never told me they were going to leave and that I would remain in Vienna. Today, parents would discuss this with their children and be honest and sincere, but I took it for granted that my parents were leaving and I was staying. If only they had said something to me, that they were sorry or that circumstances made it necessary to do this, but no it was a *fait accompli* that I had to accept. There was no other way out. Much later in life when I became a mother myself and had children I asked myself, how could they have done it, leaving their only child in Vienna, and I was very resentful. I didn't question it at the time. It's amazing I didn't, and I even went to the train station to say goodbye and did not cry, which was surprising because I was such a crybaby. It is true that I still had family in Vienna, but my parents left on the 27th of February and on the first of March my grandmother died.

My parents went first to Hungary to say goodbye to the family and then to Italy to take the boat that would take them to El Salvador. When my parents got to Genoa, they discovered the visa that my uncle had bought in Budapest was not a genuine document, but my mother said no matter she was going on this boat.

In the meantime, since my grandmother had died and one of my aunts was leaving for England, I was placed in an orphanage. My uncle started procedures to have me go to England with the Quakers. He was a strict vegetarian and pacifist and had read in a newspaper of the vegetarian movement that an English Quaker lady was coming to Vienna to take Quaker children to England. Mrs. James met my cousin Erica to take her as her adopted child to England, and I went to go live with Mr. and Mrs. Rogers in England. I was not sure that this solution would really work, so I went to the Palestine Bureau to see if I could go to Palestine, in case the deal with England fell through. Since I was Jewish and not a Quaker, my uncle was able to arrange my departure from England on the Kindertransport through the Jewish community. I left Vienna June 1939. Altogether I was in the orphanage three months. At that time, it was really a children's home, which previously had been a boarding school, but became a home for abandoned Jewish children. Although the children were not orphans, I felt like an orphan. This feeling of abandonment surfaced much later.

Considering all the circumstances, I was very lucky I was able to leave for England. I have forgotten so many details, but one thing I remember was being at the train station—there were so many children, my aunt was there with Erica who was also going to England later on. So many people, lots of goodbyes and crying. I was very calm, but I was afraid they would send me back. I noticed that I had a small signet ring and gold necklace, which I gave to my aunt, because we were supposed to give everything to the Nazis, and I was concerned they would think I was smuggling it. Many years later I did get it back. What was so very strange was that I did not cry when my parents left nor when I left. Strange.

We went first to Holland and then London. In London I was put on a train to meet Mr. Rogers at the Stroud train station and arrived at the village, where Mr. and Mrs. Rogers had a vegetarian guesthouse. I knew very little English, and the Rogers were very strange, extremist in their beliefs. Mrs. Rogers especially was very cold, and Mr. Rogers eventually was too nice. There was no question of school. They were interest in my cleaning the rooms in their guesthouse. Looking back now, it really wasn't so bad, but at the time it was very hard for me. But, it was a lovely village, and the village people were extremely kind to me. They called me the little refugee, and I eventually became friends with a German Jewish girl who worked as a cook for a wealthy family. She always fed me, because the vegetarian food at the Rogers was not enough for me. I was always lucky making friends wherever I went.

I did my best in cleaning the rooms and my other chores, but I felt I could no longer stay with Mr. and Mrs. Rogers and left when I was 16 years old and started working in the city. People used to ask me, "Where are your parents? How is it that you are in England?" That is one of the things I avoided most. I didn't want to tell them that my parents left me alone in Vienna. It was sad I was not honest. Eventually I had to face the fact that they did leave me, but in the beginning I did not want people to feel sorry for me. What helped enormously in England was the fact that my aunt, who was a well-known fencer, in fact the first Jewish woman fencer in Vienna, was in England as a domestic—the only way she could get out. Not only was she kind, generous, but also she stood by me in every way. She personally did not have any money. I didn't need money. I needed warmth and understanding. Whenever I had the opportunity and the money, I went to see her in Manchester or later on in London. I knew I was welcomed and loved. Although I felt quite independent, I did need this moral support.

When I became 18 years old, I was required to work for the War effort. There were three choices: work in an ammunition factory, join the army, or become a children's nurse—looking after children abandoned by their parents because of the war. That's what I decided to do. I never gave up the idea of seeing my parents again. Although I had a lot of resentment against them, I always expected to go to El Salvador when the War ended. In 1946, after having lived in England for seven years, I got a visa, again through the kindness of a Jewish organization. I stopped in New York first for a week to visit friends and then went to El Salvador.

It was a sweet and sour reunion. I felt as a stranger to my parents, and they thought their little girl had come back. I was not a little girl anymore. My mother expected to chaperone me. In El Salvador at that time, a young girl was not supposed to leave home alone. My mother was frustrated and hoped I would help them become part of the Jewish community, because she had difficulty getting along with anyone. I told her I was no longer a little girl and no chaperone was needed since I had been left alone for seven years. What I resented most of all was that they never had the courage to apologize or say they were sorry they had left me behind. What was it? Was it money? I know it cost a lot to go to El Salvador. But they never explained. I am sorry that I did not have the courage to confront them. It's a shame that this has stayed with me until now. I suppose I was afraid of my mother's reaction, because she had such a strong character. A friend told me once she asked my mother how she could have left her little girl behind in Vienna. My mother replied that's the way it was, and that was that.

In the beginning in El Salvador, it was hard, but I found the loveliest community of Jewish people I have ever encountered. When my mother told Mr. Eugene Liebes, the head of the Jewish community she wanted to bring her daughter to El Salvador, his reply was, why do you want to bring her here, whom is she going to marry. This was a concern of many people. As it happened, Mr. Liebes actually imported my future husband. As the owner of a very big import/

expert firm, he brought Felix Bymel to El Salvador to work for him. We married two years later and lived in El Salvador for 34 years; my two children were born there as well as two of my grandchildren. These were the happiest years of our existence up to that time. My relationship with my mother was always a little delicate and shaky. I made such very good friends, which I still mostly have.

The political situation changed, and one of our friends was kidnapped and killed in 1979. My husband Felix decided it was time to go. He did not want to leave El Salvador with the same fear he had when he left Czechoslovakia in 1940 with just a little suitcase. In the very beginning, when Felix suggested we leave, I was very unhappy. We had a lovely home, and I knew that once we left we would not have one again. I had roots in El Salvador, especially my friends. I didn't want another upheaval, but Felix made the right decision. An exodus started after the murder of our friend, and not everyone stayed.

We were one of the lucky ones who could come to the U.S., because Felix was an American citizen. Our married daughter, Diane, with her children, left first for Chicago. Diane's in-laws were also from Hungary/Germany. From Chicago, Diane and her husband immigrated to Belgium. Diane now lives in Israel. Our son, Eric, studied at the Hebrew University as a psychologist and soon after married a Sabra pharmacist from Yemenite parents. They live in Haifa and have three children.

When I left El Salvador, there was no way I would leave my parents behind, so they came to Miami with us. When we first arrived in Miami, we all stayed in a small apartment with my aunt, until we got our own apartment. I had promised my parents I would take care of them in Miami and that they would live with us, but we decided it would be best for them to stay with my aunt, who only used the apartment in the winter. It was impossible for us to live with my parents. My father died in 1981, and my aunt bought an apartment right across the street from ours. I visited my mother each day, but she was unhappy that I had not kept my promise to have her live with us.

I am very happy and grateful to live in the US, but it took a while for me to get used to my surroundings, feel settled, make new friends, and become part of the community. Although my two children and some of my grandchildren live in Israel, I do not want to leave the U.S. I don't want another change of lifestyle and learn a new language. I am happy and contented here. There is always something missing in life. You can't have complete happiness.

I go visit my aunt in England, the fencer, who is now 97 years old and lives in Wimbledon. My children and grandchildren, who visit her frequently, also share my love for this aunt.

From Dresden, Germany to Florida, USA

◆

Ruth B. Schwarz

My first memory dates back to April 1933 when my father's business was boy-cotted. I was too small to understand it all, but remember that I was anxious that something was going to happen to us when the business closed, men in uniform were standing with signs and people were screaming *"Jude, Jude!"* In May there was a public burning of all Jewish books. Jews were not allowed to practice medi-cine or law.

I think I knew my whole life had changed when I saw "Der Stürmer," the Nazi newspaper. The kids in my school told me that we were using Christian blood and I had to sit all alone on the Jew bench. It was getting worse and worse and I couldn't go to my school any more. All of us had to attend the Jewish school where all ages were put together in the same class.

One afternoon late in October 1938, I was home alone, doing my school-work, when the bell rang. Two S.S. men stood there when I opened the door. They asked for my parents. I was so frightened that I told them my father was in Berlin and my mother was shopping for food. I had to stand with the door open until my mother came back with my aunt, her sister. They asked her to pack a few sandwiches and take the passports for a passport control. My mother told them that her husband left Dresden for Berlin to try to get a visa for the United States. We all had to go with the SS. There were many people already at their office where we heard that all of us would be deported to Poland. It was a horrific night for all of us and my mother fainted many times. In the morning it was announced on the loudspeakers that those who had valid visas in their passports should come to a certain window. When he was in Italy in 1937, my father had bought Bolivian visas for the whole family. We were released and we could go home. The ones who remained disappeared and we never saw them again.

My father returned from Berlin without having success in procuring visas for us to the United States. Then Kristallnacht followed. My parents, of course, were very afraid and on December 14, 1938, they sent my brother and me on the Kindertransport to England. My youngest brother remained behind with them. It must have been the toughest and bravest decision they ever had to make.

For a long time we did not know whether they were alive and where they might be. With much difficulty, they were able to escape to Holland. While they were waiting for a boat to Bolivia, they applied to get my brother and me out of England. This was another difficult task, but with G-d's help, we all went together to Bolivia. It was a cultural and health shock, but we survived!

Although this sounds like a novel, this is how it all happened. It led us to a normal and successful life finally in the United States in 1955. It should never be forgotten how our lives were interrupted and we were uprooted. It should also be told that all three children got married and that I finished high school and college in San Diego, California. We all now live in the United States.

I had a wonderful childhood in Dresden, with so much family around, until that day in April 1933. I was frightened and feared that my life was going to change. I never realized how much.

Now that I sit on the beach in Florida, I have a feeling that I did manage to cheat the Nazis. Had I been deported, my two daughters would not have been born. They gave me grandchildren and great-grandchildren. From the survival of just one person, three generations have been created.

Child of the Holocaust

✦

Gunther Karger

This is the story of Gunther. It begins with his first six years; the only time he spent with his parents. Then it tells how he escaped from Germany and what happened to him during the Holocaust. Gunther sums up his life at the age of 69. It is a saga of a six-year-old little boy who lost all he had: his parents, his family, his little friend, his familiar surroundings, his Jewish heritage and even his native language. Virtually "shipped" off with an address tag by his parents with a suitcase containing a few clothes, a picture of him with his parents, a photo album of his family, a small cloth envelope made by his mother with a few hand-crocheted handkerchiefs, and a spoon. This little boy was sent away into the world alone who, over the next half century, with help from no one, and in the face of seemingly insurmountable obstacles, managed to become an educated professional recognized for achievements in science, named "Outstanding Young Man of America", met professionally with high ranking persons, including a Vice President of the United States, and was recognized as a leader of the scientific community during the height of the U.S. Apollo Moon program, while he raised his own family.

Gunther still has the handkerchief case and the pictures, his sole legacy from his family, in addition to being brought into this world. Gunther's story is about survival not only through the Holocaust, but survival thereafter in a tough world. It is about overcoming many very difficult hurdles over the span of a half-century that included a major hurricane, a financial disaster and even temporary death by medical error.

PROLOGUE:

We lived in Schmieheim, a small town in the western part of the Black Forest in Germany, along with about 20 other Jewish families. My parents, Herbert and

Ida, lived with my grandparents in a family house, the home of the Offenheimers for generations. My father had a clothing store and my grandparents had a small farm along the river. Schmieheim was and remains an idyllic town, nestled in the hills of the Black Forest, with a castle and a small brewery. There are no Jewish families in that town today. All, except I, Gunther, were brutally murdered by Hitler's relentless killing machine designed to purify the German race and eradicate all Jews from Europe as part of his grand plan to become supreme Führer of Europe.

As far as I know, I am the sole Jewish survivor of that town. I survived only because my parents made the ultimate sacrifice: they sent me off one night on the last train of children leaving Germany. The transport had been arranged by HIAS (Hebrew Immigration Aid Society) to gather a few more children, age 6 and under, from various parts of Germany and take them to Sweden via ferry from Hamburg. During the fall of 1939 it became clear to my parents and other Jews in Germany that either they must leave immediately, or else risk horrible suffering and probable death. As the situation rapidly deteriorated in Germany, they were unable to leave Europe at that late date. They realized that they had to send out their only child for a chance to continue the Karger family into future generations. This was already a year after Kristallnacht; Poland had been invaded and the war with England had started. The borders from Europe were closed.

Shortly after they sent me away to Sweden, my parents, along with the other 20 Jewish families were rounded up and taken to **Gurs**, a concentration camp in southern France. My parents, grandparents and other relatives were forced to work and starved to death, except for my Mother who did survive that camp. But she survived only to be shipped to Auschwitz, where she was brutally gassed to death along with the others from Gurs.

Thus ended the line of the Offenheimers, my mother's family, who had lived in that same town at least since the early 18th century. I was the only exception, as I was shipped out alone to Sweden in the far north to live with strangers. Hitler succeeded in Schmieheim: no Jews remained. But I was miraculously saved to carry on in the memory of my family.

Memories from Germany—I remember my Father playing his favorite Schubert concerto on his piano. My uncle Alfred sometimes visited us from Mannheim, driving his motorcycle with Aunt Elsie in the sidecar. Hanna Baumann was my friend, she was a little younger than me; we played while sitting on the sidewalk. I liked playing with empty cigar boxes in my paternal grandfather's tobacco store in Berlin. I remember our two-story house and the outside steps; and the white full hair of my grandmother.

During a visit to Berlin, my grandfather took me to a square to hear Adolf Hitler speak. I remember the marching soldiers, the red armbands, loud shouting and yes, even the Mercedes touring car Hitler and his people rode. Years later I saw that same car at a car show in Las Vegas where I was giving a speech.

Some things I don't remember at all: I have no memories of my Mother. I have no recollection of love and hugs or affection. Perhaps by the time I can remember anything, my Mother was already too depressed from the events in Germany. I was born in 1933, the year Hitler rose to power.

Escape to Sweden at age 6, 1939: I remember nothing about the trip from Germany and don't even remember saying good-bye to my parents or my town. To this day, this major event in my life has always been a total blank. My first recollection is our arrival with many children at a large train station in Sweden. It was like awakening from deep sleep. I woke up crying, looking for familiar faces and things, but finding none. It was almost as if I was reborn at age six in a strange place, surrounded by a strange language and strange people. From that moment on, I remember clearly all that has happened.

Someone placed a tag around my neck, an address tag telling where I was being "shipped" and put me on a train going north. I didn't speak any Swedish and I probably didn't even know in which country I was traveling. The train ride was long, and I was transferred to other trains along the way. Finally, I was taken off the train by the conductor and met by a strange looking family of tall, blond people. The Gustafson family of Stora Skedvi, a small farming village in northwestern Sweden in the province of Dalarna, had agreed to take me as part of a program sponsored by a Pentecostal Church movement.

The farm in Sweden 1939-1944, age 6 to 11: The Gustafsons were tenant farmers. They had a tall, blonde daughter. No one spoke German and I spoke no Swedish. The pastor of the Lutheran Church was the only person in the village who knew a little German. He was very nice to help me learn Swedish. I was immediately sent to school and I clearly remember my first grade teacher, "Fru (Mrs.) Anderson." First grade was in a one-room schoolhouse, next to a larger two-story building for the higher grades. Bicycle was the way to get to the school, except in the winter when we skied, as the snow was too deep for any other means of transportation. No, there was no school bus and the Gustafsons did not own a car. I almost forgot the horse. Once in a while I was allowed to ride the horse to get around.

The family lived in a small tenant house on the farm. They neither owned a refrigerator, nor an indoor toilet. During the winter, it was very cold to go to the outhouse in subzero weather, often below-40 degree weather and in an occasional blizzard. There was no bathtub in the house. During the summer we bathed down in the river and swam. The water was always cold. During the winter we used a wooden half tub filled with hot water from the stove. We often went to the community steam bath of the village, the sauna that consisted of a small hut with steam generated by throwing water on very hot stones. When finished, we cooled off quickly by going outside to roll in the snow.

I lived with the Gustafsons for five years and remember those as good years. They were nice to me, as were all the people in the village; they became my friends. I was the kid in the village and the only one with dark hair, all the others were tall and blond. The food was good, mostly vegetarian, grown right there on the farm. They made a strawberry cake for my birthday, complete with candles. They took me to church every Sunday morning and to prayer meetings at the school house Sunday nights. I remember their sleigh that all four of us could fit in. At Christmas we went to church on that horse drawn sled with fur blankets protecting us against the cold. Just like in post cards…Everyone worked hard on the farm. Early December, the family celebrated the Santa Lucia Festival with the daughter dressed in a long white dress, wearing a crown, and we all sang the traditional "Santa Lucia" song. This has remained an important event in Sweden, as it is a part of the Lutheran traditions. I remember the Midsummer Festival when everyone danced around a tall pole (Maj pole) at midnight when it was still light. We lived about 100 miles south of the Arctic Circle, in the land of the Midnight Sun. During the summer, we all worked the fields, including a horse drawn plow. The farm produced rye, potatoes and vegetables. In the winter, we were in the woods chopping down trees to be taken to the river where the logs floated downstream to a lumber mill. I remember going fishing and riding the timber logs in the spring when the ice was breaking up. During the winter it was dark most of the time; it was light around noon and dark again by 2 PM.

My parents sent me letters for a while, then cards, and then short notes via someone in Switzerland. Nothing arrived after May 1942. The letters all said the same thing…they were hoping I was well, that I was eating well and that they prayed that some day we all would come together again. The last few cards spoke of hardship, hunger and my grandparents dying. I still have these letters and cards, about 50 pieces. Their copies are displayed at the new Berlin Holocaust Museum.

Then my life suddenly changed again. Hilde Schonthal, a lady from Stockholm came to see me at the farm. She said that she knew my mother and wanted to look after me. She was very nice and brought me presents and chocolates. She even invited me to visit her in Stockholm twice. She decided that I should be brought up the Jewish way and arranged for me to be transferred to a Jewish orphanage in Southern Sweden.

So once more, my black suitcase was packed and away I went on the train by myself. I was eleven. I have bad memories from that orphanage where eight children lived in each bedroom. After a year the orphanage was closed. Once again I was shipped off with my black suitcase on a train to live with a very orthodox Jewish family in Stockholm, the Jacob Koff family.

This was a very bad time for me. Starting over again in a totally new environment, a new place, new and totally different people, and a large city. I went from a deeply religious Christian life on a farm, going to church and prayer meetings, eating mostly vegetables, to an ultra-orthodox kosher family, eating heavy, greasy, East European food that ruined my health, especially my digestive system. To this day, I must be careful what I eat. I was forced to go to Hebrew school for my Bar Mitzvah and yes, I did learn to read Hebrew a little, but never knew what I was reading. The Koff Family had a chandelier factory where I worked after school. They were nice people but I never made the adjustment from the life of simple, vegetarian, fundamentalist Christian farmers in a backwoods to a religious kosher Jew.

A digression—that shaped my entire life: In Stockholm I discovered comic books and the "Kaptain Frank" strip that later evolved into Flash Gordon. This exposed me to futuristic science and shaped my entire life as I became more and more obsessed with science and futuristic ideas. No doubt that this exposure led me to pursue a career in high technology and become one of the leaders in the development of satellite communication and related technologies, and becoming a Fellow of the British Interplanetary Society, a cherished award of recognition in the mid 1960s;—Chairman of the Cape Canaveral Section of the Institute of Electrical and Electronics Engineers (IEEE) in 1966 at age 33, the youngest ever in that elected post, and named "Outstanding Young Man of America" in 1965 at age 32. I wrote an important article in 1967: "Communications in the year 2000" that accurately described the coming of direct broadcast satellite to home

TV, wireless communication for the masses, worldwide connectivity of computers and networks for everyone, telemedicine and more. All of these have become common for everyone. I was 34 when this appeared in newspapers. Many people thought that I was a raving maniac obsessed with science fiction.

America Calls! The Atlantic Crossing: The war ended in the spring of 1945 and then a letter arrived from an aunt inviting me to come to live with her and her husband in Pensacola, Florida in the U.S.A. She claimed to be a half sister to my father.—So, why not?—I couldn't stand the greasy kosher food, the meaningless and strict orthodox rules. I felt out of place without friends. I agreed, and on August 5, at age 13, I left again by train for Gothenburg with that same black suitcase, once again by myself, to board the M S Grips Holm sailing for New York. The Grips Holm was the first diesel powered large ship to cross the Atlantic, built in 1925. She carried 1643 passengers. It was built as a luxury ship with health salons and amenities comparable to the Titanic. But, for me, it had been converted to a troop ship for the war. I was assigned to the lowest of low cabins, of course, in the 3rd Class, with four bunks, all occupied. The two-week crossing to New York, with a stop in Liverpool, which I barely saw due to dense fog, was a nightmare. I was sick almost the whole time, perhaps because the greasy kosher food in Stockholm had ruined my stomach, and the ship rolling in heavy seas didn't help.

Our ship passed the Statue of Liberty in New York Harbor. "Hello America!"—here comes Günter! Once again, with the same black suitcase all the way from Germany and with an address tag around my neck, I was met by someone speaking yet another strange language, English. No one spoke Swedish, of course; once again I couldn't communicate. I was put up at a kosher hotel in New York and yes, I remember more greasy food coming my way. The next day I was put on a train by someone from the Travelers Aid Society bound for Atlanta, where I was also picked up by a lady from the Traveler Aid Society for the night and placed on another train the following morning, bound for Pensacola, Florida. I'll never forget how hot and humid it was on arriving to Pensacola in August, after the cold Swedish climate. I was met by my aunt to begin what became a four year nightmare,…not in Germany,…not in Sweden,…not under Hitler,…but in the U.S.A.

Four years of slavery—in America: Aunt Ruth and Uncle Jack were in their early 30s. He had a good job as chief engineer at Pensacola's largest chemical plant. They had a house just outside Pensacola's large naval base and had recently adopted an infant. It was a very difficult time for me in a strange new place. The climate was hot as in an oven and there was no air conditioning in those days. I knew no English and no one knew any Swedish, hence there were many misunderstandings. Within two weeks of my arrival I was already working nearly every day as a bag boy in a local supermarket at 25 cents per hour plus tips, with all the money going to my "hosts" for room and board. Within three weeks of arriving, I started school in the 7th grade. I did speak a little English by then.

The next four years I spent going to school, working at supermarkets and other odd jobs, cleaning the house, washing dishes and their car, mowing lawns and baby-sitting for them and their friends. "Uncle" Jack constantly called me a bum, reminding me that I would never amount to anything: the best I could do was to become a farmhand. There were times when I wished I had been left at the farm in Sweden where the people were nice, even though we worked very hard on the farm and the facilities were primitive. I never had time or any opportunity for making any friends during the four years with them. I can't remember a single friend or having any fun. One day, I had just washed their car when "Uncle Jack" came screaming into the house and chewed me out for getting him a flat tire and I didn't even drive their car. I responded, "Fuck you and go to hell!" The next day I was put on a Greyhound bus for New Jersey and told never to come back. Thus ended my four years of slavery in America. It was 1950, I was 17 with a year of high school ahead to graduate.

The chicken farm in New Jersey, August 1950–May 1951: With my old black suitcase from Germany, with the pictures of my family in Germany and the handkerchief case my mother had sent with me, I was again "shipped out" to a place unknown to me, with a one-way ticket. But this time, I knew the language and didn't need an address tag around my neck. I was "shipped" to Vineland, New Jersey where Uncle Alfred and his wife, Aunt Elsie had just arrived from South America to run a chicken farm. This was the same Uncle Alfred whom I remember from Schmieheim. He used to visit us on his motorcycle with Aunt Elsie in the sidecar. They left Germany for Uruguay in 1937. He was my mother's half brother. My "Florida hosts" sent a telegram to Uncle Alfred telling him that Gunther was coming for a two-week visit. It was up to me to handle the problem of never returning, where to go after "the two weeks," and how to finish school.

The bus trip to New Jersey was quite memorable. When the bus pulled into Atlanta for a change to another bus, early in the morning, the man next to me wouldn't move to let me get off the bus. He **died** during the night.

As I arrived to Vineland in August 1950, Aunt Elsie was in the hospital having her first child. I had to face the problem of telling them about the "two week vacation;" that I had been thrown out and had no place to go, had no money and still had a year of school left. I told them the truth about Pensacola. Without hesitation, I was invited to stay to finish high school.

Thus I started another new life. I learned to clean the chicken coops. Without any doubt, it is the worst and smelliest job anyone could have. I helped with all work, as I was experienced in changing diapers, washing dishes, mowing grass from Pensacola. I went to Clayton High School in the 11th grade, where Bernie Rudberg became my first friend since Hanna Baumann, my childhood friend in Schmieheim.

An aside about Hanna: She was the last Jewish child born in Schmieheim and was killed. In 1999, a kindergarten was dedicated in her name in Schmieheim with a picture of her and me. This was one of the pictures sent out with me in my black suitcase when I was shipped to Sweden in 1939. Hanna and I went to the same kindergarten in Schmieheim.

Bernie Rudberg's parents had emigrated from Sweden in the 1920s on the Gripsholm, the same ship I had sailed on. Occasionally he invited me to his house for Swedish meatballs and small potatoes, and to speak Swedish with his parents. Bernie and I were involved in school activities. We represented our school in a WCAU TV (Philadelphia) Junior Town Meeting of the Air and on a similar radio program in Bridgeton, NJ. He used to pick me up in his old truck for some of these events.

My short year in New Jersey was a mixed experience. Uncle Alfred and Aunt Elsie were very nice to me but I couldn't stand working chicken coops and had stomach problems stemming from the greasy kosher food in Stockholm and having been exposed to lots of stress. I liked school and the teachers and was able to participate in many activities, as our class was very small, about 50 in my senior year. As in Pensacola, I had to work all the time and didn't have much time to study, but I made good grades and was even elected to the Honor Society.

I became increasingly interested in science and wanted to become an electrical engineer, but had no money for college. I was offered scholarships to two universities but they didn't provide enough money and I had no source for any supplemental money, or any help from anyone. With the Korean War the military began to draft students from high school. The Air Force advertised for electronics people and an electronics school opened in early May 1951. I wanted to go there, but wouldn't graduate until June. I convinced the school's principal to let me take all the final tests almost two months before normal graduation, so I could finally go to live my own life by taking advantage of the Air Force opportunity. He agreed as I had been making top grades. I took the tests and graduated as Valedictorian of the class "in absentia" in June. Again, I left Vineland with my black suitcase from Germany, but this time, although by train, I left on my own steam, going where I wanted to go.

My Air Force Days 1951-55—meeting Shirley: The Air Force basic training was at Sampson AFB in Geneva, NY, a small town in Upstate New York. After four months of learning military life, marching, taking orders and shooting guns, I was sent to Scott AFB in Illinois for Radio School. But instead of starting the school at once, I was assigned to manage the base pool and ping-pong hall until classes began. After a month of playing pool and getting good at ping-pong, volunteers were sought to Keesler AFB in Biloxi, Mississippi for an airborne electronics school. I raised my hand and left the next day.

On a day in September 1951, I saw a notice for a dance at the USO, sponsored by a New Orleans Jewish Girls' group and decided to go. I asked one of the girls to dance, who said that I was too short for her, but she'd introduce me to her sister who was shorter. Her name was Shirley Rosenzweig, the same Shirley I married three years later. We have been married for nearly 50 years. Over the next year, I would take the Greyhound bus or hitchhike to New Orleans to find a cheap rooming house and go out with the "New Orleans Girls." They were all in the same Jewish B'nai Brith Girls club, but Shirley was the one sent to me by a "Higher Authority." I felt that I had found **another family** when I met her parents and relatives at her 16th birthday party in New Orleans.

She lived on South Rampart Street, lined with small stores. Her family lived above the store that stayed open 7 days a week, a block from where the famous New Orleans Superdome stands today.

After graduating from the 9-month electronics school, I was assigned to a 4-month airborne radar school and then a special school for instructors where they taught me how to teach. At age 19, I started to teach airborne radar maintenance. I was transferred to Chanute AFB near Champaign, Illinois along with two other airmen to establish the first Air Force weather radar training school. As none of us knew anything about the weather, we were first sent to the Air Force Weather Equipment School and learned all there was to know about meteorology, weather forecasting and the equipment, including balloons to sample clouds. We set up and taught that course to Air Force weather students.

I lived in the barracks on the base, two to a room. My roommate was Gene Kirchner from Iowa, we have remained friends to this day. Over the years, we visited them in California and this year, for the first time, they came to our house in Miami.

In late 1953 I had the opportunity to return to Keesler AFB for a 9-month advanced course. This time, I drove my own car back to Keesler and got back with Shirley in New Orleans who was dating a violinist. We were married in New Orleans on December 5, 1954, with about 500 guests witnessing.

Although Shirley's parents were poor, lived above their store and didn't even have a car, this was possible because they invited everybody including the mailman and the milkman, but all those who came brought food. It was a "pot-luck wedding" in the synagogue that Shirley's family attended. Among all those people, only one person came from my side. I was the "stranger from nowhere" with no family and few friends. My best man was Aaron Krumbein, the brother of Jack, the husband of my half aunt in Pensacola. After I was thrown out, I still did try to make peace with my aunt and visited them a couple of times, but they refused to come to the wedding and did not send a wedding present. But I had become friendly with Aaron, who probably felt sorry for me and did come to New Orleans, the only person on my side at our wedding in front of 500 people.

The wedding was right after my graduation from the advanced radar school. After the wedding, Shirley and I drove back to Chanute AFB, Illinois, in my 1949 Mercury that replaced my first car, a 1940 Ford Coupe back. **This was an important event! I was no longer traveling alone!** We found a small attic apartment in Champaign. The bedroom was the size of a large closet without a window, so I painted a window on the wall. Shirley found a job as a keypunch operator as she had worked for the Times Picayune paper in New Orleans.

Studying to become an electrical engineer, 1955-1958: My four years in the Air Force ended in May, 1955. We left for Louisiana State University in Baton Rouge to study electrical engineering under the GI Bill. All expenses were paid plus $135 per month to live on. I was able to get lots of college credits for the technical schools in the Air Force and from the University of Illinois and Mississippi State College. This enabled me to finish a five-year course in three years by also attending summer school. We mostly lived in veterans' housing on the campus, paying only $32 per month for a one bedroom unit made of used plywood aircraft boxes from World War II. Shirley found a job at $25 per week and that's how we got through school. Shirley got pregnant and our son, Herbert, was born on March 22, 1958 and attended my college graduation as a three-month-old baby in June that year. I graduated college at age 25, married, with one son.

My Aerospace & Scientific Career—1958-1973: A tumultuous 15 year period began after graduating from Louisiana State University. My first job took us to Seattle, Washington where I became an engineer with Boeing, designing surface-to-air missiles. This was followed by an assignment to teach U.S. Marines the use of their new surface-to-air missiles at their desert proving grounds at 29 Palms, California, in the middle of Mojave Desert. The following assignment was at Bell Laboratories in New Jersey, developing a superfast cryogenic (supercold) computer magnetic memory storage system.

Northern New Jersey was the birthplace of modern communications in the U.S. I joined the Institute of Electrical Engineers and became professionally involved with such people as Allen B. Dumont, the inventor of the color TV tube; J. R. Pierce, known as the father of satellite communications; George Anderson, who managed the Edison Laboratories, originally created by Thomas Edison. I became friends with Ransom Slayton who held the patent for the original teletypewriter, and Roger McSweeney, who was Chief Engineer of RCA Communications and the person who set up modern communications in Cuba.

My interest in advanced science stemmed from the "Kaptain Frank" comics in Sweden and reading science fiction whenever I could. I had visions of a futuristic technological world and attended meetings, volunteered to help committees chaired by the industry's giants leading the Northern New Jersey scientific community. Within a short time, I was appointed to serve on a committee and within four years I rose to become Chairman of the Northern New Jersey Communications Group of the IEEE (Institute of Electrical and Electronics Engineers) at age 31. Along the way, I was invited to serve on national committees and became Editor of the IEEE Communications Group Newsletter with about 35,000 members worldwide and I was appointed to its National Executive Committee. Shirley and I frequently traveled all over the world attending meetings and conventions. Shirley became an important part in my professional society work because she accompanied me to many of the meetings and acted as my official hostess.

I had two significant assignments while in New Jersey. I left Bell Laboratories for a better job at ITT Laboratories where I was assigned to the team that developed the world's first communication satellite up/down link. The second assignment came when I joined a consulting group staffed by several companies, to develop a strategic command and control system for the Defense Department. I became the Project Manager of Strategic Command Control and Communications with the responsibility to develop a communications system that would enable the commander of an aircraft to dispatch nuclear missiles toward the enemy, Russia at that time, to areas after 100 nuclear bombs had destroyed most of the United States. The assignment was to develop a "Doomsday System" and my job was essentially to create systems I had dreamed about when reading Kaptain Frank's comics in Sweden and Flash Gordon later in America. My boss had just retired as a Director in the CIA, the President of the consulting firm was a retired Air Force General and most of the 200 people in this think tank were very senior people. The system I dreamed up was eventually funded with about a half billion dollars and later implemented. For that work I received the "Outstanding Young Engineer of the Year" award from the IEEE Communications Group in 1963.

I had worked with Fred Westheimer, a fellow Holocaust Survivor, when we engineered the first transcontinental microwave communications network. Fred was also the husband of Ruth Westheimer who became the famous "Dr. Ruth," the most famous sex doctor in TV's history. I urged her to quit her subversive activities at Columbia University as it appeared to be part of a communist cell and she was jeopardizing Fred's high security clearance that many of us needed for our jobs.

This exciting chapter in our lives came to an end in late 1964 when the consulting group's assignment was completed and the entire operation was purchased by Computer Sciences Corp. and transferred to Washington, DC. I had an offer from Cape Canaveral to work on the space and missile range communications project and I was glad to escape the cold winters, blizzards and growing traffic jams. By this time, our two sons were old enough to enjoy the beaches and have fun in the sun. We sold our house, said good-bye to everyone and left in our new 1964 Dodge Dart. This time, I did not move **alone** with my black suitcase from Germany, although I still kept it, but with my own family: Shirley and our two sons.

Florida and the Space Program: Here we come! It's 1964: We bought a brand new four-bedroom, two-bath house, three blocks from the Atlantic Ocean from where we could walk to the beach. My work focused on missiles and space programs. The word spread before we arrived and I was invited to join the local chapter of the IEEE, and quickly became involved. I became friends with Clifford Mattox, who was an "elder statesman" of the space program. Cliff was on the team that was sent to fetch Germany's top scientific team before the Russians could get to them. This included their leader, Werner von Braun, who became instrumental in developing the U.S. rocket program; Dr. Kurt Debus, who later became head of the NASA Space Center at Cape Canaveral, and others. It was quite an experience to work with these, as I was probably the only Jew on these committees in any responsible position. Cliff told me that once, in New Mexico, where the German team was taken for "indoctrination into America," the German group stood up and shouted "Heil Hitler!" when Werner von Braun entered the room. This never happened again after that incident. It's my opinion, based on personal knowledge, that for the most part, these people were scientists first and would work with any country to advance science. Von Braun, in my opinion, was a great man, not unlike General Rommel, who was first a soldier rather than an idealist for Hitler. He died for his part to assassinate Hitler.

An exception was Dr. Horst Poehler. **He did continue to practice his Nazi leanings.** During the third year in the Cape Canaveral area, I was nominated to become the chairman of the IEEE Section of about 3,000 members and was one of the largest scientific electrical engineering organizations at the height of the space program. Horst had been the Treasurer while I was the Vice Chairman during the prior year. He couldn't handle the prospect of working subservient to a Jewish person and started a petition to unseat me from the nomination and went to the press with his campaign. This led to front-page headlines in the local newspaper. Since it is unprofessional for scientists to engage in this sort of thing, I offered to withdraw from the nomination.

However, the nominating committee refused to accept my withdrawal, the election was held and I became the chairman of the Canaveral Section at age 35, the youngest ever anywhere to have attained that position. Shirley also became as well known as she was in New Jersey, as our hostess and the "Social Chairperson" of the organization.

We helped to organize the 1966 "International Space Congress" at Cocoa Beach with participants from all over the world. Vice President Hubert Humphrey gave the inaugural address.

While we were in Cape Canaveral, I joined the Jaycees that led to my involvement in the campaign for Louis Frey. He won the congressional seat for Orlando and Cocoa Beach and served several terms. Later, while we lived in Miami, Congressman Frey ran for Florida Governor, and our house was his campaign HQ for South Dade County. We drove in parades behind the mayor's of Satellite Beach and had a lot of fun. Highlights of our Space Coast life was to be included among the "Outstanding Young Men of America" by the U.S. Jaycees in 1965; inducted as a "Missile and Range Pioneer" and elected to be a "Fellow" of the British Interplanetary Society.

I was working for Pan American World Airways at Cocoa Beach that held a contract for many years to provide technical services and manage the Space and Missile Range for the Air Force and NASA. As an employee, we took advantage of the flying benefits at Pan Am. In 1965, we put our sons in a YMCA summer camp and Shirley and I went to Europe for two weeks. This was my first return. We first flew to Sweden to visit the Gustafson family who took me in as a child in 1939. We always kept in touch as I felt close to them and, in a big way, considered them to be **my family**. Then, we visited Uncle Joseph, my Mother's brother in London. He went to England before the war. He and his wife, Aunt Martha, were already old and frail; they died a few years later. We flew to Frankfurt, rented a car and drove south to Schmieheim, my birthplace. We drove past our old house that I recognized and remembered. We stopped at that city hall housed in the old castle. The mayor remembered my family and was very surprised to see me there as he thought all the Jews had been killed. There were no Jews left in Schmieheim and no Jew is living there today, in 2001. Then we drove south and toured Switzerland. It was a memorable trip.

This phase ended in 1967. Frank Borman had taken "Man to the Moon," the space program was winding down, and it seemed that many jobs would end. Expecting to be laid off along with thousands of people, I looked for a new challenge in the airline industry, which, in my opinion, was technologically trailing behind the times.

I contacted the president of Eastern Airlines in Miami; made some suggestions and was offered the job to restructure the company's engineering department. I wound up our affairs in the Cape Canaveral area, sold our house and once again we hit the road going south to Miami.

Miami—here we come in December, 1967 and we are still here: We bought a lot in an old avocado grove, had a house built on it and we are still living there. Shirley focused on raising our 8-and 9-year old sons, while I worked at Eastern Airlines. The assignment to restructure the engineering department was very difficult. I was placed in charge of a group of aviation pioneers from the days of Eddie Rickenbacker, the founder of Eastern Airlines while I knew really nothing about the airline business. Working and learning day and night, I brought the staid engineering department up to date.

I became active in innovative areas of aviation, such as supersonic transports and vertical and short takeoff commercial airliners. I worked with Scott Crossfield, Vice President of Eastern's Flight Research & Development group. Crossfield and Col. Frank Yeager were the test pilots for the X-15 rockets and technically they became the world's first astronauts.

Between 1969 and 1973, I traveled extensively, often with Shirley. The Air Force Technology Conference in Las Vegas was attended by about 1000 people. Three major dinner speeches were given by Senator Barry Goldwater, by Gunther Karger of Eastern Airlines, and by Dr. Grover Loening, who was already in his 80's and the very person who worked for the Wright Brothers to establish their aircraft engine factory in Dayton, Ohio. Dr. Loening designed the first amphibian aircraft that became known as the Grumman Goose. He and Bill Grumman founded the Grumman Aircraft Engineering Company that mass-produced them for many years. He had an aviation museum on Key Biscayne and occasionally I took our sons across Biscayne Bay on our boat to visit him. He was one of the giants of aviation. As a humble orphan survivor from World War II, I felt very privileged to be associated with him professionally. I may also be the only Jewish person who was associated with Werner von Braun and his team in the space program and with the only remaining aviation pioneer from the original Wright Brothers team.

While with Eastern Airlines, Shirley and I took many personal trips to Japan, Hong Kong, Singapore, Australia, Fiji and Tahiti. We took many Caribbean cruises and often flew to Europe for special occasions. Nearly every year we visited the Gustafson farm and the people with whom I lived during the War. We also sent our sons to spend several weeks there during summers. We once flew to Gothenburg, Sweden for a weekend to the 90th birthday party of a friend. During a trip to Sweden, our friends gave Shirley a surprise 50th birthday banquet that was also attended by a cousin to the Swedish royal family. San Francisco was our favorite weekend spot. Our son, Ken, spent a week in Cambridge, England, with our friends and our sons went on separate six-week programs to Israel where we also visited for a week shortly after the Yom Kippur War in 1973.

Again, the world changed and so did Eastern Airlines: My work was done and I considered returning to my former work in science and communications This meant moving back north from Miami and away from the warm climate. Shirley liked it here, the boys were settled in school and I was offered a promotion at Eastern Airlines, but entirely outside the engineering and technical field, but in Miami. The assignment was to develop a computer based business-forecasting system for the airline's cargo business, an important $300 million in revenues. I accepted it and developed the airline industry's first computerized cargo forecasting system and then managed it for about 15 years until September 1986 when the airline was sold and my job ended. I was "retired." That was my last full time job with a corporation.

At 53, I was too young to retire. In the late 1980s a person was "dead meat" after age 50. The more qualified, the harder it was to find a job. I had no alternative but to "hire myself" and go full time into the rocky world of stocks and investments, which I had started on a part time basis several years earlier by launching "Discovery Letter," an investment newsletter. I gave seminars at Las Vegas investment shows and appeared as a panelist several times on "Stocks, Options and Futures," a Chicago based TV program on the Financial News Network, FNN, that later became CNBC.

Shortly after "leaving" Eastern Airlines, I met the owner of a management-consulting firm who needed someone to restructure his business. We became involved with a project whereby we would acquire a company and I'd become a partner in that. Over the years we accumulated about ten rental houses and condominiums, thus we had some assets. This partnership turned into disaster. My partner failed to follow through with his commitments; amplified by the stock market crash of 1987, the project failed, resulting in a personal financial disaster. We were basically left with nothing but our house.

The next several years were difficult, but we managed to survive until 1992 when Hurricane Andrew struck and we were within the eye of the storm. Our house was severely struck; the damage amounted to about $100,000. That disaster turned into a great opportunity. Over the following year I not only personally rebuilt the house, but also used the insurance money to fund a stock investment and trading program. I rebuilt the investment business and resumed publishing the Discovery Letter, which for a time became well recognized nationally for covering small companies.

From all this stress, in addition to the residuals from the Holocaust and the active and aggressive life we had led, **in October 1993 I experienced excruciating chest pains** while I was alone in the house, as Shirley had left for some errands. I managed to get into the car and drive to the nearest hospital. After several weeks of extensive tests at various hospitals, the doctors concluded that I did not have a heart attack but a "spastic artery" that simulated the symptoms of a heart attack or blockage. I fired the doctors and sought a second opinion. Sure enough, after the second heart catheterization in three weeks, they did find a clogged artery and I needed balloon angioplasty. On December 2, 1993, at yet another Miami hospital, I was prepped for angioplasty when a nurse promptly killed me by incorrectly administering the pre-operative sedation. Luckily, Shirley and Ken, our son, were in the room at the time and saw that something was happening to me. They called for help and the hospital's "Code Blue Team" came almost immediately. I was revived; wheeled into the operating room; the procedure was performed and I am alive and well as of today.

Shirley and I had become a team in all aspects of our lives including the investment advisory business. We are known today as "Discovery Group, Inc." My earlier experiences revealed to me a very high level of dishonesty among brokers, company executives, financial columnists and TV commentators. This led me to write the book "Thieves on Wall Street—Survival Guide for the Investor" in 1995. We were widely quoted in the local and national press, I appeared on CNN's "Your Money" with Rukeyser. The CNN reporter who came to our house with her crew had interviewed Fidel Castro during the previous week. Since then, I started to write an occasional column for business journals mostly in Oregon where we still give occasional seminars. In 2003, we started to give seminars onboard cruise ships on Wall Street corruption, and as of the fall of 2003, we have gone on six cruises for a total of seven weeks on the high seas.

The return to Schmieheim, my birthplace in Germany

In September 2003, we were invited to return to Schmieheim, the small town in the Black Forest. We visited my original house, which had been rebuilt by the new owner, the gravesite of my great-grandparents and the kindergarten I once attended. There was a town gathering attended by many people, including three, who attended kindergarten with me a long time ago. Although my memory of that part of my life did not return, I felt that I had, along with my wife of 49 years, "come home" at last, to where it all began 70 years ago.

October 2003

The Refugee Girl

♦

Nellie Lee

I was born in Beregszász, a small town in Czechoslovakia, on February 9, 1936. This area had been under the control of various countries, including Hungary and Russia; it is now part of the Ukraine. The town is now known as Berehovo. My parents were Orthodox Jews who spoke Yiddish and Hungarian.

My parents had been married about two years when I was born. My widowed maternal grandmother lived with my parents. She was a strict, nervous, overprotective woman, who gave birth to my mother, her only child, three months after her husband died in a typhoid epidemic. My grandmother worked hard as a seamstress to support herself and her daughter. At an early age, mother was apprenticed as a hairdresser and wigmaker. She was self-sufficient in her own business by the time she was twelve. My father's family lived in a nearby village. All I know about his family is that he had four siblings. The only surviving photograph of my parents' wedding shows several adults and children, but their identity remains unknown.

My parents moved to Antwerp, Belgium, when I was a year and a half. I believe this move was motivated both by my father's wish to improve his finances and a desire to get away from my dominating grandmother. Perhaps it was also motivated by problems with anti-Semitism.

In Antwerp, my father had a grocery store, and my mother set up business as a wig maker at home. My sister was born when I was two, followed by my brother a year later.

There are few memories of my life in Antwerp where I lived until I was four years old. I vaguely recall the layout and atmosphere of my father's grocery store. I remember walking with a maid to nursery school. I also remember having my tonsils removed when I was about three or four. My most vivid memory is of my father's attempt to reconcile me with a teenage boy in the neighborhood who terrified me. I recall that this boy was deformed and had a very red complexion.

Whenever I saw him, I became very upset and would try to avoid him. My father attempted to bring us together and to show me that there was nothing wrong with this boy, but I remained frightened and upset by this.

In May 1940, my parents made plans to leave Belgium. My father decided to send his family away separately without him because he believed that he could sneak across the border easier on his own. The Belgian army was conscripting all men at the border and he wanted to avoid this; my father had already served in the Czech army.

My mother and aunt Toba, my father's sister, were given some money and small sacks of clothes for each child and we all were put onto a horse drawn wagon with instructions to meet my father in France. It was a difficult journey; the roads were crowded because many people were fleeing.

Upon our arrival at the designated French border town, (I don't know which town) my mother could not find my father. There were many people and much confusion. Apparently, there were some ships leaving for safer destinations. I don't know the details as to how this was decided or who was responsible for this. Luckily, we were put on a ship leaving for an unknown destination. I think the Red Cross or HIAS may have sponsored the ship. During the voyage, all three children got sick with whooping cough and we had to be quarantined for several days. We arrived in England; I was four years old, my sister was two and my brother was just under a year old.

In England the Czech government-in-exile helped us upon our arrival and boarded us in the countryside. I vaguely recall our stay on a farm with a family; and I have several small photos of my mother, aunt and us children from that time. However, my mother and aunt were very unhappy about living with a gentile family, especially because they would only eat kosher food. After a while my mother was able to get us transferred to London where there was a Jewish community.

When I was about six years old, I was sent away to a boarding school. I suppose it was for my safety and to relieve my mother. However, it was a very bleak time for me as I was in unfamiliar surroundings, lonely and separated from my family. I recall that it was winter in the countryside. There were lots of older children in that school. The women in charge wore black dresses or gowns. I think they were nuns. I felt intimidated, and I did not understand their language.

In school, I recall sitting at my desk copying words from a blackboard onto a postcard or writing paper. I did not understand what the words meant. These postcards and letters were sent to our parents. I remember that every child was given a bag of Christmas candies, but I could not find mine in my locker and was upset. I became ill with stomach pain but was too scared to tell anyone. My hair was treated with chemicals to get rid of head lice. The chemicals burned the back of my neck and I had to stay in the infirmary. After several months at this school, during which I had no contact with my mother, I was put on a train and sent home. When my mother saw that I was sick, she took me to the doctor and, soon after my seventh birthday, I underwent an appendectomy.

For a few months, my mother and I lived in Manchester, while my brother and sister were sent to a boarding school in the country. I think this was during the Blitz in London. My sister and brother have sad memories of their time at the boarding school.

While in England, my mother received letters from my father, who was hiding in Antwerp. Apparently, he had boarded a train to leave Belgium and due to heavy bombings the train returned to Antwerp. A gentile family provided him with a hiding place for a while. In his last letter to my mother my father reported that he was discovered by the authorities; he was on a train, but he did not know where it was going.

During most of the war years we considered my father missing and we were hoping to be reunited. After the war ended, my mother found out that my father was sent to the Mauthausen concentration camp, where he died. I recall her crying and burning my father's letters in the fireplace.

Mostly what I remember about London was riding the buses to school every day with my brother and sister. As the oldest child, I was in charge of handling the money and paying the bus fare. We had to change buses once in either direction, and I was responsible for taking care of my brother and sister. We attended a Yeshiva day school called *Yesode Hatorah*.

My mother obtained a sewing machine and did piece work at home. She worked at her sewing machine late into the night. We lived in one room with a small kitchen alcove. A fireplace was the only source of heat in the room, and it was cold if you were not near that fireplace. We kept our dairy food cold outside on the window ledge because we did not have an icebox. My sister and I shared a bed. My mother and brother had their own bed. We shared a bathroom with several tenants in the building. We had to insert coins into the hot water heater for a bath. My sister, brother and I often shared a bath in the same tub of hot water to save money.

There was an air raid shelter dug into the dirt in the backyard. It had steep stairs leading down into a small, dark area with wooden benches on the sides. We often slept with all our clothes on, so when the air raid siren sounded; we could run out of the house into that shelter. Sometimes we slept in the shelter. One night, the door of the shelter flew open and we saw a big fire outside. When the air raids became more frequent, we would take bedding with us to the Underground train station and spread the blankets on the cement walkways to sleep there for the night. Despite the noise from the continually passing trains, many people slept in the Underground, because it was safer. One night my sister got on a train and was lost for a while; we were very upset and worried until she was found. In 1945, after the war ended, my mother contacted her mother's sister in New York City. My great aunt, Esther, had immigrated to the U.S. before World War II. She sponsored my mother, aunt Toba and us children to come to the US. We were on a waiting list for two years before we could sail to New York in December 1947. We arrived in New York harbor on the M.S. Battory, a Polish ship.

We lived with my great aunt in a three room walk-up apartment on the sixth floor of an apartment house in the Bronx. In January, just before my twelfth birthday, I was enrolled in Roosevelt High School. I had started high school in England the semester before and thus qualified to enter high school in New York. I attended that school only for one semester. Although I did manage the academic requirements, I did not fit in socially with the students, who were much older and more mature. After living with my great aunt for several months, my mother moved to her own apartment on Delancey Street on the Lower East Side of Manhattan.

Once we settled in our apartment, my mother got a full-time job in a wig shop and also started her own wig making and styling business in our apartment. We lived in a small, four-room, walk-up apartment with the bathtub in the kitchen and a small, separate toilet. Gradually, my mother built up her home business and quit her full time hairdressing job to work at home. Her customers were the local orthodox Jewish women; she styled their wigs.

I graduated with a commercial high school diploma from Bais Yaakov High School in Williamsburg when I was fifteen. I lied about my age and soon got a job working full time in an office. During that summer, when I was fifteen, I met my husband George, who was sixteen. We both were members of the local B'nai Akiva Youth Group. About a year after I graduated from high school, I started to take additional classes in night school to qualify for college. I continued to work full time and attended night classes. Eventually, I accumulated about a year of college credits at Hunter College while working in an office during the day.

In December 1954 I married George Greenberg in an Orthodox wedding ceremony. He was attending Brooklyn College and was also a rabbinical student at

Rabbi Jacob Joseph Yeshiva on the Lower East Side. In 1956, we moved to Durham, North Carolina because George had received a scholarship to attend the graduate program in psychology at Duke University. I continued to work and attend college, earning a B.A. in Education from Duke in 1959. George received a Ph.D. in Psychology in 1960. Our first son, Avram Jeffrey was born in Duke Hospital in April 1959. We lived very modestly and worked hard during our four years in North Carolina.

In 1960 George accepted a job in Massachusetts, where we lived for a year and a half. In 1961 we moved to New Jersey, where our second son, Leon Marc, was born in April 1962. In 1968 we bought a small home in Leonia, New Jersey. I continued my studies and earned two master's degrees, one in social work.

George Greenberg and I were divorced in 1975. I married Martin Lee in 1977, and we lived in Leonia with his two daughters and my two sons until 1980. In August 1980 Martin and I moved to Miami because he received a good job offer. Martin Lee left Miami in 1984 and our marriage ended in divorce.

My mother remarried after her three children had left home. She became ill with cancer and had several surgeries. She and my stepfather moved to Israel, where they lived for several years. They are buried in Bnai Brack, Israel.

I am now living in Miami, semi-retired, working part time as a social worker. My two sons are married; one lives in Las Vegas, Nevada, the other in Teaneck, New Jersey. My brother and sister, and their families, live in New York and New Jersey.

October 2003

Campkid

✦

Anna Blitz

I was not born in a cabbage, as children are commonly told in Europe, but in a hospital in Brussels in 1938. I found myself living with a whole bunch of people: my parents, my sister Lily, who was seven years older than I, and my paternal grandmother Oma. Hitler didn't know my family, yet he was threatening to kill us all. Evil's "logic"! So we had to flee and did so in 1939. We first went to Spain. My Dutch father knew Spanish, having worked there previously.

It was just after the Spanish Civil War; the country was in chaos. So we moved to Lisbon, Portugal. My maternal grandmother Oma Line joined us there. My father, a metallurgist, resumed working. Life seemed to become normal again, but there were rumors that Franco might join Hitler, as did Mussolini. My parents looked for a safer haven.

My father, being born in New York, applied for immigration to the U.S. The young couple and their children were accepted, but not the grandmothers. Under Roosevelt's immigration policy younger members of the family were allowed in the States while the older ones were to be left in Europe to Hitler. It was inconceivable that my father, a quiet man of strong principles, would abandon the older members of the family. Instead, in 1941, we boarded a ship for Indonesia, a Dutch colony at the time.

New arrivals were temporarily interned in a transfer camp while their documents were examined. My grandmothers and my sister Lily were soon released. Lily went back to school for a year. My father, who had a German name, was born in New York and had not done his Military Service in Holland at 18 as he was already becoming deaf, had to have his papers checked further. My mother and I remained interned with him. My first memory is actually from this transfer camp. We lived in a beautiful house surrounded by a large verandah and well kept garden. Mothers were given daily a cup of milk per child. My mother would make a little pudding, turn it over on a plate and watch over me while I ate it on the verandah. It was a quiet moment of nurturing between mother and child.

After 6 months we were finally released and moved into a little house in Bandung, Java. Mom was now very busy, tending to all of us. She had become tense, irritable, and ordered me around abruptly. I turned to Oma, our cook. There was a large table in the middle of the little kitchen. I played under the table while Oma worked around it. She would also take me to the park to play in a sandbox. From time to time, I would raise my eyes to her, feeling good seeing her sitting on a bench, chatting with others. To and from the park, Oma would hold my hand and chat. I couldn't understand it all, but I agreed whole-heartedly with whatever she said. We were peacefully connected, much more than by our hands.

When the tropical rain season came, I loved standing under the gutter, the rain pouring over my head. I would undress and put my clothes away carefully, folding them on the side with my ribbon on top. But time after time I forgot to take my shoes off. It utterly frustrated my mother: shoes were hard to come by in wartime.

We were living in that little house, on a slope, when the Japanese invaded Java. The Japanese army trucks would roar down our street. I was not allowed to leave the garden. Our street was my world and I knew that the "ends of the world" were located at the top and the bottom of the street. One day I decided to explore it. I opened the gate and walked up the street. I discovered a circle with many streets crossing it. Wow! The world was so big! I was absorbed in that exploration. But suddenly I couldn't find my way back home. There was a moment of panic but then I heard the roar of Japanese trucks, coming up to the circle and roaring down. I smiled, now I knew my way home. My mother, however, did not smile. I was a lively and mischievous child, and she was burdened enough already by all our circumstances.

The Japanese, as the allies of the Nazis, incarcerated all Dutch citizens. We were not. My father was fair-skinned and had a heat rash. A medical certificate stated that he had a "skin disease." The Japanese referred to VD as "Skin Disease" and were very frightened of it. Instead of incarceration, we were quarantined in another house…with a garage, where my father lived isolated from the rest of the family. To avoid incarceration, my parents played their roles. I was not allowed in the garage or to touch him. I would stand in the front of the entrance, watching him walking up and down the room before he'd sit down at his desk. I was hoping that he would notice me, but he didn't, and I felt totally ignored. At night he would occasionally sneak back into the house and sometimes smile at me and hold me on his lap. It was confusing; I didn't dare touch him anymore.

The house and the garage surrounded a large patio, with an entrance to the kitchen. Two Indonesian women cooked under my mother's supervision. The food was then packed in pails. My sister, who was 12, would load them on her bike and take them to the camps where the food was sold. My father never complained, but it must not have been easy for him to be forced into such a passive role, when he had always provided for "his women."

Being four, I saw that my mother was now very busy and irritable, as was my sister. Oma was withdrawn and remained so until liberation, and my father was absorbed at his desk in the garage. I played in the patio, mainly riding my tricycle, feeling lonely, unloved and rejected.

I turned to the two Indonesian cooks. They were always placid and good-natured. They wore multi-layered sarongs. When in need of comfort, I would find my way in between the skirt's layers and rest there for a while. Later in life, I tended to trust simple, dark-skinned people. This lack of discrimination was going to have disastrous consequences.

The Japanese would unexpectedly come to check that all was in order. On one such occasion, my mother had some pimples on her arm. She ran toward the Japanese, appearing very distraught, crying: "Look what he has done to me!" They fled in a great hurry, the family bursting into loud laughter. I laughed too but wondered what was funny. Eventually, the Japanese did find out that my father did not have VD and we had to be interned. But it meant that we were well fed for a whole year. It probably saved my mother's life and my own as we were both starving by the end of the war.

We were interned on my fifth birthday. I was very sad: I had to leave my tricycle behind. We all entered the Bloemenkamp (Flowers Camp) in the vicinity of Bandung. Each family lived in a little house. My mother had to do chores that she had never done before as she had always had domestic help. She was washing sheets by hand and looked utterly exhausted and despondent. My grandmothers were not much help. Everyone was self-absorbed, and I was increasingly left on my own.

As in all tropical climates, siestas were the rule. The children were told to stay at home for that period, because any child found in the streets would be caught and eaten by the patrolling soldiers. Of course, one day I went out. I wandered around the hot, deserted streets when I suddenly saw a Japanese soldier. I ran for my life, wondering why the soldier was so slim after eating so many children. I was sure he was following me, and I was terrified. Looking over my shoulder, I saw that he was just walking in a very relaxed manner, barely looking my way. I thought he mustn't be hungry, having just eaten another child. I went back home thinking how lucky I had been…In retrospect, I can now see that at that time we hardly had any contact with the Japanese soldiers, who were always described as bad.

We were moved to Familie Kamp, where we shared a house with another family. Oma Line, my maternal grandmother, ran a little kindergarten that I attended. My mother was calmer and reappeared in my life. But after settling in, we were uprooted once more.

We were sent to *Vrauwenkamp* (Women's Camp). Instead of a little house, we only had one room per family, with several families in one house. As a family was living in the hallway, we would enter the room through our window using a board from the ground to the windowsill. I didn't mind it, but I don't think my two grandmothers enjoyed it very much. Life was more crowded, but interesting with so many children around. However, lack of food was becoming a very serious matter.

We were notified that men and boys over 10 were going to be sent to a camp for men. The women in the camp were in utter despair. Everywhere I looked, someone was in intense pain. My father was a quiet, strong and always optimistic man. But that day, while standing three abreast in a row of men, he was looking down defeated and resigned. I could not believe it! My powerful father was helpless! This was going to be the only time in my life that I would see my father discouraged. I was in shock. I knew that this was a major catastrophe. The men, all looking down, slowly marched out of the camp, and my mother, Lily, the two grandmothers and I were left alone in our room. I felt very sad, abandoned and unprotected.

It was in this camp that the women were asked to fill out a lengthy questionnaire, with a question about our religious affiliation. As the Japanese were allies of the Nazis, my mother's first reaction was to lie. But she gave it further thought. The Japanese had such a different way of thinking! She felt that she could not predict their reactions. Therefore, she decided to tell the truth, unaware that the Japanese considered Jews to be Middle-Eastern, closer to them than the Dutch. As such, we were sent to the best camps together with some other privileged groups. This too probably saved my mother's life and mine.

The straw fence that surrounded the camp collapsed under heavy tropical rain. A few soldiers came to repair it. It was hot and they were perspiring. One of them looked at me and said, "Western women are so rude! Not one of them has brought us a glass of water." Puzzled, I went up through the window to ask my mother why she didn't bring some water to the Japanese soldier. My mother looked at me stupefied. "We are their prisoners and we should bring them water?"—she screamed. I saw that she had a point, too. I was struck by the fact that two people would look at a situation so differently.

The soldiers had not yet finished the fence, when a jeep drove up and stopped in front of us. Next to the driver was "The Bad Japanese," a fat man with a thin horsewhip. We, the children, knew him as "The Bad Japanese." Two little boys and I were watching the jeep, when "The Bad Japanese" suddenly became furious, jumped out of the jeep and ran toward one of the little boys. We all ran away and I found refuge in a hole under the house. The Japanese caught the little boy and started whipping him. The child screamed, but the Japanese continued whipping him rhythmically. From under the house, I could see the women in the next house all coming to the verandah to look on. None of them approached the Japanese to tell him that it was enough. He kept on hitting him, and the child's screams became weaker. I was terrified, thinking that the other boy and I would be next. And I also knew that no one would come to ask him to stop. Finally, "the Bad Japanese" left. The women lifted the little boy from the ground and brought him inside. I then found out that the man became angry because the boy had made a face, a grimace. It had not been as arbitrary as I first thought. The child remained sick for a long time. I remained disappointed for life that not a single adult tried to calm down that man.

The children hungered for revenge! We could not accept this brutality without hitting back. We talked for days about possible retaliation. Then one of us had a brilliant idea that was unanimously acclaimed. That night, I would not allow myself to fall asleep while lying in bed, one of the most difficult things I have ever done in my life. I waited until the family was asleep and sneaked out. We all met in the garden and went to the kitchen, located in a separate building. The door was closed, but a window was always left open. We helped a child climb through the window and he opened the door for us. Four of us carried away a gas stove on our shoulders. It was a night with heavy tropical rain and the stove weighed heavily on my left shoulder. We went to the back of the garden, where the land was uncultivated, up the slope and then, with all our strength, threw the gas stove down the hill. We watched it with great satisfaction as it was tumbling down. What an achievement! We returned to the garden, washed our muddy feet under the spigot, telling each other not to say a word to any parent about what we had done, in case they would tell the Japanese. Suddenly, I got scared! I knew I wouldn't say anything, but I also knew that some children were closer to their families than I was and one of them might talk. The next day, the Japanese retaliated. A group of women, each holding a gas stove, had to walk under the sun. They were red-faced and exhausted. I felt sorry for them, but I had a strong inner conviction that we did what we had to do. Life resumed as before, but whenever I saw the Bad Japanese, my legs weakened, making it hard for me to flee.

My sixth birthday came. My mother and grandmothers were already quite weak and did not interact much with me. But my mother always celebrated my birthdays, no matter what. For this one, she looked for someone who could sew a doll. She was made from rags, had two yellow braids, and I called her Lisje, Little Lisa in Dutch. My mother paid for the doll with food, and later I heard her say repeatedly that she did not know what was more important for a little girl: food or a doll. My mother was weak, but she put quite some thought into that decision. And yes, receiving Lisje was important. I loved her more than I ever loved any of the beautiful dolls I received after the war.

We moved to a new camp, Adek, near Jakarta. I remember very little about it. Then we were sent to Tangerang. Each time we moved, we had to walk from camp to camp for hours in the dark of the night, because it was too hot during the day. We carried a small bundle of clothes, our only possessions. I felt sleepy and very tired. So did my mother. She walked slowly, with obvious effort. Once a soldier yelled at her and pushed her. I thought he was going to hit her and I screamed out of sheer terror. The man looked down into my eyes, and I saw that he was sorry, he didn't mean to frighten me and didn't know how to calm down a screaming child.

In Tangerang, there were many women in each room. We slept on raised wooden platforms, our heads toward the wall, with little space among us. The women were very hungry now and lying there the whole day to save energy. Lily, who was only 13, had to take turns to clean the Japanese soldiers' quarters, without any food in return for the expenditure of her energy.

One day, a little boy died in our room; his mother was lying down on the platform. A Japanese soldier approached and stood in front of her, holding the hand of another little boy. He said in Indonesian, the language used by all: "You no child. Child no mother. Take child." She raised her head and rested it down again. The soldier waited and then repeated the same words. Again, the woman raised her head and then rested it.—I thought the Japanese soldier had a good point.—This continued for a long time until nightfall. The soldier became restless and at last, left with the child. The woman quickly sat up and exploded: "Can't he understand that it is my child I want?"—I realized that she had a point, too. Again, one situation and two different interpretations.

I found life interesting, plenty of children to play with. A Japanese soldier gathered the children in a quiet section of the camp and taught us Dutch songs. He wouldn't teach us Japanese or Indonesian songs, only Dutch ones. I wouldn't miss a session for the world. The Japanese man came at the same time each day, judging by the angle of shadows made by metal poles stuck in the ground. One day, I saw that the shadow was further away than usual, there was time, so I played a bit longer away from our group, arriving late for the singing. I was so upset that after that episode I always came early and waited no matter how long. If one made a mistake while singing, the Japanese soldier would silence that child with a sign for a few minutes until the next nod. I loved that man, and whenever I saw him in the camp, I would flash him my biggest smile.

I liked Tangerang, but we had to leave again. We walked at night for a long time until we boarded a train. We were back in Adek. I was relieved to be in a familiar camp. It was hard to adjust each time to a new situation. The closeness with the Japanese, which had started in Tangerang, further developed in Adek.

Some of the children "had a Japanese," or one became "the Child of a Japanese," meaning that we became buddies. Flipje (little Phillip) was the son of my mother's friend in the camp. In the children's terminology, Flipje and I were the "Children of a Japanese Soldier," he was "Our Japanese." He was a thin man with big ears. I would sit on his lap, twisting his ears forward, saying "Flip" and then backwards, saying "Flap," so he became our Flip-Flap. The Japanese culture emphasizes respect. This was very disrespectful, but he didn't mind. He would sit on a bench with his legs stretched forward, watching us play in front of him. He built us a seesaw under a tree and would move it around to keep it in the shade. One day he was happily waving to us from a distance. He was excited, which was unusual for this placid man. He had brought us some bananas and clearly enjoyed sharing them with us!

One day Flipje, another little boy and I found a large feather. We took turns to squat, push our pants aside a bit and stick it in our butts, jumping around while making noise like chickens. We were laughing our heads off. Flipje was by far the best chicken. He was so funny! As we were laughing, a woman came by and angrily said: "Vies…vies…"—it's dirty! We stopped for a second and then Flip-Flap burst into laughter with us for quite some time. The Japanese would say that the Westerners were always angry and I started to agree with them.

Twice a day, we had to assemble in the large courtyard. Flip-Flap would look at me there, completely expressionless, and I looked back at him the same way. I knew that, there, he wasn't "My Japanese."

We all had to wear a metallic number. I wore mine on the right side of my panties, my only clothing. The metallic number would often drop off and get lost. I had to go to a hut where a Japanese man would make me another one. He soon recognized me and would get very angry. I was terrified. But he never did anything harmful. Eventually I stopped being afraid of him, even while he was angry. I used to stand next to him for long stretches, watching him skillfully make numbers and other metallic objects.

One day, at the assembly, the officer in charge was angry with the prisoners who weren't wearing their numbers. They had to stay put, while the others were allowed to leave. I did not have my number and was really scared. So much so that my mother, who was already very weak, reluctantly gave me her number and stayed there instead of me. The officer let the children leave at once, but the women had to stand in the sun for a while. I waited there feeling very guilty. My mother was furious with me, saying that she had known that I would not be punished. The women seemed to know that the Japanese weren't usually cruel to children.

As long as we obeyed, they were not cruel.—A child once stole some thread from the sewing hut. He was punished by having to stand in the sun, which is not only hard but also dangerous in the Indonesian climate. He was standing in front of the kitchen, where some women were working, while a Japanese soldier stood guard over him. Two of the women came out of the kitchen holding a large pot of water and waited. It was unusual and I wondered what was going on…The Japanese soldier slowly turned around, looking away in the opposite direction, while the women poured the water over the child. The soldier then turned back, facing the boy again. I was surprised that he did not appear to see the water at the child's feet. They repeated this several times. By then I understood that the soldier was turning away deliberately, against orders. I truly admired this man for his courage.—But not all the children were so lucky! Another child had to stand in the sun and suffered a heatstroke; he never recovered and became brain damaged.

The women complained about the Japanese hitting them. Whenever seeing a Japanese, as a sign of respect, we had to bow. Some women, who would only barely bow or not at all, were slapped in the face. A delegation of women prisoners went to the officer in charge, requesting the slapping to be stopped. The officer, surprised at first, replied that he would even hit his wife if she were to be so disrespectful. And they were only prisoners! Back in the room I heard the women ridicule the officer's answer. I understood that Dutch women did not want to be slapped, but the point made by the Japanese was also understandable. I bowed to them happily and never got slapped.—The Japanese were saying that Western women didn't know respect, were rude and always angry. It was clear even to a child like me that these two groups did not understand each other at all.

Indeed, the Western women often seemed unreasonably angry. There was a group of German women in our camp who had been incarcerated by mistake. No one spoke to them. Everyone was angry with them. Yet, to me, they looked just like us. Another ostracized group was "The Women with Lipstick," who went to the Japanese section at night. We heard their laughter and the sound of eating and drinking. It sounded great! I asked my Japanese soldier to be allowed to come too. He frowned and sternly said, "*Malam tidur!*"—At night you sleep! For me, that was the worst possible answer. I begged him again and again, but his angry reply was always the same. I was surprised. It was actually the only time that he appeared angry. What was the big deal?—Flipje and I decided to sneak in there, as we also wanted to eat, drink and laugh. We looked for an opening in the wall, but there was none. We couldn't go over the wall, as it was too tall. I came up with the idea to go to the gate and sneak in while there was a change of guards. As we approached the gate, the guards, who were not supposed to move at all, chased us away while making dreadful, angry faces. We tried our luck with another shift with the same result. We were far from being unnoticed and finally gave up. But I thought that the "women with lipstick" were very lucky, and could not understand why the other women were so angry with them. Perhaps the Japanese were right about Western women always being angry.

One night, the Japanese flag was removed and replaced by a huge panty. I thought it was funny, but the Japanese didn't think so. At the morning meeting, we had to stand in the sun until the person who did it would step forward. I looked around and knew that no one would do that. The Japanese did not punish us without reason, but they were very tough when there was one. I was afraid. We could get sun struck while standing there. We stood as the sun was rising and the heat intensified. We were thirsty. It was hard to keep on standing. There was no escape, no running away. We were surrounded by armed soldiers. I thought: "Better wait and see what happens…" I wondered whether it was the end? I looked at "My Japanese," but at that moment he was not my Japanese, just another soldier. We were very tired standing in the increasing heat of the sun. The Japanese were also standing, but didn't appear tired. Then all of a sudden the officer let us go. I couldn't help thinking that the Japanese were not as bad as my mother and all the women were saying.

At another assembly, my mother, sister and I were standing in the front row—my grandmothers did not have to attend. A Japanese officer walked up and down and stopped in front of my sister. He looked at her silently for a while and continued walking. My sister, then fourteen, was already a very beautiful girl. When the assembly was dismissed, my mother and the other women exploded in anger against that officer. I thought it was most unfair, as I didn't see what was wrong with someone looking at a person. I tried to explain that, but they ignored me. For quite some time my sister wouldn't leave the room alone. She would only go out with two women, one at each side. When she needed to go to the toilet, Lily would stand by the door. Slowly, a woman would get up and stand at one side. Another woman would drag herself to the other side and they would march, waiting for her outside and then escorting her back. They bitterly complained that it was the officer's fault. But the poor man didn't give such an order; he never even said one word. I knew it: I was in the front row, almost facing him. I began to see that the Japanese were right: Western women were indeed angry people.

My mother was exhausted as my seventh birthday rolled about. She could barely stand, but she organized some games for the children. Seeing that, one of the soldiers started jumping and making funny faces. All the children fled. The soldier burst into laughter. He thought it was funny and so did I. On the other hand, I could understand my mother being furious. It had taken her a lot of effort. I felt confused. It was rather nasty and nastiness is confusing.

Life was indeed confusing at times. My mother was telling me that we would win the war, return home and everything would be wonderful. Flip-Flap was saying that they would win the war. I had no idea who was right. He showed me a photograph of a large Japanese family. I don't know if he told me that he would take me with him after the war, or if I only assumed it, but I wondered how the Japanese family would feel about me coming to live with them, looking so different.

In Adek, we were also sleeping on wooden platforms. Our platform neighbor was a young woman with a baby. She had long blond hair and used to spend the day, sitting cross-legged, with a blond baby-boy on her lap. He would cry a lot and she would lift him to her breast. The baby would suck a bit and then burst out crying, frustrated by the lack of milk. She would spend hours motionless, looking down at her baby, obviously depressed. I knew that she deeply loved her baby. I would stand there, looking at her for a long time. I was fascinated by the love of this mother. She didn't talk to anybody and I felt that there was nothing I could do to get closer to her. One day she disappeared. She must have left for another camp. The other women were happy—a bit more space for everyone! I missed her.

On the platform, in front of us, was a mother with two children. She would sit up and talk to them with joy and excitement. She was also starved and weak, but despite that she did enjoy her children. I looked at her with fascination. Flipje was an only child, and I could see the closeness he had with his mother. I knew that I wasn't loved the way those children were and I was sad about it. To be loved once a year on your birthday just wasn't enough. Later, facts confirmed my assumption beyond any doubt.

I felt totally unprotected, totally on my own despite having a family. I could rely only on myself, and I was always on alert, aware of the dangers. I even developed a sixth sense. Occasionally small, poisonous snakes appeared, and we had to be careful not to step on those with our bare feet.

I was left to my own devices. But at night, Lily would chase after me to come home and tell me to wash my feet before going up the platform to sleep. I felt she had no right to tell me what to do. She was always irritable, her life was difficult and I caused her more trouble. She was going to be angry with me for years.—Was she another angry white woman?—Lily had far too many responsibilities for a child of her age. She was only 14. She was worried—and not without reason—that our mother was near the end, she would pass away, leaving her the full care of two grandmothers and a little sister.

One day, while I was playing, some people came running; shouting that the war was over and that we had won! I was surprised, as the Japanese seemed much stronger than us. Everyone was jumping up and down and shouting with joy. I joined in as well, but I wondered about Flip-Flap.

When I saw him, he was aloof and ignored me. He seemed to be the angry one now. I didn't think that it was my fault that we had won the war, but I walked beside or behind him with my head down as if I were guilty. I followed him until he reached the Japanese section that was closed to us. Sometimes I waited for him there. Eventually he would appear but he continued to ignore me. I thought that at some stage he would stop being angry with me.

I had to go back to the infirmary with malaria and dysentery—the little brain-damaged boy was there, too. People were dying of starvation and disease, as there was no medication. I learned later that my mother and I were near the end. We are alive, thanks to Hiroshima that brought about the Japanese surrender. That night there were celebrations, the loud sounds of happiness and the smell of wonderful food, but I was not allowed out.

One day, the Camp's gates opened up and strange foreign soldiers arrived in a large convoy of trucks. They were Americans and didn't speak either Dutch or Indonesian. Everyone was overcome with joy, including me, but again, I worried about Flip-Flap.

There were big, big changes. The first big one was a large barrel that appeared out of nowhere, next to the kitchen, and was always full of rice…and we could eat as much as we wanted. After I ate, I felt a strange sensation of well-being. I remembered that feeling from a long time ago, an old feeling coming back. I savored it. For a couple of days, the camp was silent. Women would walk slowly toward the rice barrel, take some, then sit somewhere and eat it. I could not understand how the barrel always stayed full, so I sat under a tree, watching. Periodically two women would come from the kitchen with big pots and pour their contents into the barrel. But I still didn't know from where the rice was coming. Previously, the Japanese brought food in the morning. They often killed a pig and its screams sounded very human, like our own cries. I felt the animal's despair. We saw the food brought into the kitchen. But where was the rice that no one brought, coming from? I asked someone how long we were going to have rice, how long before we would be hungry again? The answer was that from now on, there would always be food. I knew this couldn't be true! Everyone knew for a fact that there was not enough food to go around. I asked again and got the same response. I couldn't understand why they kept telling me something that was obviously impossible to be true!

But not all was good! Some new people came into the camp. They made us sit on stools with our heads turned back and poured a painful fluid on our hair. I didn't like it; fleas were very natural to me, and much less painful than those burning fluids. Another day, we had to stand in line in front of a tent. Inside, some children were crying. Something very painful was going on. Then it was my turn. Without a word, an indifferent looking woman vaccinated me in different areas. I didn't like it, but it wasn't as terrible as I had expected. Then I had to get on a truck. An exceptionally nice man sat me on a chair, opened my mouth, and hurt me quite a lot. He gave me a little picture, and promised me another one when I return. Despite that promise and his kindness, I did not want to come back. I hated having the many cavities in my teeth filled.

Strange things were happening in the camp. The Japanese were slowly disappearing, replaced by those newcomers. I still quietly followed Flip-Flap until he also disappeared without a goodbye, without a word. It was unexpected and painful.

One day I was told to go to the Japanese section that was now open to us. I entered a long room, and at the other end my mother was standing next to a man who looked familiar. My mother was smiling, relaxed, suddenly appearing very feminine. I walked toward them, wondering who the man was. He looked like the man on the photo, on the platform, next to where my mother slept. I was still thinking about it when the man suddenly rushed forward and grabbed me. For a second I was scared, but then I realized that this was a very warm hug and I relaxed. When he finally let go, my mother said that my father had come back. I was overjoyed! My mother was a rather distant person, and I was hoping for a close relationship with this new man as I had with my Japanese soldier.

The Indonesians were seeking independence from the Dutch and guerrilla warfare began. A kind of Molotov cocktail was thrown into our meeting place while no one was there. I was told not to get out of the camp, but the world outside was fascinating. Another little girl and I went out and picked some flowers, which I put in my father's room, away from the women's camp. When I returned, my mother was hysterical. She tied me to a doorknob, but my father was laughing. He always laughed when I was mischievous, but in this instance I felt betrayed, because he did not acknowledge the flowers in his room.

Things were very different in the camp. The children would line up each day for a small bottle of Coca-Cola. Those bubbles seemed miraculous! They also gave us beets, and I couldn't believe how red those were! I had never eaten anything that good! But on the whole, things didn't feel right...The Japanese had almost all left, and I felt unsettled. We were going to be repatriated to Holland.

We were taken to a large port, where a huge boat was waiting for us. I wanted to escape, but there was no place to go to. The boat was fascinating, but an epidemic broke out from the rats hiding below. A third of the children died. There was chaos everywhere. A mother who had lost a child was screaming endlessly. I can still hear the sound of her desperation in my ears. My sister fell sick and then it was my turn. The nightmares were horrible! I would wake up and struggle to keep my eyes open, because I was afraid that I might never be able to open them again.

We arrived in Rotterdam, and I awoke on the pier. A blond girl on a stretcher, next to me, was very agitated. I fell asleep again and when I woke up, a blanket covered her face. She was not from our camp. I didn't know her, but my tears were running down into my ears. I was also angry with her for not fighting harder to stay alive. We were taken to a hospital in Hilversum. My sister was in the room. At night I woke up. Two nurses were sanding beside my bed, looking at me: "Another one that will go tonight"—said a nurse. I saw it, heard it and understood it, but had no emotions. I couldn't feel anything. I woke up the next morning, clearheaded, seeing every detail around me, and knew that I was out of danger. When I told my sister that I almost died, she laughed and told me not to be silly. For two decades, I thought that she didn't care until she told me that she had laughed to reassure me. The Dutch nurses were unbelievably rigid and insensitive. I was thirsty from the fever but they refused to give me water. I might wet the bed and they threatened me with huge injections that I saw again in my nightmares.

We had lost everything during the war. A stepsister of my mother took us into her home. Oma went into a nursing home and I only saw her occasionally after that, but she was always very kind and understanding. She was deeply religious and I loved her.

I had to get used to wearing a coat and shoes, which were very uncomfortable...and scary because it made it difficult for me to run. That was the way we protected ourselves in the camp. I started school, where everybody knew how to read and compute. I didn't, and felt humiliated during that first year, although everyone was kind to me there. Later I heard that in some schools we were called "Campkids," a rather derogatory term. Indeed we had "no manners." I remember once sitting on the floor, cross-legged, at a bus stop with my beautiful new coat, people staring at me and I wondered why?

After our return to Holland, my mother learned what had happened to her very large family and to Jews in Europe. She became extremely depressed. I would come home from school and find her in her robe, staring at the wall motionless. I would call her. She would look at me for a second and then stare at the wall again. This went on for some time. I also felt sad in Holland without knowing exactly why. Too many changes!

After six months, we moved to Brussels for a year. I attended a French-speaking school, where I still felt lonely and different, but both my mother and I were recovering. My father couldn't find any work until he was hired to be the representative of a Benelux steel company in Madrid. In eight years, we had moved 13 times, but we settled down in Spain at last. As a result of all this, it has been relatively easy for me to move to another city or country, and yet it's still painful. I find it difficult to feel that I belong somewhere and then leave behind the people I had become attached to. But I found a way to cut off relationships.

In Madrid, I went to the Lycee Francais, where again I felt more comfortable with the simpler and darker skinned Spanish girls than with the French ones. By now I was used to Europe and didn't feel sad any longer. Lily also resumed schooling. At 14 she had missed a lot. She was tense, irritable and suffered from intense migraines…until she finished high school. She decided to become a nurse because in case of a war, nurses are needed and never go hungry. She understood the situation in the camps better than I did and it was more traumatic for her. My father served as president of the Jewish community for ten years. The 1492 decree prohibiting Jews from exercising their faith was still in force. In secret, the community conducted forbidden Sabbath services in two small basement rooms. My father met with Franco to request to have the decree abolished. These two short bald men, with big stomachs, hit it off. Since the change would take some time, Franco gave an immediate interim permission for a synagogue. Jews were able to move to a beautiful large flat, in the open, on the first floor, and money was raised for the first synagogue in Spain since 1492: "Beth Yaacov" in Balmes St.

After the war, my father, in his early fifties, had to start from scratch, which he did with his usual optimism. He worked very hard and kept very busy with community affairs. But at home, he would turn off his hearing aid. I didn't feel that I was having much contact with him. Before the war, my parents had been close, but now they weren't. My mother had always been distant from me. Now it was worse as "I looked like my father."

We had two live-in maids and frequently entertained members of the community. After a meal, conversation often turned to the war. Everyone had a story. Yet my father never spoke about his own war experiences—I know nothing about his two and a half years in camps. I was greatly affected by these stories. In class, I wondered what my classmates would do if Franco became anti-Semitic. Whom could I trust? I made a conscious decision to give people the benefit of doubt, despite a deeper layer of mistrust.

Through the Jewish Community I met a Moroccan student of medicine. He was dark, simple and distant like my mother at a time when I thought that to be a good quality. He appeared very stable and I was in much need of a secure relationship. We immigrated to Israel, got married and had three children. He was indeed stable, but also chronically deceitful, dishonest, envious and vain. He played well the "victim" game ending up believing his own lies while being the aggressor—a little Arafat! He sabotaged me professionally in every way he could. He also managed under a false pretext to bring me "temporarily" to a small Moroccan town where I was isolated for years. That "concentration camp" was more traumatic to me than the first one. I escaped, once the children had grown up a bit. It provided them with a stable childhood and despair for me. I needed to develop spiritually as is often the case in crisis.

Despite of all this, I was able to become a clinical psychologist. That is what I wanted to be since the age of 14. My childhood had prepared me for my profession. Having been exposed to different cultures and ways at looking at an event; the experience of pure Evil through the stories of the Holocaust heard around the dining room table; trying to understand what was deep down inside people; the determination to resolve my own problems and help my family resolve theirs, kept me determined to study and work in my chosen field.

Two of my sons are dyslexic just as my father was. They were poorly coordinated and accident-prone. At the time, there was no provision in the Israeli Army for such cases. I succeeded in moving the family to Australia despite my husband's initial opposition and usual unfulfilled promises. If I had had a more constant and secure childhood, I might not have become as independent and self-reliant, and my children would never had been born.

For twenty years, as a young woman, I had recurrent dreams of giving birth to an Asian baby-girl. There were different interpretations, but it shows the depth of my attachment to Flip-Flap. After my divorce, the recurrent dream changed for one in which I had an intense connection with a man who would invariably lose interest in me. In one way or another, I had been "abandoned" by parental figures: Dad, Mom, Oma, Flip-Flap. It's only very recently that my dreams end in a positive manner: the connection being maintained. It seems that it is only now that I am ready to find my life's companion.

In some ways I am what's called a "first generation" (born before the war) and in others I am "second generation" (born after). I have such strong feelings of being a survivor that I wouldn't always seek refuge in a shelter when we were bombed in Israel. On the other hand, while writing about the transit camp in Bandung, I would suddenly feel exhausted. I realized that in a typical "second generation" manner, I had internalized my mother's depression at that time. In the camps I was alone, yes, but not crashed.

Paradoxically, on the whole, I gained through that experience strength and vitality. This can happen: a crisis can make you or break you. I am well aware that we have been very lucky, we were blessed. All of my immediate family survived and my own family that I created is doing very well. That's a lot to be thankful for and I am thankful, indeed!

Lost Yesterdays

❖

Ruth Glasberg Gold

This is an abbreviated version of Ruth's published autobiography: **Ruth's Journey** [1]

At the folds of the Carpathian Mountains, along the bank of the Prut River, surrounded by ancient forests rises Czernowitz, the capital of Bukovina province,
where I spent the most impressionable years of my life. Over the centuries, its
earth was stained with the blood by conquering Tatars and Ottoman Turks. It
endured the Austro-Hungarian Empire, became part of Greater Romania, was
annexed to the Soviet Union in 1940, recaptured by the Romanian Fascist army
in 1941, and retaken by the Soviet Union in 1944. North Bukovina is now part
of independent Ukraine. During my childhood, Czernowitz with its parks and
squares, elegance, culture, and language evoked a feeling of *Gemütlichkeit,* of
coziness, a small Vienna. The large yet closely-knit Jewish community of about
fifty thousand people represented half of the city's population. Czernowitz bred
many prominent Jewish, intellectuals; the town was the home of many poets, art-
ists and writers, making it a vital center of Jewish and German culture. I was five
when we moved into this beautiful town. Although the area was part of Greater
Romania, German was its predominant language. The Romanian government
was frustrated and posted signs: "Speak Romanian!"

Ironically, I never learned Romanian until I entered elementary school, and
Mama never mastered it at all. In addition to German, Mama also spoke Ruthenian and Yiddish, and Papa also spoke Yiddish, Hebrew, Polish, and Romanian.
Perhaps my facility with languages came from being exposed to such a wide variety, although my brother and I spoke only German with our parents.

---

1.   Ruth Glasberg Gold: *Ruth's Journey—A Survivor's Memoir,* University Press of Flor-
      ida, 1996.

Every year from June to September, my mother, my brother, and I would spend the summer on my grandfather's farm in the village of Milie. This was always the happiest time of my childhood, one I looked forward to and day-dreamed about for months in advance; I liked to go with my brother on his expe-ditions in search of rare plants and flowers for his herbarium. I also helped him chase the brilliantly colored butterflies that he preserved in his collection. He tol-erated his little sister well and never had any harsh words for me. I felt very privi-leged as a child.

The affection missing in my parents' relationship was supplanted by devotion to their children. In my eyes, Papa was more than God. He was all that God was supposed to be; only he was real and present for me, an absolute idol, a fountain of inspiration, goodness, love, intellectual stimulation, humor, kindness and devotion. Oh, how I worshipped him...

Facing Romanian Anti-Semitism

In 1937, I was seven when dark clouds gathered over our pleasant lives. For the first time, I heard the word *anti-Semitism*. Although Papa explained to me that it meant hating Jews, I had difficulty understanding its implication. Romania is a country with deep-rooted anti-Semitic traditions. During the late 1930s the fas-cist movements reached their height of popularity. The Iron Guard, a Nazi-type party in Romania, was funded by the Gestapo and taught the Nazi methods of genocide. The *Goga-Cuza* government, with an anti-Semitic platform, laid the foundation for the persecution of the Romanian Jews.

As a child I overheard adults whispering the name *Cuza-Goga*. It was the first openly anti-Semitic government. Although it lasted only a few months, their fol-lowers continued the systematic oppression of the Jews, aiming at the eventual destruction of the third largest Jewish group in Europe. Each day new decrees were issued, limiting Jewish activities and prohibiting access to certain areas and buildings.

In school everybody knew who was a Jew, not based on physiognomy but on names and such revealing clues as not kneeling and crossing oneself during morn-ing prayers or whether one attended the Jewish religion class. I did not experience any insults, but my brother did.

He went to a predominantly Gentile high school and was often humiliated by students and teachers alike. I remember Bubi sharing with us one such incident. As an outstanding student he often came up with the correct answer. But because he was Jewish, the teacher, instead of praising him for his knowledge, said to the class with contempt, "You see, even though Glasberg is a *zhidan* [kike] he knows the right answers."

Gradually the government stripped the Jews of citizenship, seized their businesses, and barred them from jobs and education. Czernowitz was less affected by the decrees; Papa was still working, we still spent the summers in Milie, and, come September, Bubi and I returned to school.

In 1939, there was talk of war, but it was much too remote for me. I spent a lot of time at Ilse's, not only because our games were a lot of fun, but also because they had a radio. We enjoyed listening to music, regardless of its genre. But much of the music was replaced then by the aggressive speeches in the angry voice of Adolf Hitler. Although I did not understand their implications, they scared me.

Often the music was interrupted by shouts of: *Uwaga! Uwaga!* Papa told me it meant *Attention!* in Polish, a warning of an oncoming air raid in Poland.

I could feel the uneasiness in the air, and, watching Papa and Bubi anxiously pore over the newspapers; I grew more and more frightened. As I sought comfort, my father always reassured me: "Don't worry, everything is going to be fine."

But I was not so sure. The adults spoke of war but did not share the details with me. I sensed imminent danger lurking around the corner, threatening my happy childhood.

August 1939. The German and Soviet foreign ministers, von Ribbentrop, and Molotov, signed a pact that included the return of Bessarabia to Soviet sovereignty. A year later when the Soviets occupied these territories, they also claimed North Bukovina, including Czernowitz.

◆   ◆   ◆

June 1940. Romanians, ethnic Germans, and some Jews decided to leave before the arrival of the Soviets. It was a sad exodus driven by uncertainty and fear. I experienced the first pains of parting when my friend Ilse and her family said good-bye to us.

For us, children, conversion to the Soviet system was a welcome change. Gone were the private and segregated schools. Boys and girls mixed for the first time. There were no more separate religion classes for Jewish and Christian children, no more morning prayers in class. In its place came a daily dose of communist ideology: fraternity, equality, and liberty, regardless of religion or race. Justice for all fulfilled my childish optimism, but I couldn't erase my patriotism for Romania and my love for the king and the prince.

I was assigned to a new, school, slightly farther from my home. Mingling with children of all ages and being with my cousins and some of my friends who had gone to private schools before was especially exciting.

We were encouraged to become Pioneers, future communists, a privilege given only to top achievers. The school also provided social activities, unlike the Romanian schools. I had no problem mastering Russian in a short time and soon became a Pioneer. My loyalty to the Romanian monarchy, once expressed in patriotic songs and poems, was switched to Stalin and the Soviet regime. I proudly belonged to the elite of the school, although I did have a problem with one aspect of Soviet education: atheism. Having come from a religious home with a strong belief in God, I could not easily accept such a radical theory. I was not alone in that predicament.

One day our Russian teacher became exasperated with the class and exclaimed, "*Bozhe moy!*" ("My God!") I seized the opportunity to confront her.

"Comrade Teacher, excuse me!" I said sheepishly. "How come you just called on God, but you insist on teaching us that He does not exist?" Before she could answer, there was a collective murmur of approval from my classmates.

"Well, children, you have to understand that it is a habit, a matter of speech," she answered unconvincingly.

While the children liked the novelty of the Communist regime, our parents were worried, particularly since the economic situation was getting worse. There was no money and little food. The Communists started to limit the living quarters of each family, crowding several families into one apartment. Total strangers had to share kitchens and toilets; an inconceivable notion for my mother. One day we came face to face with this. The doorbell rang several times; Papa went to answer it. Several Russian-speaking officials told him they were bringing new tenants to share our apartment. Papa apparently did not understand what they meant, but let them in anyway. Mama, on the other hand, who spoke Ruthenian, similar to Russian, did understand and went berserk. She started screaming in German, "*R-a-a-a-us! R-a-a-a-us! R-a-a-a-us!*" ("O-o-o-ut! O-o-o-ut! O-o-o-ut!"). They ignored her and entered the living room. Mama planted herself on the sofa, teeth and fists clenched, eyelids shut, and kept screaming: "R-a-a-a-us, r-a-a-a-us!" I had never imagined my mother capable of such an outburst. We could not reason with her. She just kept repeating: "R-a-a-a-us! R-a-a-a-us!" I pleaded, crying, "Mama, please. I'm scared! Stop it!" But to no avail. She went on and on. It scared not only us but also the commissars; after a few more minutes of high drama, they left, threatening to return. It took Mama hours to calm down. We came to understand how strongly she felt about our home and to what extremes she would go to protect her territory.

◆　　　◆　　　◆

The German and Romanian Army, code named Barbarossa, launched a surprise offensive against the Soviet Union, attacking Bukovina and Bessarabia, heavily bombarding our town. My childhood came to an abrupt end on June 21, 1941, the first day of summer and my eleventh birthday. Instead of celebrating, I had to hide in a bomb shelter. Words like *camouflage*, *blackout*, *air raid*, and *all clear* began to enrich my vocabulary. When we heard the sirens, we put on gasmasks, ran to the poorly lit shelter, and sat on benches along the walls. I fought the mask mainly for fear of suffocating, but I had to comply.

With each explosion a shudder ran down my spine. I covered my ears, closed my eyes and clung to my father, who kept saying, "Everything is going to be fine."

The Romanian army advanced toward our town, leaving behind a trail of blood throughout the small towns and villages where they massacred Jews in the most barbarous ways. On July 1941 the Romanians and the German *Einsatzgruppen* marched into our town and the ethnic cleansing began.

I overheard snatches of conversation about more murders in the streets, labor camps for young men, and the relocation of the entire Jewish population of Bukovina and Bessarabia to Ukraine, where the Jews would be given some land to cultivate. That last rumor I did like. I tried to turn a deaf ear to the rumor that we would all be deported and killed.

October 11, 1941. The governor of Bukovina decreed the formation of a ghetto just a few blocks away from our street. Within twenty-four hours, fifty thousand people were sent to the ghetto with only what they could carry. The ghetto was surrounded by barbed wire, and armed soldiers guarded the gates day and night. An area that could hold ten thousand people now housed fifty thousand in addition to the Christian population that had already lived there. The authorities either enlarged or dismantled the Czernowitz ghetto, thus enabling us to return to our apartment to be shared with other families.

For a while life almost returned to normal. But 30,000 Jews from Czernowitz were deported before the transports were stopped. I learned many years later how things actually developed.

Dr. Traian Popovici, one of the few righteous Romanians, had the courage to speak out against evil. Popovici desperately appealed to the governor to dissolve the ghetto and stop the deportations, warning him about the paralysis the city would experience if professionals and those dedicated to culture and the arts were deported. After his intervention, joined by Jewish and Romanian personalities, as well as the clergy on a national level, Antonescu, Romania's dictator, exempted about twenty thousand Czernowitz Jews from deportation. The governor authorized the mayor, the German consul, and General Ionescu to screen who would stay and who would be deported, but reserved the right to sign all authorizations.

Popovici, a Righteous Gentile, personally signed four thousand authorizations for highly skilled Jews to remain in the city; they were called "The Traian Jews." Popovici personally brought the good news to the ghetto to bring a ray of hope. The screening committee ordered the leaders of the Jewish community to prepare the lists. Desperation led to bribery and corruption; money became more decisive than justice. The rich could buy their freedom. Thousands, including our close relatives, bribed corrupt Romanian officials. The Romanian *baksheesh* system was saving lives; the same process would have been inconceivable in Germany.

The hunt for Jews without authorizations began. Romanian soldiers raided the streets, herded the Jews into columns, and chased them toward the railroad station while looting the abandoned homes.

Although I had lost my sense of security, I still saw a sliver of good in all this upheaval, an adventure. I kept telling myself that it would be another train ride to the country in the company of my friends. I tried and sometimes succeeded in blocking out all the adult worries about hiding, escaping, and bribes to avoid deportation.

Sadly, we did not make Traian's List. My father was not indispensable and we did not have money for a bribe. This prompted fierce debates with our relatives. My mother was defiant: "They're playing tricks in order to take our money, but in the end they won't deport anybody." We remained in our apartment with everything packed into knapsacks and bundles: one per person, as ordered. Because I was small, Mama sewed a knapsack for me from an old brown dress. Chaos, panic and fear of the unknown were ripping apart my secure childhood. My family's misfortunes began to avalanche.

Deportation

November 1941. Zero hour struck! That morning soldiers pounded on *our* door, yelling and screaming obscenities. They ordered us out of the apartment onto the street. With knapsacks on our backs and some luggage in our hands, we left our home forever.

Terror-stricken, I silently watched the pandemonium in the once peaceful, familiar streets of my childhood. There was merciless shoving, swarming, panic and shouting; horses neighed and reared. We were surrounded by chaos: people of all ages and walks of life, women carrying wailing babies, sick people aided by children, the elderly with their backs bent under the weight of their packs. Others struggled with heavy bundles. Some pushed wheelbarrows with valuables and trinkets stuffed inside the bedding, weighed down by bundles of clothes hastily bound by rope.

For a fee, a few horse-driven carts would ferry luggage and passengers through that sea of anguish. My parents propped me atop a cart full of luggage. From there I could see the immense caravan; as I would later learn, some two thousand people. The cries of women and babies, and loud shouts of *Shemah Israel* (Hear, O Israel), I began to realize what was happening. To me it looked like a grotesque funeral cortege…our own. There were heartbreaking scenes of parting families, cries, wails and moans. The soldiers led the caravan to a railroad, different from the familiar main station.

A long train of about thirty cattle cars with open doors stood ready. The surrounding area overflowed with bayonet-wielding police and soldiers shouting:

"A year ago you welcomed the Russians! For this treachery, Transnistria will be your reward!"

At first I could not believe that these cars were for us. But there was no time to think. The soldiers screamed at us to get aboard. We did so, and filled one car: ten, twenty, thirty people…and more and more until there was no more room. It was so crowded that we were suffocating. There were close to eighty people packed in each wagon. I held on to Papa's hand silently; I wanted to cry and say something, but couldn't. I took a last glance at what used to be my beloved Czernowitz. After a few shrill whistles, the soldiers struggled to slide the heavy, wooden door shut and bolted it from the outside. We were trapped. I thought it was our end. We tried to settle as best as we could. Most people sat on the floor leaning against their bundles, while others remained standing, pressed against the locked doors, perhaps hoping to escape, should those be opened again. But it did not happen. Instead, there was a whistle, the smell of the engine, and the screech of metal against metal as the train lurched ahead toward the unknown.

◆   ◆   ◆

At last, we arrived. Up to this point, my brother was clutching his violin case in the hope of playing again, somehow, somewhere. To our great relief, the inspectors either didn't notice it at the checkpoint, or thought nothing of the violin. A few minutes into our march, one of the guards noticed the violin and kicked it out of Bubi's hand:

"Dirty kike, your yearning to play the violin will soon be gone!" he shouted. Bubi watched helplessly as his cherished instrument was defiled in the mud. I felt his humiliation and was choked up. I felt like screaming, but I had already learned to keep quiet and to hold back my tears for fear of being beaten or shot. I looked at my parents and saw the pain etched into their faces. I guessed their thoughts: Their gifted son who was to contribute to the world's culture, was forced to watch his violin brutally torn out of his life. Papa was only fifty-five, but he was suffering from a double hernia and could not walk far.

From the small reserves of money my parents had hidden, they paid for letting my father and me perch on a luggage cart where only small children, the old, and the infirm were allowed. To our guard Papa looked too young for such pampered treatment, so a short way into our journey he stopped our cart, hurling insults at Papa and ordering him to get off.

"What's the matter? You too lazy to walk? Get off, you dirty kike or I'll kill you!"

Papa begged him: "Please, Mr. Gendarme, I am old and sick, I can't walk much." That infuriated the Romanian Nazi even more. It was a miracle that he did not shoot him; instead, he hit Papa viciously over the head with his rifle. The blow sent Papa tumbling down from the cart, screaming in pain and bleeding from his temple.

Seeing the pain and degradation of my father made me tremble with rage. In tears, I climbed down from the cart and rushed to Papa's side, my fallen hero twisting in agony and humiliated—my pillar of strength destroyed before my eyes. With Mama and Bubi, we helped him to his feet. Without thinking of the consequences, and hoping for some kindness from this soldier, I begged him:

"Please, please, let my sick father ride on the cart, and I will walk instead."

"Shut up, you dirty seed of kikes. Get back on the cart or I'll kill you," he said, and drove the barrel of his rifle into my shoulder.

Defenseless, and in severe pain, I watched Papa gather his last ounce of strength and join the rest of the column in line with Mama and Bubi. Silently crying, I climbed back on the cart and kept looking back to see my family as they desperately tried to keep pace with the convoy.

How Papa did it, I will never know. I prayed that none of them would fall behind, convinced that I possessed a power to shield my loved ones as long as I kept my eyes fixed on them.

Under a barrage of humiliations and insults, this human caravan of all ages fought the mud, their hunger, thirst and their fear. With their heads bowed and their faces distorted by pain, they trudged behind the overloaded carts under the gray, unfriendly skies of that November day.

Following a catastrophic flood of the Dniester in the summer of 1941, the primitive dirt roads were extremely muddy. The heavy rains and the unusually early winter had made the mud deep and sticky. We passed through as many as ten villages.

Little by little our assets dwindled and so did our caravan. About two weeks after we left Czernowitz, we approached a town named Bershad.

Hell

Our thinning column barely dragged itself along toward Bershad, where we hoped to find some relief. But Bershad was not intended to be our last stop. We would have to walk for another forty kilometers, then cross the River Bug to be delivered to the German S.S. By then, everybody knew that the other side of the Bug was synonymous with death. But we heard that a bribe to the Romanian commander would allow us to stay. The bribe, in the form of jewelry and cash, was collected from our group and we were allowed to stay.

Following the transaction, the exhausted and emaciated people were herded into an area surrounded by barbed wire. This was the Bershad ghetto-camp. A primitive place, partially in ruins, yet it had some sense of normalcy compared to all the other places we had passed through. It is difficult to describe Bershad. My recollection of the place is vague, as hunger dulled my senses. I was too sick to roam around and see for myself, others said that it was a small area where the local Jews had lived before the war.

The camp consisted of about twelve narrow, unpaved streets, two wider main streets, and a few hundred tiny, low mud houses. Within its perimeter, some twenty thousand people had to find room—often just enough space to sit on the floor.

Bershad was the largest and the most infamous of more than a hundred Transnistrian camps. It soon became notorious for the worst conditions, for the greatest number of victims, and for having had, in the beginning, the most sadistic administrator, Florin Ghineraru. The Romanian Fascist government chose it as a site for mass murder. Many thousands had already been executed by the time the mass executions were halted in the fall. We learned, later, that after this change of policy, no new scheme was devised to provide housing or other accommodations for the tens of thousands who would be arriving. These new deportees were to be abandoned without any sustenance, to perish on their own.

Some of the local Jews fled with the Soviets before the town fell to the Nazis, but many of those who stayed were murdered, only a few families escaped the massacre. These Jews were allowed to stay in their homes inside the ghetto. But the majority of the Jewish homes were abandoned and in ruins from bombing and shelling. Normally a ghetto is a part of a town for a minority to live but have access to the outside. But the ghettos created by the Nazis in Transnistria, Poland, and Lithuania became concentration camps. Instead of barracks, the people stayed in overcrowded houses. We were imprisoned, surrounded, and watched over without even minimal provisions of food and water. We were expected to expire slowly and quietly, but our jailers still went on sporadic killing sprees, depending on who was in command.

As our caravan entered the narrow, snow-covered streets, everybody was trying to find shelter in the homes of the few local Jews. We also knocked on many doors. Curiously, I do not remember ever seeing a human face; all I recall is hearing the word *"Tief!"* meaning Typhus, from behind the locked doors. We soon got the impression that the local Jews were using this excuse to scare us away. That left my family no choice but to settle down in the rear room of a partially demolished house. Our rear room had already been turned into a shambles. Its back door and only window were missing, frames and all. A vacant crib stood in a corner of the room. My mother immediately claimed it. We took turns in squeezing ourselves into this crib, two, sometimes three at a time. That way at least some of us were protected from the ice-cold dirt floor on which the others slept sitting on blankets or some garments. But at least we were under a roof and protected by four walls, even if we had to share that space with twenty other people.

Even by the wildest stretch of imagination, it would be impossible to visualize the conditions. Twenty of us packed into a small room of a half-destroyed house with a leaky roof, without doors or windows, not to mention electricity, running water, and toilets; luxuries unknown to the locals. They did not even have outhouses; the back alleys were used instead. The fatigue from the two-week march, in addition to the freezing cold, was cause enough for despair, but the ferocious hunger was the worst. Papa, already a skeleton with a short, gray beard and deep, sunken eyes, became totally apathetic.

We were rooming with total strangers, except for the Sattinger family from Czernowitz. We learned to adapt to a situation where privacy and human dignity were forgotten.

In the beginning, people slept sitting, semi-reclining on their bundles, or leaning on each other. To stretch out was a luxury, allotted by turn, possible only after a corpse was taken out. The more corpses removed, the more space to stretch out.

Quietly, without any commotion, those around us died one by one. They were too feeble even to moan or complain. For days, the bodies would stay in the same room with us until picked up by the undertakers.

Every so often I would hear a bell. At first it reminded me of the joyous sounds of sleigh bells. I could daydream of gliding through Czernowitz on a sleigh with the bells of the horses cheerfully chiming. It was close to Christmas, but the bell was not a sound of joy. It was followed by a man shouting: *"A meth?"* (A corpse?) Someone would show where the corpse was. Two men would grab the body by the feet and arms, and drag it away. I still did not comprehend what was happening until one day I looked through the windowless window and froze in horror. In a wooden sleigh, with two high poles at each side to hold more bodies, lay naked skeletonlike corpses of men, women, and children, their limbs dangling between the poles. This macabre scene became a daily occurrence.

There seemed to be no escape from death. It was everywhere; we inhaled, smelled, and watched it all the time. These undertakers made their daily rounds, filling their sleigh. But as more people died, they stuck in the poles to hold more corpses and avoid multiple trips to the cemetery on the outskirts of town.

Later, they came only every few days due to growing demand and to the intense frost, which froze the soil, preventing the digging of graves. So they just piled up the corpses on the frozen soil without burying them at all.

◆   ◆   ◆

The terrible living conditions quickly led to infestation and disease. Weeks passed without a bath or a change of clothing. The outside temperature was below freezing and our shelter was not much warmer. Water was brought in from far away, which only the few healthy and fit could reach, leaving the majority without it. When there was no other water, we melted the snow and drank it. Water was so scarce that we preferred to boil and drink it rather than use it for washing. We only scrubbed our hands and faces with snow. Lice began to feast on us and typhus broke out at a frightening rate and became the number one killer, followed by starvation, dysentery, freezing, and sporadic executions.

My father was an easy target. He probably had no immune defenses because of his obsession with cleanliness and sterility. I never realized how sick he really was until one day I tried to shake him out of his apathy and make him talk to me.

"Papa, tell me everything is going to be fine," I begged. Through great effort, he managed to whisper,

"Yes, my Muttika, don't worry. All is going to be all right." I did not know that these would be his last words.

Papa and Bubi, who were both very sick by then, occupied the crib in the room, while Mama and I, the relatively healthy ones, slept on the floor. One morning in December, my brother called out from the crib in a frightened voice:

"Mama! Mama! I think—" I did not understand what his unfinished sentence meant. Only after Mama got up to look at Papa and turned to us in horror that it struck me like thunder. I felt I was choking as I approached the crib and saw my father's open, expressionless, blue eyes.

I got hysterical, and screamed, "Papa, Papa, answer me, please!" His serene face and slightly open mouth, as if smiling, gave me the impression that he was pretending not to hear my screams. I touched his face—it was ice cold. My screaming was in vain. He was dead. My god was dead! He died silently, unnoticed, extinguished like the flame of a candle with the expression of his goodness frozen forever on his face.

Without a word, Mama and Bubi pulled me away from the crib. Nobody stirred or showed any compassion, nobody offered a word of consolation or a hug, as if death was expected and was just a matter of one's turn. I continued screaming for some time, until numbness took over. An icy sensation crept into my whole being, and I could not cry.

Somebody closed Papa's eyelids without covering his body and put him on the floor with the other corpses. I stared at the lifeless body of my beloved father. Rebellion, anger, pain and fear—were slowly suppressed. I became emotionally numb; I was watching all the madness as if it did not concern me at all, as if it were a film from some other world, one I had no connection with. I could survive only by pretending it was an awful nightmare, disassociating myself from reality. As I learned not to speak, that very numbness protected me. Then as now, no words could do justice to the horror of what we witnessed.

The undertaker's bell took on another meaning for me; it was *my* father who would be dragged out like a log. Three days later, it did happen. Papa was gone forever, and along with him went a part of me.

As mortality was rising, the corpses were picked up less frequently. It was every few days, then weeks. One wall of the room became a makeshift morgue with corpses piled up from the entire house. The wait for the undertakers became almost an obsession for the living, who had to share the room with the dead. Nobody accompanied the bodies; nobody knew what happened to them once they were taken away. Few had the physical strength to follow the sleigh on foot to the outskirts of town. The undertakers were free to claw inside mouths, pull out gold caps, rip off clothes, and simply drop the corpses on the ground at the Jewish cemetery without digging graves in the frozen soil.

A few weeks later our overcrowded room of twenty held only six: the two Sattingers with their two-year-old girl and the three of us. While the Sattingers crouched in one corner of the room on the floor, we occupied the baby crib in the other corner, sitting up, our knees bent.

Although I do not recall all the conversations among the adults, I certainly do remember the exact dialogue between my mother and Mrs. Sattinger that started right after my father's death.

"Frau Sattinger, remember what I am telling you," my mother said.

"Everybody in this room will die except Ruthi and the two of you." She articulated this premonition with an air of authority. She knew. But how?

Mrs. Sattinger reprimanded her: "How dare you say such a thing, Frau Glasberg! Its a sin."

She tried to change the subject by engaging my sick brother in a conversation about the future. My mother insisted: *I* was to be the only survivor in our family.

She wanted to die in peace, assured that somebody would look after me, and that "somebody" was to be Mrs. Sattinger.

"Frau Sattinger, please promise to take care of Ruthi when she will be left alone."

"I am not going to promise anything because you are not a clairvoyant. And stop scaring your children"—said Mrs. Sattinger.

But Mama would not give up. I sat there listening, not believing, and hoping for her to be wrong. I was petrified; my starving, freezing, gaunt body intensified that fear. How could I survive? I could barely stand on my feet.

As Mama and Bubi were so desperately ill and I was unable to walk, we were totally dependent on the mercy of the Sattingers and the Menschels. Dr. Menschel's family lived in the front room, and, being a physician, he was given permission to go outside the ghetto and treat Ukrainian peasants, who paid him with groceries. We survived on the fringe benefits of his fees in the form of a once-a-day meal of salty water in which their potatoes had been boiled. We looked forward to that with great anticipation. It was a lucky person who accidentally fished out a fragment of a real potato.

This kind of nourishment could not keep the Sattingers' toddler alive for long. Soon the little girl died. Sick as she was, Mama, sharp and as resourceful as ever, seized that tragic moment to get assurance from the grieving mother.

"On the corpse of your dead child, you must swear to me that you will take care of Ruthi so that I may die in peace"—she insisted.

There was no answer. All night long Mrs. Sattinger clung to the dead child, and only in the morning, before she placed her on the floor, did she comply with my mother's request. Repeating Mama's words, she said in a solemn voice:

"On the corpse of my dead child, I promise to take care of Ruthi."

I was caught in a drama with increasingly bizarre twists. The house had three rooms: a well-preserved front room for the Menschel family, a small, middle room teeming with people, and ours—the worst. Because of its back entrance, our room also served as a makeshift morgue. Thus, the hideous corpses from the other rooms were brought into ours and piled up against the wall next to the door opening.

Bubi stopped to talk. He sat with hunched shoulders and head, his chin on his chest, his eyes partially covered by a fur hat that was too large by now and slipped over his forehead and eyes. I thought that he did it to avoid seeing all the suffering.

Mama sat motionless opposite Bubi but said that she could not see anything; she also claimed to be unable to move. She was fully alert and coherent but refused to take the potato liquid. She refused everything, including water. It was beyond my comprehension how she could become blind and paralyzed at the same time.

"Ruthi, check on Bubi!" Mama asked me.

"Why don't you look at him yourself?"—I replied.

"I can't see anything and I can't move," she said. Bubi was directly in her field of vision, yet she said she could not see him. That really intrigued me, but I obeyed and checked. Lifting the fur hat slightly, I could only see a pair of glazed eyes.

"Ruthi, how is he doing? Is he breathing?" Mama inquired.

"Yes, Mama, he's breathing. But he doesn't answer me," I reported.

"Give him the hot water with a spoon," she instructed me.

"You do it, Mama, please," I begged her.

"I can't. Don't you understand?" No, I did not really understand. I obeyed, but every time I tried to put a spoonful of water into Bubi's mouth, it came back out with froth. That infuriated me. I thought he was playing games with me. I was also angry with my mother for not doing things herself. I sat at the side of my brother watching his agony, not knowing that he was in a coma. As a child, I reacted with irritation, suspecting that everybody was playing games with me. I was trapped in the middle between my silent, non-responsive brother, and my "unseeing" paralyzed mother, while I could barely stand on my feet.

Weeks of starvation had sapped my strength, and the events of the past weeks must have also done something to my mind. I do not know what kind of chemical or electrical changes take place in the brain when a child is faced with such unspeakable trauma and loss, but changes surely do take place.

Nearly two weeks after my father's death, my brother, who had been motionless and silent for many days, suddenly screamed,

"Ruzena-a-a-a!!!"

This was his last word. I was shattered that of all the things he could have been dreaming about, it was our cow in Milie.

Many years later, I came to understand that in his tortured moments, and in a nearly comatose state, he had chosen to return to Milie and relive the joys of his earlier life. I hope he was transported there in spirit and died with happy memories.

After a few days the sinister bell was heard. *"Meth?"* Someone went out and flagged them down. They pulled out my Bubi with the other corpses.

"Who would be next?" I asked myself. Every day the death toll rose in the camp. In a matter of a month all that remained out of twenty people in our room were four survivors.

I did not know what was going on outside. Here and there I heard fragments of information about cruelties and killings, but they did not affect me; I saw the results of the "other method" and that was plenty. My world was confined to that morbid room, and I never ventured far for lack of physical strength. I hardly had enough energy to go out and take care of my bodily functions behind the house. There, men opened their trousers to urinate into the snow, while I squatted in the freezing cold.

After a while the Sattingers moved to better lodgings with a local Jewish family. Our neighbors in the adjoining room were sick and rarely appeared, so Mama and I remained alone in the morgue-like room with the corpses. Outside the wind was howling, blowing the cold air through the missing window and door.

The snow was piled up to the window. Inside, there were just the two of us…and corpses. There was no food, no heat, and no hope. I clung to my mother in despair, hoping for a word of encouragement. Mama began to prepare me for being left alone.

"Ruthika," she said, "you have to understand that having lost Bubi—my only hope and purpose in life—I can't continue. You are the only one who will survive." Then she began preaching sermons about life and values.

"People are kind and will take care of you. Be good, obedient, honest and well-behaved and everything will be fine. One day you will return home where your aunts and uncles will watch out for you. You will be Aunt Anna's child. And remember, all our assets are at Aunt Cilli's. That will help you to survive until you grow up."

Such talk frightened me, and I begged her to stop it.

"Mama, Mama, please don't leave me alone," I repeated over and over again. For two weeks my mother talked to me about nothing else but her imminent death and my future thereafter. I rebelled and tried to persuade her to make an effort for my sake. But she only replied that when a mother loses a son, there is no reason to live. The implication that I was not worth living for hurt me deeply. What she did not say was how desperately ill she was. But at least she talked and that was a small consolation, the only straw I clung to in order not to drown in anguish and sorrow.

Each day I begged her not to die and leave me alone, but she continued talking about her death until one day she could talk no more. I realized at that point that all my efforts were in vain. Yet I redoubled my efforts to keep her from dying. I stayed awake day and night for two weeks, shaking her periodically and calling.

"Mama! Mama!" to which she responded with a faint,

"Hmm, hmm." It sounded as if she was in another world, but it was the only sign that she was still alive—the last ray of hope I clung to. Gradually, my stamina began to fade. Stubbornly, I suppressed my need to sleep for two whole weeks for the sole purpose of keeping my mother alive. To block the unspeakable, I closed my eyes for short periods and imagined myself back in the tranquil surroundings of Milie. The cold, dark, and desolate room seemed to be closing in on my dying mother and me. I thought it was the end of us, when some people from the middle room took pity and moved us in with them, crib and all. They helped put Mama flat on her back with knees bent to fit her into the crib, and I continued my vigil from a sitting position near her head.

"Mama! Mama!" I called out, remembering my vigil.

"Hm, hm," was all she could murmur. On the fourteenth sleepless night, my willpower was crushed and I fell asleep. But the obsession with my vigil crept even into my dreams. Startled out of my sleep, I woke up and shook her calling out:

"Mama! Mama!"

Silence.

I shook her some more, but she did not respond with her usual faint "Hm, hm." She chose to die when I stopped for a while to call her and keep her from dying in peace. She took advantage of the silence to slip away from that mad world.

I touched her ice-cold face and screamed:

"Help! Help! Please, somebody help me!"—There was no answer. Death was so common that it evoked no emotion anymore. People had grown numb, and I must have grown numb as well. But now I became like a wounded animal. I yelled at my dead mother:

"How could you leave me alone in this crazy place?" Then I cried out,

"Dr. Menschel! Dr. Menschel!" Through the closed door, came his muffled response:

"It's too late now. There's nothing I can do." The doctor did not even bother to come and take a look. Nobody cared; their souls were dead after all they had witnessed. Everyone was waiting for his turn. I sat clinging to my mother's cold body, screaming at the top of my lungs, hoping that somehow she could be revived. Doing so I felt that I was still not totally left alone. I had lost all sense of reason. Later, the people who shared the room with us, came to our crib, took a good look at her, and with that typical expression of resignation and helplessness in their faces, confirmed her death.

As I clung to my mother's body, conflicting thoughts raced through my mind: I could not let go, while I also wanted to flee from her cold, lifeless body.

I cannot recall who finally took Mama into the morgue. As she was placed with the other corpses, I did not shed a tear, though inside me reigned a hideous turmoil. *Was Mama right in her predictions about my survival? Why wasn't I the one to die from hunger and cold?* The lifeless body of my mother lay on the dirt floor, a bundle of bones held together by her transparent skin. I hoped that the gravediggers would pick her up soon. I was bewildered by the senselessness of it all and amazed at my own survival against all odds.

To my great surprise, Mrs. Sattinger kept her vow to my mother; three days later, she and her husband showed up. They told me that there was not much they could do except take me to some women from our hometown, who were willing to give me shelter and some nourishment in exchange for items stuffed in my bundle.

In my present frame of mind, I could not have cared less what they wanted.

◆   ◆   ◆

In spite of the improved lodgings, my thoughts were constantly with my mother's abandoned body, which I knew had not yet been taken away. I was very weak, but I did venture out every day to see her. It was so cold that I could see the white clouds of my breath. Alone in my grief, I went back to the gutted house; some force drew me to my dead mother. I understood she was dead, I saw that she was dead, yet I could not let go. I still wanted to see her. I could not find peace of mind until she was taken away and, I hoped, properly buried.

By that time I understood what should be done with the deceased. The pain almost totally consumed me. It now seems impossible to imagine the grotesqueness: a bald, emaciated eleven-year-old girl, in the bitter cold, standing alone in deep snow outside that makeshift morgue for hours, staring at the dead body of her mother through an opening that used to be a window.

Something eerie baffled my already bewildered mind. Every day I found her body in a different part of the room. It gave me the shivers. I could not understand what was happening. If she was dead, why wasn't she in the same place all the time? In my childish fantasy I had invented a multitude of explanations—from the ridiculous to the most macabre.

I asked my "foster parents" about it. They explained to me that aside from the hungry people, there were plenty of hungry dogs around that helped themselves to abandoned corpses. That unraveled the mystery! Horrors of all horrors! My mother was being dragged around and perhaps even eaten piece by piece by ravenous dogs!

How could I prevent it? Why hadn't the undertakers picked her up? From then on I began to crusade for my mother's burial. Each time I visited my mother's corpse, I would follow the gravediggers, trying to run after the overfilled sleigh, begging the men to collect my mother's body. I could barely walk, yet my desperation somehow made me run. I was out of my mind, obsessed by the thought that they would never get there. They were making up to fifty trips a day to the cemetery with full loads, and every time I caught up with them, they either had no time or no space for her.

For two long and painful weeks I went back and forth to see Mama. I looked into her lifeless face, afraid to enter the room or to get near her. Every day I stood in front of that window space for hours until I almost turned to ice. Only then did I leave with a heavy heart, fearing that in my absence the dogs would devour her. I knew I had to persuade the diggers to pick her up, but who would listen to me, a "skeleton-child"? Perhaps they expected a bribe to collect her corpse, but I had nothing.

On the fourteenth day, I set out to see her as usual. At last, she was gone. I felt a mixed sense of relief and sadness. I felt like a stab in my heart when I realized that it was final, and now I was really and truly alone. I was no one's child anymore. There was no one to love me unconditionally anymore, no one to care about me.

An ice-cold sensation settled in my heart. With my head bent and with frozen tears on my cheeks, I walked back to my foster home.

January 27, 1942. At age eleven, I was left alone in the world.

Epilogue: Ruth's survival is described in her book: Ruth's Journey—A Survivor's Memoir. Following her liberation, she returned to Romania, from where she joined a Zionist group to go to Israel. After much struggle, she became a nurse, married a Colombian businessman with whom she had two children, Michael and Liana. Ruth lives in Miami, her children are grown; Michael is a physician and Liana is a nurse practitioner. Ruth's great delight is to spend time with her two small grandchildren. Ruth's autobiography has been translated into Hebrew and Romanian. A new edition of her book, "Lost Yesterdays," is scheduled for publication by YoNa Books in November 2003. "Ruth's Journey" is out of print.

My dream in Hassag

✦

Tova Goldszer

1. Before the War

My name now is Tova Josefzohn, but it was Guta when I was born in Poland on September 20, 1928.

My mother passed away a week after my birth and my father was left all alone to raise three daughters—12-year old Jadzia, 10-year old Rachela, and a newborn. Brokenhearted, father could not find the strength to care for us. The family pitched in and took turns helping us. After the first year, my father married Sara Levin, who soon assumed the role of wife and mother.

I have fond and loving memories of Sara from the time I was a tot. No one had ever told me that she was not my biological mother. She has always been my mom.

In 1934, my father fell ill. He could not work and the medical bills began to pile up. My sisters were already in high school and I was attending the first year of a public school for Jewish kids.

One morning in February of 1935 I was awakened by screams of sorrow. My mom was crying. I remember that I was very afraid; and my sister took me to a neighbor's house. The following day I was told that Dad had died and gone to heaven.

Because I was so scared, I stayed with the neighbors for several days. I do not know which was worse, the fear of death or the fear of dying. I could not understand why we die and how we get to heaven. There was no one who could explain these to me.

At home, the sadness was overwhelming. A procession of friends and relatives was coming to visit. Candles were lit and prayers were said for my Dad's soul twice a day.

Mother cried a lot during the days of Shiva, the seven-day mourning period. After the Shiva, my sisters and I went back to school. Mom was struggling with financial problems. All the money was spent on father's medical bills. There were no more maids around the house—mother had to do everything, but she never complained.

My sister Jadzia met Adek Brzoza and they were soon married at the Nozyk temple in Warsaw in February 1938.

The situation in Poland got tense with rumors of war. In August of 1939, German propaganda was preparing the public for a war against Poland. War preparations were intense in the schools.—Jadzia and Adek fled to Russia.

At 5:45 in the morning of September 1, 1939, German troops entered Poland, bombed our airports, destroying almost all Polish aircraft.

The Germans only met resistance at the Modlin fortress in Warsaw. Surrounded by artillery and bombed, Warsaw surrendered on September 26.

2. The War

The persecution against Jews became vigorous and gruesome. The Nazis drastically curtailed our freedom. Jewish schools were closed; Jews were not allowed in parks and were forced to wear armbands with the Star of David.

One day, after mom had waited in line for hours for a piece of bread, she came home empty-handed and worn out. She was so depleted that she just died right in front of me. I was alone with her and sat there, crying, until my sister arrived. She called the "funeral home" and a man showed up with a wheelbarrow to transport her body for burial—God knows where he took her.

The ghetto was closed in November 1941. Jews from neighboring cities were all sent to the Warsaw Ghetto. Posters warned that Jews faced the death penalty if they left the ghetto. A census showed 433,000 Jews—men, women, and children—packed in the small ghetto.

Systematic starvation was the first weapon of mass extermination. Lack of hygiene and the consequent spread of contagious diseases killed hundreds of people every day.

The German terror discouraged any attempt of organized resistance. They also formed the *Judenrat (Jewish Council)* with the purpose to control the population of the ghetto. The Jewish police provided the Germans with work groups and chose people to fill the quotas for deportation to extermination camps.

Adam Czerniaków, the president of the *Judenrat*, committed suicide in his office on July 24, 1942. He could not stand to collaborate with the killers of his people. His death forced the Jews to face the tragic reality: the Germans aimed to isolate and spiritually destroy all Jews. Their plan was total annihilation in the ghetto and in the extermination camps. There were rumors circulating in Warsaw about a "death factory."—The Jews began to refuse to show up for transfer.

One day, while crossing the street on my way to work, a policeman grabbed me by the arm and forced me into a horse-drawn trolley, the means of transport to *Umschlagplatz* and to Treblinka. The trolley was filled with men, women, and children. I stood on a step and the policeman held on to my hand so I would not escape. Suddenly I bit his hand and he gave me a shove. I fell off the step, got up and started running as fast as I could. I hid in a building on Nalefki Street that had a passage to Ciepta Street. He couldn't find me. Miraculously, I got away that time.

3. Life in the Ghetto

My sister Rachela came up with the idea to join a cleaning crew in the ghetto that returned to Prosta Street every day after they had cleaned the apartments of Jews deported to death camps. Rachela wanted us to work in a uniform factory, and we pretended that we were part of the cleaning crew.

Even though we worried that someone would discover us, we joined that crew and began to walk toward our unknown destiny. We arrived at the uniform factory in the afternoon. At the gate I got separated from my sister and went to look for her. A German crossed my path and asked,

"Where are you going?"—I was frozen with fear, stared at him but could not answer.

He yelled again: "Do you work here?"

"Yes,"—I managed to answer, shaking.

"What can you do?"

"Sew buttons."

"Excellent!"—he seemed pleased, and then added.

"Come to see me tomorrow morning on the second floor!"

I woke up very early the following day, took a bath, washed my hair, cleaned my only pair of shoes and went to see him. I was so afraid that I could hear my heartbeat and felt sweat running down my face. Then the German arrived and took me to a large room, where men and women were sewing buttons on uniforms. He told a supervisor to give me some work and said that I would get a card to receive food. Tearfully I managed to whisper *"Danke Shein."*

I began to sew buttons. The same afternoon I met my sister Rachela and my mom's brother, David Sztajner with his wife and two children, Eva and Ala. He took us to live with them. We were all working from 7 am to 7 pm for many weeks until one morning the loudspeakers blasted:

"*Alle yuden raus!!! Alle Juden raus!!*"—(All Jews outside!)

My uncle, his wife and Ala went down. Eva had a broken foot and stayed in bed. Rachela found a ladder and hid me and an elderly neighbor in a tall bathroom closet that covered a whole wall. Rachela hid the ladder in another apartment and ran downstairs.

I don't know how long we were hiding in that bathroom closet. The German soldiers passed through several times, looking for people. I heard a shot and wanted to get out. The lady whispered in my ear:

"Don't get out or they will kill you."—Was she my guardian angel? I don't even know her name…

In the afternoon my uncle and Ala returned without my aunt and Rachela, who were taken by the Germans along with others. Eva was shot in the head. Uncle David cried all night long. The following morning he went to *Umchlagplatz*, and asked to be reunited with his wife.—They were sent to Treblinka…

Several days later Rachela showed up at the factory, frail and weak. She jumped off the train to Treblinka and hid in a Catholic cemetery for several days until she was able to return to the ghetto.

4. Time to Fight

The first grim reports of the mass extermination of Jews in the death camps were arriving via Polish messengers. The effect was the dramatic unification of the Jewish fighters.

On Erev Pesach, Monday, April 19, 1943, General Himmler ordered the acceleration of the destruction of the Warsaw Ghetto. The gates were opened on Stafki and Nalefki Streets during the night and the SS troops, under the command of General Stroop, were ready to take the last Jews left in the Ghetto. The troops were 'welcomed' by heavy gunfire from the roofs. Some German soldiers fell dead or wounded; the others ran from the Ghetto in panic.

Only in the afternoon, reinforced by artillery and tanks, the Nazis began to bomb every block, every house, leaving behind rubble. Lufthansa planes dropped incendiary bombs, transforming the Ghetto into a sea of fire.

The struggle continued in the sewers and shelters, with men, women and children crammed together, suffocating and hungry, but resisting bravely. The Jewish fighters, dressed in German uniforms, ventured out at night to bring back weapons and food. General Stroop expected the destruction of the Ghetto in three days, but it took 42 days.

In all history few battles are comparable to the incredibly unmatched forces fighting in the Warsaw Ghetto. The last dwellers of the Ghetto, disheveled, exhausted, and debilitated, were able to hold the German Army at bay for forty-two days.—A glorious page in our history!

We received the news promptly about something strange taking place in the Great Ghetto. From the roof, we could see the sky blackened by smoke and fire, and hear the bombs and gunfire. But we did not know that the commotion was an uprising led by Mordechai Anielevicz. They did not fight for themselves, as they knew they had no chance of winning. They fought to show the world that the blood of the Maccabees was still running in their veins—defying death and sacrificing their own lives to save the honor and dignity of our people.

5. To an Unknown Destination

On April 29, 1943, SS troops entered the uniform factory and told everybody to leave quickly and line up. The loudspeakers blasted warnings: Anyone who tried to hide or escape would be shot. In 25 minutes, hundreds of men, women, and children started to march, followed by SS troops, towards the unknown.

We passed by the large ghetto at Mila, Nalefki and Zamenchofa Streets. All we saw were ruins, smoke coming out of buildings and several bodies along the way, burnt beyond recognition. We finally arrived at the *"Umschlagplatz"*—a building that had been a vocational school before the war and became a part of hell. The stairs were covered with blood. SS soldiers holding bayonets hit us and yelled "Run, run faster!" Suddenly, a soldier grabbed an elderly man by the arm, opened the third-floor window and told him to jump. The man stood on the windowsill, paralyzed. The soldier pushed him out. I closed my eyes and ran to the other side of the room, where hundreds of starving people were piled up—denied water, thrown on the floor like human rags. I don't remember how long we had to wait; it seemed like an eternity.

The death commandos, with their black uniforms and the skull and bones symbols sewn on their caps, were frightening. They spoke Ukranian and Lithuanian, and ceaselessly hit and shot people. The nights were dreadful. I was too scared to get up and use the bathroom. One morning they started pushing people down the stairway. The screams and cries of the children were horrifying. There we were, without any food, shadows of human beings, walking skeletons. Those of us who could not climb down the stairs were executed.

I ran down in despair and was pushed into a cargo train with many other people. I tried to stay close to a window so I could breathe. It took a while to load the train with its human cargo. Then we heard a loud whistle and the train began to move.

I don't recall how long we traveled on that train. I know that night fell and I slept. Sometimes I woke up to the cries of children, but fatigue would overcome me and I would fall asleep again.

I woke up when the doors opened to an awful sight: a half-dead column of people marching away to Majdanek; ghastly witnesses of the atrocities committed against them.

We walked for several hours, followed by female SS soldiers with machine guns and ferocious dogs. Worn-out, hungry and weakened, at last we arrived at the Majdanek Camp.

An electrified fence surrounded the camp. The guards, perched atop high towers, had powerful searchlights and machine guns.

A guard opened the gate and we entered the camp, walking toward a huge shed. There were several benches inside. We were told to leave our clothes and jewelry on top of the benches. Everything was very organized. Minutes later, we entered the bathroom. I thought that was the end. I thought about my parents, my mind was in turmoil, my lips were dry from thirst. All of a sudden, water began to pour from the showerheads. It was water, not gas! I cried and laughed at the same time. My tears were washed down by the shower and left a sour taste in my mouth.

Moments later the doors of the bathroom opened and we entered another room, filled with clothes. Several SS women distributed pieces of clothing for us to wear. I got a long, black dress, a blue short-sleeve wool sweater and wooden clogs.

Then we went to a huge patio, in rows of five. It was a beautiful day, the sun was shining, but the wind was so cold that my body, still quite wet, started shivering. It was May 3, 1943, Polish Constitution Day—what an irony…

The SS women, with whistles and whips, told the Jewish women to leave the shed and stand in line. We moved like cattle, quick and organized. Then German soldiers began to count us to make sure nobody had escaped. Among the hundreds of women I spotted my sister Rachela, but I was too scared to leave my place in line. Finally, they finished the count and we all ran to barrels filled with boiled potatoes with their skins. I was dizzy with hunger and thirst, and used the last bit of my strength to reach the barrels. Then my sister approached me with potatoes in her hands and gave me some. I hugged her tight and started to cry. I was happy! I had found her and felt relieved for not being alone anymore.

We heard a whistle and the SS women told us to stand in line again for the assignment of chores.

I was standing there when Brigida, a German woman, pushed me toward a tank full of manure that was to be taken to the fields. Six of us pushed the tank, fertilizing the soil. We spent several hours working on it and came back to the camp tired, dirty and hungry. We received bread with margarine and got into the shed. I lay in bed—a straw mat—fully dressed.

It was almost morning when I woke up with the SS women shouting, *"Raus!"* ("Out!") I jumped out of bed and ran to the patio. Light rain was falling and it was very cold. We stood in the rain until they told us to run to the potato barrels, which were also drenched by the rain. I was nauseated, but my lips were shivering from hunger and cold. I needed to eat something, and there were only potatoes. I pushed some people and managed to get to the barrels to grab some. I was eating quickly when they told us to leave for work. Once more we went to work in the fields to fertilize the soil.

The days and weeks went by slowly, the routine was the same. One day, my sister Rachela met Mrs. Gaal, the mother of one of Rachela's school friends. She worked at the hospital—only for Christians—and was called the "Angel of Majdanek." She was Jewish with false documents.

Mrs. Gaal told Rachela about a transport leaving for a work camp, but she did not know where it was going. She just said:

"Go, and tell all your friends and relatives, because nobody will leave this place alive."

Later, several women ran toward a building to enlist for the transport and we followed them. It was a huge building with about 20 Germans seated behind many tables, selecting women who were parading nude in front of them. I saw my sister from a distance and was scared to think that I might not pass the selection process. A cold shudder went through my body—I did not want to die! I kept walking, like a robot, until I stopped in front of a German soldier who asked me how old I was. I lied: "Sixteen and a half "—I was just shy of fifteen. He pushed me toward an exit, where hundreds of people were walking to another building. I followed them without any notion of where I was going until I got inside and saw Rachela. She ran to me with tears in her eyes—she thought I had not been chosen. Five hundred women were chosen to board the salvation train.

6. Train to Salvation

At the train we received a piece of bread with margarine. We boarded the train like cattle and were thrown on the floor. The doors closed and the train started to roll. Once more, we were propelled toward the unknown.

My body ached, I was thirsty and nauseous. I closed my eyes and fell asleep on my sister's lap. I woke up when the train stopped. Through a little window I saw a sign with the town's name: Skarzysko Camienna. The train rolled on for a few minutes and then stopped. The doors opened and we were ordered to get out.

Several armed soldiers accompanied us to the Hassag ammunition factory. It was a huge building with horribly noisy machines. Suddenly, the machines stopped. It was the 20-minute break for breakfast. We received a piece of bread with marmalade and black coffee.

The supervisor spoke for a few minutes. The work schedule was from 7 am to 7 pm, in two shifts. No talking during work. Any attempt to escape meant execution.

Janek, a young Polish man, told me to follow him to his work area. There were 16 machines called Real Machinen. We were quickly told how to control the quality of the bullets. I was happy with my work and time passed quickly as the machines were running.

They distributed a watery beet soup at 7 in the evening. The beets were as hard as shoe soles, but I was so hungry that I had no choice but eat them. The night-shift people arrived and we were taken to the barracks. I fell on the bed with my clothes on; my body ached from head to toe. I stretched out on the hard mattress and fell asleep.

I woke up at sunrise, cold and hungry. I jumped out of bed, washed my face and tried to comb my hair with my fingers—I had neither a comb nor a toothbrush, and only one change of clothes to wear. I thought it was better that I did not have a mirror. I left for work running.

For two days, I could not find Rachela. On Sunday, I met her at the patio. She was working as a nurse and sleeping at the infirmary. She was all right.

Days and weeks passed with the same routine. Winter came and with it, snow. I wore my open-toed wooden clogs without socks. Many times, lying in bed, I would ask God to give me the strength to endure it all. One evening I arrived at work with a headache. Janek gave me some medicine and I went to the bathroom to wash my face. I sat on the toilet and sleep came over me. I do not know for how long I slept, but I was awakened by bangs on the door. A German woman pulled me out of the bathroom and pushed me into a small room. She told me to lie on the floor while she took a whip from the wall. I closed my eyes and covered my mouth not to scream. I still remember the first lashes. When she finished, I could not get up. They threw water on my head and I opened my eyes. I tried, but could not stand up. I do not remember how I got back to the barracks. Someone told me to lie on my belly and applied cold compresses to my back. I slept for a few hours and woke up feeling better.

I tried to get up, but my legs were still weak and my head was swimming. I did not want to stay alone in the barracks, I was afraid they would kill me. With a lot of difficulty I went to the infirmary where my sister was working and asked for her. Dr. Zaks gave me some anesthetic cream. I went back to the barracks when it was time to go to work.

For the next several weeks I thought about what had happened and wanted to write about it, write a song or something like that. As I was working the night shift, I wrote during the day, at the barracks. The result was this song:

My dream in Hassag

It happened once during a nightshift spell
Quite by surprise my heart began to swell
If I was asleep I cannot tell
I was strangely relaxed, I felt so well,

In my dream that occurred
I was not in Hell
I was not in camp für Juden
Nor in a cell

It was Eden itself, all honey and sweet
No watery soup no bread, breaking teeth.
I was clad in fashion, head to feet.
Thick warm soup with noodles and meat.

And "Hassag" our prison was fully in bloom
With lilacs and roses filling each room

Wine of all kinds washed out the gloom,
Humor and laughter, like Eden, I assume…

Until suddenly I am shoved back to my rut
The boss awakes me with a punch in my gut
Fire in her eyes, she took me to a hut
She ordered me whipped square on my butt.

And "Hassag" our prison was fully in bloom
With lilacs and roses filling each room
Wine of all kinds washed out the gloom,
Humor and laughter, like Eden, I assume…

The song *My dream in Hassag* was a huge success and quickly spread throughout the camp. Everybody would sing it—in the barracks, at work, in the bathrooms. I can say that the song saved my life. During breakfast, I received an extra piece of bread and, in the evening, an extra spoonful of soup. The following day, a German soldier gave me a ham sandwich. I started to feel safer and had a greater will to live. Months went by. We heard rumors of being transferred to another camp. It was the end of Spring in 1944. The trees were in bloom and the sun was shining against the blue sky. The world seemed wonderful.

The Germans gathered everybody on the patio and told us that we would be transferred to another camp the following day. Janek, who worked with me, ran to tell us what he had heard on the radio that he was hiding:

"The Germans are losing the War!"

He asked whether I wanted to go to his house and hide in the basement. I answered no, because I was Jewish and had a sister whom I did not want to abandon. Janek came closer and hugged me goodbye. He said,

"Who knows, maybe we will meet again one day…"

"Who knows…maybe…"—I answered.

The following day, we got up very early and stood in line at the patio. The Germans followed us to the train station. The embarkation took several hours, because there were so many of us. Suddenly someone called my name: "Gutka, Gutka!"

I stood up and waved. A tall man approached the train and threw me a loaf of bread, saying:

"I loved your song, God bless you!"—I never learned who he was.

We heard a whistle and the train began to roll, once again toward the unknown. We were thrown in the cargo cars like cattle. However, I was not sad. I remembered what Janek said:

"The Germans are losing the war!"—It was probably true. Joy came over me and I started singing my song. Everyone on the train sang along. Then we shared the bread; others shared some potatoes, and a young woman who had worked in the kitchen shared some soup that she managed to take with her.

I had not felt so happy and hopeful in a long time. I could only think about Janek's words—"The Germans are losing the war!"

I wanted to scream, but clenched my teeth, closed my eyes and fell asleep. I woke up with the sun shining. I tried to look out of the window, but could not see anything. The train was slowing and then it stopped. The armed Germans got down from the train's roof to take us to an ammunition plant similar to the previous one. The patio was smaller, surrounded by barbed wire, with high towers manned by guards armed with machine guns.

We stopped in front of the plant and a tall German soldier, Batenszleiger, interrogated every one of the new arrivals. When it was my turn, he asked me if I knew how to peel potatoes and I answered that I did. I was sent to the kitchen. I was hungry and thirsty. The kitchen supervisor placed a huge bowl of potatoes in front of me and told me to peel them. The smell of food made me dizzy. I asked the supervisor for a glass of water, which I quickly drank. I also sprinkled my face with some of it. This was my first day at the Warta camp, in Czenstochowa. At night, we received potato soup and a piece of bread, which I saved for the following day. Days and weeks went by quickly. I continued working in the kitchen and was happy. I always got some extra soup and potatoes, which I took to the barracks to share with Rachela.

One night, the Allies' planes came at short intervals, bombing and destroying what was still left. Nevertheless, the concentration camp kept working normally—with its fences, towers, and guards with their machineguns. A few days later, Wehrmacht soldiers entered amidst turmoil and the guards disappeared from the towers.

The Red Army was approaching the city. On January 14, 1945, a Russian tank tore down the gate of the concentration camp and several soldiers jumped out, yelling,

"You are free, you may come out!"

For a few minutes, no one moved. I held on to Rachela and cried tears of happiness.

7. Freedom

Night fell and Rachela would not go out with me in the dark. We decided to stay. In the morning, we left without any direction, looking for shelter. It was snowing and we were cold and hungry. I spotted an abandoned military coat on the floor and picked it up. It was long and big, but I wore it because it was very warm.

We walked for several hours until we arrived at Warszawski Street. We stopped at a building and asked whether there were any empty rooms? An armed Russian guard let us go inside to look. The fleeing German army abandoned the building. We found a small room with beds, chairs, and a writing desk. We opened the desk drawer and found some money that was probably German. Rachela grabbed the money and put it in her pocket.

We were both worn out and promptly fell asleep on the beds. The following morning we woke up to a sunny day and went out. A lot of people were wandering the streets aimlessly, like us. We met reporters and war correspondents, and some soldiers of the Jewish Brigade who took us to a makeshift hospital, where food was distributed.

The future in Eastern Europe after liberation from the Nazis appeared gloomy. The only way out for us, survivors, was to go to Eretz Yisrael. The first Israeli representatives arrived in October 1945 to establish escape organizations and start the flow of survivors across the Czechoslovakian border. This was the first organization for illegal immigration, the *Mossad Alia Bet.*

I joined a group of young survivors who were anxious to leave Poland and go to Eretz Yisrael. Motek was our supervisor, who taught us Hebrew, sang songs, and talked about the importance for the Jews to have a country.

We were getting ready to cross the border early in 1946. We had fake documents stating that we were returning to Greece. We learned a few words of Greek, like *"Kalimera!" (Good day!)* and *"Kalinista!" (Good night!)* and were forbidden to speak Polish. There were about 50 people in our group.

We rode in cargo trucks to Prague. We stopped at the train station. Each of us had to buy a ticket. I stood in line, shaking with fear. When it was my turn, I showed the fake document and spoke some Greek: "Saloniki". The agent gave me the ticket and I felt like jumping for joy.

At that moment, a man arrived, speaking Greek. Obviously I did not understand a word he was saying. A Russian police officer wanted to know what was going on, but our group was already embarking. I grabbed my ticket, showed it to the police officer and yelled: "Greek, kalimera, kalinista!" and ran to catch the train!

We arrived at the German border that night where a man was waiting for us at the station. He told us to walk single file, in silence. We walked for hours until we arrived at a small village where a truck was waiting for us. It was morning when we arrived at Degendorf, where there was a refugee camp. We got a change of clothes, towels, coffee, bread, jelly and some American chocolate. After coffee, we were assigned to our rooms with bunk beds, pillows and blankets. There were even hot showers. After five years in hell this was the first time that we were treated as humans. We received a lot of help while staying at the refugee camp for several months.

Only a portion of the credit should be assigned to Jewish influence. Most of the credit is due to American religious and political traditions, which portrayed the migration of surviving Jews to Israel as a fair and natural movement.

In September we left for Marseilles to await the ship that would take us to Eretz Yisrael. We were quartered in a huge house that looked like a castle, surrounded by trees and a waterfall. A supervisor explained that they did not know how long we would have to wait for the ship, and the other people already there had arrived a month earlier.

The following morning, I woke up to a beautiful day. I got dressed and went out to the garden. Several people were setting long tables for breakfast. I did not know anyone but I was sure that those people were part of the group that arrived before us. Opposite to me at the table sat a tall, blond, blue-eyed young man, who stared at me incessantly. I wanted to talk to him, but did not say a word. When I got up, he followed me and started a conversation. We strolled in the garden for several hours, chatting. I felt as if I had known him for a long time. From that day on we became inseparable. It was love at first sight. The days and weeks passed by quickly. I was happy with Paulo and sure that, for the first time in my life, I was in love.

8. Voyage to Israel

Our entire group of about 250 embarked on the *Latrun* in November, 1946. The ship was anchored at a deserted beach. The embarkation took several hours. All of us got into bunk beds; a South American flag was raised and heavy curtains covered the ship. It was already dark by the time the ship left the beach.

I fell into a heavy sleep that night. The following day volunteers were distributing bread with Toddy that we could not drink because the water tanks were not washed properly and salt water was left inside. I got out of bed but could not stand up. My head was spinning, I felt nauseous and did not know what to do. I spotted Paulo, who was looking for me. He did notice that I was not well and brought me a bottle of water that I drank to the last drop.

It took us 14 days to reach Israeli territorial waters. Two British cruisers were trailing us and, through loudspeakers, asking questions. Our ship kept going until the cruisers hit her bow, opening a crack and water began to pour in. There was no alternative but to surrender. The supervisors opened the curtains, took down the South American flags and raised the flag of Israel. We sang the *Hatikva*—Hope. It was November 25, the anniversary of the Balfour Declaration.

The British towed our ship to the port of Haifa. From the distance, hundreds of people were shouting slogans against the British government.

When the soldiers boarded the ship to start the disembarkation, our young men jumped on them, hitting them and screaming. The soldiers threw tear gas bombs at us. I fainted and fell to the floor. I woke up in a hospital bed in the British ship that would take us to Cyprus. An English doctor took care of me. He was Jewish and could speak Yiddish. He asked how we mustered courage to travel on a ship like that, as he would not even transport cattle in that. I told him that we had nothing to lose and began to cry. He gave me an injection; asked someone to bring me some soup and promised to come back later. I fell asleep and only woke up as we were arriving in Cyprus.

The huge area, surrounded by barbed wire and towers manned by British soldiers reminded me of the concentration camp.

Despite the difficulties, illegal immigration had been successful since the end of the war. More than 69,000 illegal aliens had arrived in Israel, and their number kept rising.

I do not remember for how long we remained in Cyprus. The night before our travel to Israel Paulo and I went for a walk. He proposed to me and we kissed for the first time. I was enthusiastic, wanted to have a home and forget the past. We decided to get married in Israel. The following day, we left for the Promised Land.

We arrived at Atlit, the city where we received identification cards. Paulo stayed with some relatives in Tel Aviv and I was sent to an agriculture school in Afula. I missed Paulo, although he would visit me sometimes during the weekends.

During the weeks before the declaration of the State of Israel, some local friends were concerned about the predictions of experts that a Jewish state would not survive an attack by Arab armies and was condemned to annihilation. Nevertheless, the People Administration did not hesitate and made the state a reality.

Friday afternoon on May 14, 1948, the State of Israel was born. Ben-Gurion read the Declaration proclaiming the Republic of Israel and rabbi Maimon gave the traditional blessing, thanking the Lord Almighty for allowing us to see that day. The Philharmonic Orchestra of Tel Aviv played *Há-Tikva*, the national anthem. Thousands of people gathered in front of the museum. I hugged Paulo and cried. I was very afraid. At midnight, the Egyptian, Lebanese, Syrian, and Trans-Jordanian armies invaded Israel.

We spent the night at a shelter. Despite the war, we decided to get married as scheduled, on May 28, 1948. The wedding was held at the house of Paulo's cousin. The rabbi and some guests were present. Everything was done in a hurry because of the situation. At 6 p.m. sirens blasted and we ran to the shelters. There have been few events in the history of mankind like the birth of Israel. A new state was born, with worldwide public opinion approving it and with the support of the major powers: the United States and the Soviet Union.

9. The War of Independence

Israel was constantly attacked from the moment of its creation. Many nights we had to sleep in antiaircraft shelters—it was a nightmare…

The campaign against the invaders lasted four weeks. On May 17, Acre, the city that Napoleon was unable to conquer, surrendered to the *Hagana*. After the truce of June 18, there was another ceasefire, this time with unlimited duration, as required by the United Nations.

During the ceasefire, Paulo was able to rent a small apartment for us. We could only fit a twin bed there, but we were happy.

A month later, Paulo found a job at Lod Airport with Shell. We were delighted! It was a miracle to find a job with the ongoing massive immigration.

On March 30, 1949, our beautiful baby girl was born, whom we named after my mother—Sara Zilda. It was very difficult to take care of the baby during the first months. I had no experience with newborns and was weak from the delivery. Paulo helped me during his time off, and a nurse from the *Tipat Halav* program *(Drop of Milk)* for babies born in Israel, was also a great help.

During the first years, it was very hard to accommodate immigrants. There were no jobs and the salaries were very low.

There were also difficulties educating the children of the immigrants. Adult education was also critical.

The country needed a lot of money to solve all those problems. North American Jewish representatives launched the "*Bons*" campaign. Large sums were collected by the United Jewish Appeal to welcome entire Jewish communities from Yemen and most of the Jews from Iraq.

Slowly, things began to improve. My husband was still working at Lod Airport and I took care of the house and our daughter, Sara.

One day I woke up feeling ill. Paulo immediately took me to the hospital and the doctor confirmed that I was three months pregnant. We panicked, as our home could only fit a twin bed and Sara's crib. Aside from that, food was rationed and Paolo's salary was far from good.

There was a joke going around. Prime Minister Ben-Gurion had met President Truman and the former asked:

"How much does a worker make in the U.S.A?"

The President answered:

"1,200 dollars a month, more or less..."

"How much does he spend?"—asked Ben-Gurion.

"Around 850 dollars"—answered Truman.

"What does he do with the rest of the money?"—asked Ben-Gurion.

"We are free to do whatever we want."

Then it was President Truman's turn to ask:

"And how much does your worker make a month?"

"Seven hundred and fifty lire"—answered Ben-Gurion.

"How much does he spend a month?"

"Nine hundred."

"Where does he get the rest?"—Truman wanted to know.

"We are also free to do whatever we want..."

It was lucky for us that Paulo was an optimist, young, a hard worker, and had great faith in God. We were able to move mountains.

On October 2, 1950 our son, Jacob Tzwi was born. He was named after Paulo's father, who along with his wife died in Treblinka during the Holocaust.

We were desperately looking for a bigger house to accommodate our two children. We found one in Kfar Ono, now called Kiriat Ono, which, at the time, was a village with 100 families. We moved there immediately.

In January of 1952 Paulo lost his job. Under pressure from the Arab countries Shell left Israel. We were desperate. Paulo spent days looking for work. Weeks and months went by, and the little money we had managed to save was almost gone. We had no hope that the situation would change in the short term.

In 1953, we decided to move to Brazil. My father's sister, my aunt in Brazil, sent us tickets for the voyage. In November, we boarded the ship for São Paulo with our last one hundred dollars in our pocket.

10. Brazil

With two small children the trip was very tiresome. We could not be careful enough. At last, the ship arrived at the Santos port. I did not know that part of my family as they emigrated before I was born. Paulo got hold of a piece of cardboard and wrote my aunt's name on it—Regina Rosset. We left the ship together. My two cousins were anxiously waiting to meet us. It was very emotional to meet my family again. We were not alone in the world! My sister Rachella had gone to the United States and married but I had not received much news from her.

On the way to my aunt's house, a trip that took more than an hour, my cousins asked many questions, especially about the Holocaust and how we were able to survive. We were the only ones among our big family to escape with our lives. However, it was difficult to explain how or why we had survived. Only God has the answers.

We stopped in front of an old building in a section called Bom Retiro. My children and I ran up the stairs. My aunt was waiting for us at the door, and we hugged, crying. It was a very emotional moment.

We stayed with them for a while and then moved to a rented house. We put the children in daycare and began looking for jobs. I found work as a Hebrew teacher at the Shalom Aleichem School and Paulo began selling linen. It was tough in the beginning, especially because of the language, but little by little, life got better.

One day, at the Hebrew Teachers' Congress, I was offered a job in Campinas, a town 55 miles from São Paulo.

Paulo accompanied me to the interview. The Jewish community was small and the town was quiet. They offered me a house and a monthly salary of Cz$2,500. It was an excellent salary for the time and we could not reject the offer. We were very excited.

In March of 1956, we moved to Campinas. I worked at the Beith Jacob School for two years. Paulo opened a clothing store and I decided to work with him.

We managed to buy a beautiful house. The children were studying at the public school. I had a live-in maid who helped with the children.

We worked for several years and with God's help were able to improve our lives. In 1960, my sister visited us with her daughter. We were very happy with their visit and promised to see each other again soon. Unfortunately, this was not possible because in 1962 I gave birth to another daughter, 12 years after Jacob.

The baby brought us a lot of happiness and we named her Céfora after Paulo's mother. Céfora was a beautiful baby, who slept and ate very well. I hired a lady to take care of her while Paulo and I continued to work together at the store.

In 1963, we celebrated Jacob's Bar Mitzvah. It was a wonderful party at the Sears banquet hall in São Paulo. After the Bar Mitzvah, we began to realize that the environment was not the best for the kids. Beith Jacob closed and many of the families moved to São Paulo. We also moved back to São Paulo at the beginning of 1964.

We sold everything in Campinas and bought an apartment in the Higienópolis section of the city and opened a store in Brás, another area.

We stayed in São Paulo for 25 years, living in the same place. We managed to marry all our children; even our granddaughter was born there.

Meanwhile, all our children had moved to the United States and we decided to follow them.

We arrived in Miami in 1991 and bought an apartment in Aventura. Everything was perfect, but our happiness was short-lived. Paulo was diagnosed with Alzheimer's and suffered with the disease for five and a half years. He passed away on June 29, 1999, a Saturday. The Saturday *paracha* was Pinchas, his name in Hebrew.

Paulo is sorely missed by all of us. Our love for him is eternal.

Facing Mengele

◆

Magda Bader

I started my memoirs so that my family, my children and my grandchildren would know something about my childhood and me. I was born on April 17, 1930 in Munkacevo, Czechoslovakia, with eight feet of snow still on the ground around our house. Our town was in the Carpathian Mountains where Slovakia, Romania, Hungary and the Ukraine merge. All those languages, as well as Yiddish were commonly heard in that area, but while the others are still spoken there, Yiddish is gone, probably forever. When I was nine, our little town of about 30,000 people became part of Hungary and was now called Munkács. We became Hungarians.

My parents were born under the Austro-Hungarian regime; my father on August 31, 1879 in Svalava (Solyva in Hungarian) in Carpathia, and my mother in Munkács on March 14, 1885. My mother, Franceska (or Fáni) Bleicher, was 18, and my father, Julius (Gyula) Sternberg 24 when they were married in Munkács. They lived in the same house almost all their married life, except for a short episode during World War I, when they had to evacuate to Bratislava, where Eugene was born, and in April 1944, when we were forced to leave our house within 24 hours. We had had a relatively nice life in Munkács until then. My parents were very wonderful, kind people, always quiet and hard working. I never heard an angry outburst from either of them. Even today, when I think of them or talk about them, my eyes fill with tears and in my heart I revert back to being 14 years old. That was the last time I saw them.

Hitler's army occupied Hungary, Germany's ally, on March 19, 1944. The persecution of the Jews moved to a new plateau. When we were ordered by the Hungarians to leave our home in the middle of April 1944, we had to leave all our possessions behind, except for what we could carry in our arms. We moved to the Ghetto in Munkács that was a street guarded by Hungarian fascists. We moved into some relative's crowded apartment with other families. We were forbidden to leave the Ghetto, but my sister, Klári, and I took a chance and secretly went back to our wood shack, behind our house, where we kept firewood for the winter. The night before our departure from our house, mother had dug a hole under the woodpile and hid silver trays, candlesticks and other items of value. When we returned to the wood shack the very next day, everything was gone. My mother sewed the rest of our jewelry in our jackets thinking that we would be able to exchange the jewelry for food at some later date.

We stayed in the Ghetto for a few weeks. An order came from the *"Nyilasok,"* Hungarian Nazi collaborators, the "Arrowcross" party, to vacate the Ghetto and march to the outskirts of town to the local brickworks. Cattle cars on railroad tracks were waiting there to take us to our "destination." We had no clue where that might be. Many people from other ghettos were also brought to the large outdoor space at the brickworks. This was the gathering place for the region. We stayed at the brickworks for a few days, sleeping outdoors, with very little room. It was the middle of May. As we were marching from our ghetto to the brick-works, my grandfather, Bernard Bleicher, who was about 85, could not walk fast and fell. My mother tried to help him up. The Hungarian guard hit her with the butt of his rifle and forced her to leave her father on the ground and move on. That was the last time I saw my grandfather.

At the brick factory, there were guards watching from lookout towers and shooting randomly, so that no one would even think of escaping. On the day we were loaded into the cattle cars, my biology teacher from my freshman high school class was shot on the ramp. Her body was removed, and they proceeded with loading the people, about 100 to a cattle car. It is hard to describe the smell, the hunger, the thirst and the terribly confined space. After a few days, we arrived, still hoping against hope that our immediate family would stay together. This hope was immediately shattered. My 58-year old mother, my 64-year old father, my sister Sári with Fricike, her little girl, my sisters Lili, Klári, Hanci and I were together until that moment. When the SS guards opened the heavy iron doors of the cattle car, we were ordered to march in the direction of a group of officers who were giving out orders. We could not stand up, let alone walk fast. We could not see well, because we had been in the darkness of the cattle car. We arrived in front of an elegant SS officer, who told us to separate, mothers and young children in one direction, old people in another, young adult women yet in another direction. His words were kind and calm, assuring us we would see each other again. Later we learned this officer was Dr. Josef Mengele. I held my mother's hand and one of my sister's. I let my mother's hand go, and I went with my sisters, Lili, Klári and Hanci. We never again saw mother, father, Sári and Fricike.

We marched along an ugly road; both sides had tall concrete fences with barbed electrified wires. Behind those fences, people with sad eyes pointed to the things we still held on to for dear life, they wanted us to throw those to them. We did not do so. We needed them; those jackets had jewelry sewed into them that we might trade for food—so we thought. As we arrived at one of the barracks in Auschwitz-Birkenau, we were ordered to disrobe at once and place all our clothes and other belongings in one large pile. We were standing naked, waiting to have our heads shaved. After that the disinfecting showers were waiting for us and some dirty old clothes; we did not know where those came from, but those were there for us to wear. No shoes, no underwear; none of our personal belongings. Next, we went to our new home in the C lager in Birkenau. This barrack had shelves, three-tiered wooden planks for us to sleep on, ten people per shelf and about a thousand women in one barrack. We were told by the *"blockelteste,"* a Polish Jewess, who followed orders from the SS, what to do and when to do it. Our days consisted of getting up at 4:00 or 5:00 a.m. to line up along the side of the barrack and wait and wait and stand and stand. The Selection took place at that time. The SS officers picked out persons from the line who looked sick, weak, young or whatever they were looking for at that time. I was picked out of the line as I stood in a row with my sisters, Lili, Klári and Hansi. The SS did not know we were sisters and we did not want them to know, because they would have separated us to inflict even more pain and suffering. They picked me out, because I looked weak and younger than most in the barrack. During the night we were able to exchange me for someone else who was also separated from a sister or a mother.

We were always hungry and cold at night, and we were covered with body lice that we periodically picked off each other. The worst was not knowing what had happened to our mother, father, Sári and Fricike. The smell and the heavy dark smoke from the chimneys of the crematoriums were very frightening. When the SS guards finally selected all four of us sisters to go on a transport, it did not matter to us where we were taken. We all thought that no place could be worse than Auschwitz. We were put into the disinfecting barrack again and we were given a different pile of rags to wear. After a few days we were finally put in cattle cars and left Auschwitz. After a few months in Auschwitz we were now on our way to another camp.

The train took us to Northern Germany. After a few days without food, drink or bathroom facilities, we came to a campsite called Tannenberg, not far from the towns of Falling Bostel, Celle and Unterlus. These were small towns. We were to work in an ammunition factory compound about 8 km from the Tannenberg camp. There were 500 women in this camp from Poland, Romania, and Hungary. They gave us blue and gray striped uniforms and wooden clogs, but no underwear and socks. We were very cold all the time. It was winter, it was snowing a lot, and the wind blew through my uniform. The snow landed on the ground and turned into ice, then it melted and froze again. My dress was like a sheet of ice against my body. One day I found an empty cement bag and wore it under my dress to shield me from the wind. As we returned from the day's work, we were frisked and a female SS guard beat me for wearing that cement bag. Despite this incident, this camp was an improvement over Auschwitz. The barbed wire fences were not electrified, and the food was a little better. We were locked in our barracks at night. We slept in bunk beds, on bare wooden planks, without covers, of course.

Lili became the camp's medical person, and she ran a small infirmary in a room; Hansi was her assistant. Klári worked in the SS kitchen with a German civilian cook and I worked outdoors at the Krupp factory, braking up stones to pave the roads. It was the Reinmetal Borsig factory, a part of the Krupp conglomerate. The Krupp factory was producing war materiel then. Now they are making coffee makers and so on. Lili was saving people from getting really very sick. She kept them in the infirmary, away from work, but when the supervising SS doctor arrived from Bergen-Belsen and found the same person in the infirmary twice in a row, Lili got into trouble and was warned that she would be taken to Bergen-Belsen. That meant certain death. Typhus and typhoid were rampant and not one person ever taken there from Tannenberg came back alive. When people got sick with pneumonia or dysentery, they became dehydrated and Lili could not do anything for them, except keep them out from work for short periods.

As the SS guards locked us up at night, we could hear the heavy bomber planes flying above. I was hoping that whatever might happen, my sisters and I would be together. I was very afraid to be separated from my sisters.

As the heavy bombers flew over our barracks night after night, we knew that either the Americans or the British were now fighting the Germans over Germany. Meanwhile, the SS guards were telling us not to hope for survival. They practiced how they would line us up, shoot us, and we would fall in the prepared ditches; or they would load us on to trucks and take us to the death camp at Bergen-Belsen, where typhus and typhoid fever were rampant. According to the SS, there was no hope for our survival.

One night, a miracle happened. The SS guards escaped with their dogs to save their own lives and left the camp unattended. It was only for a short time, because the local civilian militia arrived with guns to finish what the SS guards had planned, to take everyone by truck to Bergen-Belsen by force. Between the time that the camp became unattended and the civilian militia arrived, the civilian cook for the SS officers told my sister, Klári that this was a good opportunity to escape. So Klári, Hansi, Lili and I with two other people managed to jump from a kitchen window and then crawled on our bellies in the mud until the militia would not be able to see us. Other women had similar ideas, but they were shot, dragged out and forced onto the trucks to be taken to Bergen-Belsen. We stayed in the woods for a few days. We were cold, hungry and sick, so we returned to our camp to look for food. From a distance we saw fighting and fires. We reached the main road, the same road we had used to go to work, but now we saw American soldiers. That is how we realized we were free. It was April 15 1945.

The war was still going on. The American soldiers went on to other parts of Germany, and the British soldiers became the occupying force where we were. Major Mitchell became the mayor of the town, and he found an apartment in a German house for us. We finally had enough food and a place to live, but now began the really difficult time to cope with reality. We could not find any information about our parents or our sister Aranka, who was last seen in Prague, and our sister Sári and her child Fricike. We never found any information about them. Our hometown, Munkács, was now occupied by the Russians and became part of the USSR.

Our brothers, Bill, Morris and Marci were part of a forced labor group that was captured by the Russians. After the war, they returned to Munkács and found our house occupied by people who claimed that it was their house. Our old family pictures were the only things that Bill could get back from them. My brothers did not stay in Munkács, but went to Prague. Meanwhile, one of the British officers was able to find our brother Eugene in England. He was the only one in our family who was able to finish his studies in Cambridge, England, during the war years.

After the war ended, my sisters and I stayed in Germany for another year. Lili worked as a medical officer with UNRRA (United Nations Relief and Rehabilitation Administration), Hansi also worked with UNRRA, Klári worked as a social worker with the Red Cross, and I was an interpreter for the British Red Cross, traveling to displaced persons' camps as I spoke some of the languages needed to be helpful: some English, Hungarian, Hebrew, Yiddish, a little Polish and German.

In the summer of 1946, Hansi and I went to England. We spent some time with Major Mitchell's family in Somerset. Later we went to London where we stayed with friends of Eugene and Marci. When I arrived in London, we stayed with an English family, taking care of their household. We also worked at various jobs and went to night school to improve our language skills. I also studied shorthand and typing, and briefly worked in an office typing invoices.

Meanwhile, Hansi and Klári got married. I was 17 when I passed the entrance examination to the Central School of the Arts. Each day, before I went to my art classes, I prepared breakfast for 30 girls as I was working in a girl's dormitory. I had the good fortune to meet people who were helpful and kind to me. I stayed at the Art School for three years. I traveled to Italy before coming to the U.S. on a foreign student scholarship to the University of Denver, where I received a BFA in 1952. After graduation, I became a fourth grade teacher in Long Beach, California. My interest in art was always strong, and when I received two grants to the Columbia University Teacher's College, I left California for New York. I earned my MA in a year, and it was great to be near my sister Hansi, my brothers Morris, Marci and Bill, and their families.

All my brothers reached New York before me. Eugene came to the United States in 1946. My sister Klári remained in London with her family for a while, and Lili stayed in Belgium until 1962 when she moved with her son, Michel, to Israel.

I taught art in a high school in Roslyn, Long Island from 1954 to 1956. Toward the end of the second year of teaching, Sam and I got married. We lived in New York City for a very short time and then moved to River Edge, New Jersey for five years. In 1962, we moved to Boston and lived in Newton Center for three years; then in Englewood Heights, NJ for three more years; and in the winter of 1969, we moved to Miami, Florida, where I have lived for 32 years. Our children, Annie and Julia, were born in New Jersey in 1957 and 1960. They moved away from Miami after graduating from high school to study at out-of-town colleges.

I remember my family, my parents, with great love, and after all these years I still have tears in my eyes when I think of them. What we suffered can never be forgotten, but in spite of the horrors of the war, I was very lucky. I have a wonderful family, children, six grandchildren: Joshua, Naomi, Esti, Briant, Kismet and Noah; two sons-in-law, and I have my sisters and brothers. Four of my siblings are still alive: Klári, Hansi, Eugene and Bill, with their families. I have nieces and nephews, the children of my brothers and sister who are no longer alive. I had a teaching career of more than 26 years, teaching art at all levels from kindergarten to college and at museums. I was Teacher of the Year three times at the Biscayne Gardens School where I taught for 20 years. I still teach in an adult program at Florida International University. Art has always been my passion. I play tennis every day and love to be with friends and family.

Sam and I met at the tennis courts in New York City's Central Park. We were married on April 27, 1956 and lived together for 45 years. Sam was born in Rozdal, Poland on October 29, 1912, the youngest of eight children. His father came to the U.S. first and sent for his wife and children to follow him in 1922. His family was very poor, and Sam was a true self-made man. He was very proud of his achievements. He helped his brothers' and sisters' children to succeed, too. Sam was quite well until his late eighties; he played tennis and also earned a GED.

Sam died on September 6, 2001, and as a war veteran he was to be interned in Arlington National Cemetery near Washington, DC on September 11, 2001. Due to the tragic events on September 11, our plane was not permitted to land in Washington, DC, and I could not attend the event that was delayed until September 12. Despite all the bad things that happened, I live with the hope that I will be able to enjoy life in a peaceful world, where people care about one another and that our children and grandchildren can live in a safe environment in the future.

Special Eyewitness for the March of Death

✦

George Klein

My name is George Klein[1]. I was born in 1928 to a well-to-do Jewish family. My grandfather and my mother, Sida owned free and clear 1000 hectares of land. Jews were allowed to own land. My aunt Rosa received 1000 hectares of land as her wedding present. Life in Hungary for most Jews was very good. In our part of the country there were no pogroms or anti-Semitism until 1937, although a generally non-violent form of anti-Semitism was common in the country, especially among university students in the 1920s. It often did result in acts of violence. There was the *Numerus Clausus*, the first such law in Europe in modern times that limited the participation of Jews in education and in many professions.

In April 1944 the Hungarian government took orders from the Gestapo and Arrowcross fascists and our small town of ten thousand people was cleansed of all Jews in two hours.

We were taken by train to Kassa—Kosice—a town in the present Slovak Republic—to the ghetto that was established for Jews. In less than a month, we were rushed to Auschwitz to be part of the final solution. Our horrible train ride

---

1.   George Klein was born in a small community in Northeastern Hungary. He was 14 years old when his entire family was deported to Auschwitz-Birkenau during the summer of 1944. George was the sole survivor of his family. George is married to Gloria. Their two sons are now grown. Jeff, their younger son and his wife presented George and Gloria with two grandchildren, a boy and his younger sister, the brightest points in the lives of their grandparents. Eugene and his wife live in New Zealand. George has been active in his synagogue in Miami and had served as its president and vice president for many years. He has also been active in many ways to defend the Jewish community and Jewish causes against physical and emotional harm.

and the deplorable conditions were no different from the thousands of horrible stories described by other survivors.

As I arrived in Auschwitz, I was robbed of all the love of my immediate and extended family and friends forever. Everyone except my father was gassed and burned. The biggest loss I suffered was parental guidance that I have never been able to overcome.

I had suffered the same as thousands of other survivors who have written about their experiences or personally described those to you. My father survived the original selection process. He passed away on April 28, 1945, ten days before the end of the war.

I do not want to take up your time with my personal story. However, I want to give you eyewitness testimony of the Auschwitz Uprising and resistance, an attempt to blow up two of the crematoria. It was from the collaboration of male *Sonderkommando* workers and Jewish women, led by Roza Robota of the Union Munitions Factory, who along with some of her coworkers, under the threat of immediate death, smuggled small amounts of gunpowder, hidden on their bodies, to help create a bomb.[a] Lowenthal and 45 other people made the attempt in October 1944 that was only partially successful. Everyone was murdered. Roza Robota was singled out and tortured in solitary confinement and finally hanged in Auschwitz, Poland, in front of all the other prisoners, in January 1945.

I don't know exactly how many people were physically present but I was there. All the prisoners in the camp were ordered to witness the executions. These people died in their attempt and they are my heroes of Auschwitz. In Roza's own words: "Vengeance will follow!" *Heil Roza!*

I provide my eyewitness testimony truthfully and to the best of my ability, as I am the only witness to live to describe it.

◆   ◆   ◆

Death March of Auschwitz as described by George Klein, on January 18 and after, from 20 feet up in the air.[2] I saw every last person following a group that was shot automatically, left frozen on the side of the road. Women prisoners were

---

2.   During the first weeks of 1945, George was in a separate camp from his father; the camps were about 15 km apart. George was hiding in a hayloft for about four days during the days as the march was getting started and he watched from that loft, 30 feet above ground, the unfolding of that great human tragedy. He rejoined the prisoners when he and his father were accidentally able to reunite. *(Based on a conversation with G.K. on Oct. 6, 2003.—P.T.)*

ordered to lie on the ground and machine-gunned on the order of Dr. Mengele[b] and Höss[c], the camp's commander.

I say at this point: Never again!

The Aftermath of the March on Foot: We were forced to board a train filled with snow in freezing temperature and taken to Weimar, Germany, to the Buchenwald concentration camp. Within the Buchenwald camp was a completely separate, fenced area that was called the Little Camp. I am a survivor—*B.H.*[3]—of that Little Camp. I have no idea how many more are like me. As if the conditions in Buchenwald were not bad enough, the Little Camp of Buchenwald was created for the sole purpose of making people die from beatings, complete starvation and thirst. The meager rations given in the large camp were cut to less than half and there was no water supply. I do not know how I managed to drag myself around while I was there.

◆   ◆   ◆

The Ghetto of Lodz was emptied of boys of the average age of eight or less and set up in the Little Camp to starve. With the help of *Hashem*, I was moved there in May.

◆   ◆   ◆

There is a special meeting at the Kennedy Center in Washington, DC, to commemorate the Little Camp in Buchenwald. The rest of my story is very much like everyone else's, highlighted with all the sufferings.

◆   ◆   ◆

My story is too painful and too depressing. I am No. A-10267, one of three survivors of Babitz-Auschwitz/3 when counted in 1945, and now one of two still alive bearing the tattoos from A10,000 through 13,000. I was a participant of the 1998 March of the Living from Miami, Florida, an eyewitness to the march of death and the march of the living. Ever since I returned from the March of the Living in May 1998, I have felt compelled to tell my experiences in the Holo-

---

3.   Baruch Hashem—Bless the Lord

caust. It is my duty to talk to young people so that they remember what I tell them.

My talk to high school and middle school children begins with a brief introduction of my personal history. The audience is made up of children who were typically raised as Christians. I ask them whether they knew that Jesus, Mary and the Twelve Apostles would have been marked for death had they lived in Hitler's Germany in 1939? They were all Jews. Hitler's laws defined anyone a Jew who had at least one Jewish grandparent. At this point the children understand that all Christians are Jews in a certain sense. Silence follows and then they listen to me very attentively.

I have been talking to students at various schools in our area at the rate of about once a month. One of these talks was at Miami Senior High School. The notes that I received from the students at that school prove that I have achieved my goal that the Holocaust will never be forgotten. I spoke to them on July 23, 2001. With God's help, I reached these students, and I have their promise to talk about my testimony. NEVER AGAIN!

Here are some excerpts from the letters I have received:

"It was interesting to meet a real life survivor of the Holocaust. I would also like to recommend you on your strong courage, it was a horror for me to hear about the Gestapo, Nazis, the camp Auschwitz (Oswiecim) and what happened to you and your family. I was shocked to hear when you said that Jews weren't the only ones sent to death camps…It is sad to hear that people say that the Holocaust did not happen, and you try to convince them and they don't listen and it's hard. I'm glad that you keep on striving…when I start a family of my own and inform them about the Holocaust they won't have a great real life survivor to speak to them the way you did, so I took full advantage that I could…" (Judith Oriental)

"I can't explain how a human can treat another human without any respect…no one should be treated like that no matter what race or religion. We all are human beings with feelings…." (Hector Lopez)

"…all the innocent people that suffered and died…." (Francisco Villanova)

"…now I know something new that I'll never forget." (Jerlyn Lara)

"Sorry that you lost your friends and family…I didn't know that 6 million people died." (Trenecie Daws)

"I felt extremely sad when you were telling us about your experience and I felt anger that humans could be so cruel." (Julie Rozo)

"You came to the United States of America you were 18 years old and now you are 73 years old." (Ivan Goins)

"…it's unbelievable that there was so much hatred and racism in the world…It's one thing to read about it but it is so different to hear it from a victim. Thank you for talking to young people and helping us understand history so that next time it doesn't happen to us. The hatred of one man killed many…and I hope that it never happens to anyone else. I wish that in the 1940s the Jews and all those in camps had the freedom we have today. But I can't change the past. All I can do is tell future generations about you and your story." (Adileu Aguila)

"You mentioned that so many men, women and children were killed right in front of your very eyes. I have no idea as to how you cope with yourself everyday." (Myrlande Simeon)

"What occurred was a tragic experience for you, and young people like us need to know what happened in the past…thank you very much for the knowledge you embedded in our memories." (Javier Pozo)

"It is the prejudice and exclusion of minorities and those different from the rest that lead to violence. Your emotional presentation helped me realize that." (Lindy Lan)

"I am a Jehovah's Witness, and as such, I understand what it is like to be persecuted for your nationality or beliefs, because my parents were persecuted…brothers of my faith are being tortured right now in Russia for their beliefs." (Hector Ramos)

"…though some people deny that the Holocaust took place…their ignorance can't hide everything that happened in Auschwitz. Your speech…makes me feel all the sadness and anger that you are feeling right now." (Cindy Tahuico)

"You confirmed many things that I saw in movies and read in books to be true, like the women who were hung and left up as examples. It took a lot of heart for you to tell

us about your two year Holocaust experience at Auschwitz…I would like to give you another big thanks because you said after talking to us you will go into a deep depression. I am hoping our letters will help…" (Danitra Rogers)

"I will also like to let you know that I know it is hard growing up without your parents and family members, but remember that you have us your admirer and we love you!" (Yoima Garrin)

"You gave me the key of life, because the new generation we think everything in this life is a joke…you have made me think about how grateful I am for the reason that I have my family with me." (Maier Conizales)

"I could never even imagine a 16 year old being 65 lbs…If I went through that I wouldn't have the strength to talk about it…I didn't know about the camps." (Vanessa Morales)

"I'm sorry…my family for not helping you people out." (Alfonso Dahl)

"These are just a few things I learned: The Holocaust between 1933 and 1945…consisted of homosexuals and disabled people; 60,000 people were killed by gas chambers…December 1939, all Jewish homes were confiscated." (Jerlana Phillips)

"I knew about the Holocaust and felt sympathy for the Jews. Now as a result of you, I feel resentment towards the corruption and apathy that human souls are capable of." (Jacqueline L. Pradere)

"When you said about that they did to the babies tears almost came out of my eyes. I hope you know that you and your story have changed my perspective towards the Jewish." (Gigi Morera)

"You have really changed the way I think about the Holocaust because now I would never forget it. You made me realize that if we just forget it happened, it will just happen again." (Juan Nunez)

"…about your father, I think it was pretty tough having to stand…and see your father being killed." (Donald Valverde)

Notes:

[a] **Roza Robota** was a young Zionist in Ciechanów, Poland. She was deported to Auschwitz in 1942 where she collaborated with the Jewish underground to supply small disks of explosives, stolen by women prisoners from the Weichsel Union Metalwerke within the camp. On October 7, 1944, prisoners *(Sonderkommando)* blew up one of the crematoria and began a prisoners' uprising. The Gestapo followed a trail of clues to Roza and brutally tortured her to obtain other names of the participants. She never revealed any information. Along with three other women, Roza was publicly hanged on January 6, 1945, she was 23 years old. For further details, refer to

> **Encyclopedia of the Holocaust,** (ed.) Guttman, I; Macmillan, 1990; Vol. 3, p. 1286
>
> http://www.datasync.com/~davidg59/rosa.html
>
> http://www.shtetlinks.jewishgen.org/Ciechanow/Robota.htm

[b] Dr. Josef **Mengele** was the infamous Nazi doctor and SS officer. He was assigned to the Auschwitz death camp where he performed prisoner selections *(Selektionen)*, deciding who was to be exterminated immediately among the prisoners, making life and death decisions on the basis of a quick glance at a prisoner. Mengele also performed cruel medical experiments on prisoners, especially on twins. He is often referred to as the "Angel of Death."—At the end of the war Mengele disappeared and was rumored to live for several decades in South America. He was never apprehended for his crimes. For further details:

> Enc. of the Holocaust (pp.971-2):
>
> http://www.candles-museum.com/mengele.htm

[c] **Rudolf Höss,** (1900-1947) was the camp commandant of Auschwitz. He was chosen by Himmler to carry out the "Final Solution of the Jewish Question" in Auschwitz. The following is cited in the Enc. of the Holocaust (p.691-2), based on a report written by Höss in a Polish prison. Himmler told Höss:

> "... *The Führer has ordered the 'Final Solution of the Jewish Question.' We, the SS, are charged with the execution of this task. I have chosen the Auschwitz camp for this purpose, because its convenient location as regards transportation and because in that area it is easy to isolate and camouflage the camp...I am herewith charging you with the task. This is a strenuous and difficult assignment that calls for total dedication, regardless of the dif-*

*ficulties that will arise. Further practical details will be conveyed to you by Sturmbannführer **Adolf Eichmann**...'"*

The Story of my Life

✦

Jack Baigelman (Beigelman)

I was born on August 19, 1927 to Samuel and Ita Baigelman in Lodz, Poland. We were a conservative, middle-class Jewish family. My father was a professional musician, a violinist with the Lodz Symphony Orchestra. This was his main occupation, but he also played saxophone at exclusive hotels and clubs as a sideline. During the off-season he played in summer and winter resorts in Zakopane and Krinica, Poland.

My mother was a devoted wife and an excellent mother who would do anything for her family. Before marrying my father, she was singing at the Yiddish Theatre in Lodz. I was their only child for seven years when my brother Abram was born.I had a very good childhood. We lived in a one-bedroom apartment on Gdanska 20. I will never forget being in my playpen on Friday evenings, when my mother would give me a piece of butter kuchen and a glass of milk, a real treat for me at that time. My family wasn't rich, but we lived comfortably. When I got older, I remember playing games with friends in our back yard. I remember Michal and Basia, a Christian girl, the daughter of the superintendent of our apartment building. We had a lot of fun.

My fondest memories were of my father taking me to the movie theater, where he and a pianist would play for the silent movies. My father had to adopt his own music to fit the movie. I will never forget the times my mother, father and I went to the mountains, to Zakopane in the winter and Krynica in the summer, where my parents stayed at luxurious hotels. I skied in the winter and climbed the mountains in the summer. That was the life I remember before I turned seven. Our lives changed after that, we didn't travel or have much fun anymore.

I started public school at the age of seven. Most of the Jewish boys attended a *cheder*, a religious school, but I did not because we were not orthodox on account of my father's profession. My parents were not very religious, but respected the traditions.

My school was within walking distance; it was only for Jewish boys. It was segregated from both, Jewish girls and Christian children; they had their own schools. In addition to all the required subjects, we had a class once a week in Jewish religion and the history of the Jewish people. I did enjoy school.

I have very fond memories of my maternal grandparents, uncles, aunts, and cousins. We were a very close-knit family before the war with about thirty-five to forty members. Not all of them lived in Lodz. Most of the men were also musicians, as my father. The women were either singers or were connected to the Yiddish Theatre. I will never forget the Passover seders at my grandparents, where almost the entire family got together. None of them was Orthodox, but they all followed Jewish traditions. I remember my grandfather taking me by my hand on the Shabbat and the High Holidays and walking to the temple together. I felt so proud to walk with him. Never having attended a *cheder*, I never learned how to pray. Later in life I was sorry for that.

My mother never had to change her maiden name because she married another Baigelman. My grandfathers were brothers, thus my father and mother were first cousins. My paternal grandparents lived in a small town, Ostrowiec, Kielecki; my father was born there. During summers, I remember my mother taking me to visit my grandparents, whom I loved, but I must admit that I didn't know them as well as my maternal grandparents. I do remember my father's brother and sisters, and some of my cousins. Some of them also lived in Lodz.

All that good life, education, freedom and everyday fun ended abruptly after Sept. 1, 1939, when the war began in Poland. German planes began to bomb our city. Our family of four, along with other tenants in our building, was crowded into a bomb shelter in the basement. The bombing was very intense and kept up for two nights and a day. As a young child I did not know much about the world at that time and didn't understand what this really meant. My little brother, Abram, and I were very frightened; we cried and cuddled with our parents who were trying to calm us down as much as they could. When the bombing finally stopped, we came up to the street. What I remember from that day was a very impressive German army on motorcycles, tanks, and on foot. They looked triumphant and proud. They were impressive to a young child like me. The Polish army never looked like the Germans at any time I had ever seen it. But little did I—or anyone else among us—know what was yet to come. Soon, the Germans issued a proclamation ordering every Jew to wear a white armband with a yellow

Star of David at the center. This way all the gentiles could recognize that we were Jews. This caused us tremendous grief; we were often harassed and mistreated; we felt like branded cattle. Jewish men were picked off the streets every day and taken out of the city to perform various kinds of hard labor. They were beaten and threatened not only by the Germans, but also by gentile Poles. Often those captured men were also killed.

Another proclamation, early in 1940, ordered all the Jews in Lodz to leave their homes. We were ordered to take along only such belongings that we could carry and report to the worst section in the city, the Baluty, assigned to be the ghetto. The four of us arrived there and were given a room about twelve by fifteen feet. We found two bunk beds with wooden slats and a potbelly stove in the center of the room for cooking and heating. There was neither an icebox, nor any refrigeration whatsoever. The sanitary facilities were very poor: there was no running water, but a hand pump outside. We used pails and wash pans for everything. There were outhouses in the back to be shared by all the tenants of the apartment building. We were lucky to take with us blankets, pillows, some pots and pans, plates and silverware. We also took along some clothes. These items provided some comfort for the time being.

As it turned out, the four of us spent four and a half years in that miserable room. Miraculously we escaped deportations, personal persecution, selections and other types of harassment. Several of our relatives and friends weren't that lucky. Some died from starvation and disease, others were deported to unknown places.

Soon after I arrived in the ghetto, I was ordered to report to a leather factory that manufactured products for the German war effort. I worked there twelve to fifteen hours, seven days a week. They gave us very little food. For breakfast, a small piece of black bread and a cup of watered down black ersatz coffee. Lunch was another small piece of black bread and a small bowl of watered down soup perhaps with a potato peel floating in it—if you were lucky. We were kept on a starvation diet. A ration card was the reward for our labor that allowed my mother to receive a very small amount of food. The rations didn't include any meat or other necessary nutritional items. Occasionally, they gave us some shirts and pants. Others say that they received money, but I can't remember getting paid.

At the age of twelve my formal education stopped, my normal life was turned upside down. I was living with the constant fear of being deported. We were very hungry; food was on my mind all the time. The only good thing in the ghetto was that our family of four was still together. My father managed to keep us out of trouble, especially my little brother, who had escaped all the deportations of children under twelve.

I witnessed the death of many friends in the ghetto from typhus, starvation and other diseases. I also became very ill one time. I don't know how, but my mother did manage to nurse me back to health.

The Lodz ghetto was unlike other ghettos: it was sealed off from the world with a fence around its perimeter. There was no news coming in or going out. The ghetto was sealed on May 1, 1940, when it had 164,000 inhabitants. By the time the ghetto was liquidated in 1944, 60,000 had died of starvation and disease. The Wehrmacht,[1] the Gestapo,[2] and the Kripo, the Jewish police, guarded our ghetto. The Lodz ghetto was self-governed. The Germans appointed Chaim Rumkowski the leader, "the Eldest of the Jews." Thirty members of the Kehila, the ruling Jewish party, assisted him. Rumkowski ruled the ghetto. Hans Bibov, the German commandant and his staff supervised him. The ghetto, at one time, even had a symphony orchestra. My father and several other members of my family played in that orchestra, but the orchestra was eventually dissolved.

All in all, life in the ghetto was boring; there were no books, no opportunities for recreation at all. Thinking back, even if there had been such things to do, we would not have had time for those. It was work and home, nothing more for young people who needed nutritional nourishment, as well as mental and educational challenges. But our lives depended on Hitler's war and the Nazis' plan for the Jews.

On August 13, 1944, just before my seventeenth birthday, another of Hans Bibov's proclamations ordered the liquidation of the Lodz ghetto. We were to be moved deeper into Germany to work at the same trades as usual. The liquidation was to be conducted in an orderly manner, street by street. Everyone should pack all the belongings one could carry, and be ready to leave at any time. We had no choice but obey the orders. We still had about twenty-five of our close relatives in the ghetto. Our turn came the next day. We were first marched to the market place along with thousands of people and then to the railroad tracks where we were herded into cattle cars, packed tight like sardines. They gave us some bread and water. There were no toilets. It is very difficult to imagine this train ride lasting two nights and a day. People were screaming and dying around us. I will never forget the stench as long as I live. This trip seemed to take forever, into eternity. Finally, the train stopped. When the doors opened, we discovered that

---

1.   The German Regular Army
2.   The German Secret Police

we were told a lie; we didn't arrive in Germany, as promised, but at the now infamous gates of the Auschwitz death camp. The "Arbeit Macht Frei" sign[3] stood above the gate. I had never before learned about this camp and what it stood for.

Those who were still alive among us were ordered to get off the train. We were lined up facing toward the beginning of the line and moving forward. As we moved closer, my parents told me that no matter what happens, I am to stick with my father. My mother was to take care of my little brother. As we got to the front of the line, an SS officer stood there, who directed my father and me to go to the left. My mother and Abram were ordered to go to the right.—I found out later that the SS officer was the infamous Dr. Mengele. That was the last time I saw my mother and my brother. I learned later that they were sent into a gas chamber and cremated in Auschwitz.

Dr. Mengele acted like God and decided who shall live and who shall die. My father and I temporarily escaped the gas chamber. We were ruled to be capable to perform free slave labor for the Nazis. They planned to squeeze out the last drop of our strength and then kill us.

We were ordered to undress and leave all our belongings in a huge pile in the center of a room. They shaved our heads and then ordered us into a very large room. There were many showerheads mounted in the ceiling. To everyone's pleasant surprise, instead of Zyklon gas,[4] water poured forth from the showerheads. We showered without soap or towels. Then in another room we received striped prisoner uniforms and wooden shoes. The next order was to gather in a large empty area, the *"Umschlag Platz."* We had to stand at *Appell*.[5] The SS men immediately started to lay down their rules for us, all the while threatening, harassing, degrading and denouncing us. They took some prisoners out of the lineup at random and began to beat them beyond recognition. They dragged them away later, most likely to the crematorium. They kept us standing at attention for at least two hours.

After they got through with us, they took us to long barracks, which were lined with two-tiered bunks on each side of the room; there was a line of benches at the center. They told us to find spaces to lie down. My father and I climbed to a top bunk and lay down very close to each other. We were packed as tight as sardines. That night we had nothing to eat or drink. It was still dark when they woke us up the next morning. They ordered us out to the *"Umschlag Platz"* and

---

3.   Work makes one free.
4.   The commonly used poison used in the gas chambers.
5.   Headcount or roll call.

we got the same treatment as the night before. Then they ordered us to enter the barracks for a small piece of dry black bread and a cup of coffee. We were fed once more each day: a small piece of bread and a small portion of watered-down soup, practically all water. This routine lasted for about two weeks. One day after *Appell,* we were told to line up for a "selection;" none of us knew what this meant. The same Dr. Mengele was at the head of the line, who had sent the people to the right and to the left at the railroad station. This time he was selecting prisoners for labor camps. I was sent to the left and my father, who stood behind me, was sent the same way. We were then given a new identity, a number tattooed on the left arm. My number was B 6507. If you sum up the digits, my numbers add to 18. Jews believe that 18, referred to as *Chai,* life, is a lucky number. It turned out to be lucky for me. My father's number was B 6508. We were branded like animals, stripped of our real identity, dignity and honor.

I became only a number to the Nazis. It was then that I realized that the Nazis' goal was to keep us alive as long as we can work and produce for them at minimum expense.

That same day we were loaded onto trucks and taken into Germany to Gleivitz 4, a labor camp. Once we were unloaded, they ordered us to gather at the new *"Umschlag Platz,"* where we received the same treatment as in Auschwitz-Birkenau: insults and beatings, as before. After a long lecture, we were assigned to barracks, given some food and told to lie down and rest for the night. It was still dark when we heard shouts to line up in front of our bunks. They ordered us to go outside for Appell. After a long series of lectures, we were divided into separate commandos for various work details. They loaded us onto trucks and sent us to the town of Gleivitz. My group was assigned to dig ditches for sewers and water mains.

We worked from early morning till late evening, seven days a week. The reward for our labor was a small piece of dry black bread, a bowl of watered-down kohlrabi soup and a cup of coffee. It was late in the fall and the weather was very cold. We still only had our original prisoner uniforms and open wooden sandals. I looked for something to wrap my feet and found some paper. Paper helped to keep our skinny bodies a little warmer. We had no protection for our hands against the cold, we had no gloves. It was unbearable; life was very bad.

One day my father became ill with dysentery. He was granted permission to stay at the camp and he was to see the nurse. I went to work as usual. When I came back to the camp someone told me that my father was in the hospital. I had to find out the reason. Someone told me that he was severely beaten by our cook, a German political prisoner, a criminal, who was known to hate the Jews; he was a sadist and a murderer. He was serving time at our labor camp. On that day my father was assigned to work under him. Having dysentery, he had to run frequently to the outhouse. The cook accused my father that he did not want to work. He beat him with his hands and then threw barrels at him. My dad passed out; later, he was carried away to the so-called nurse's station or hospital.

I had to ask for special permission to leave the barrack. That evening I saw my father. He was still alive. I spoke to him for a short while. We held hands. I was numb. I was told to leave. When I left, I knew that I would probably never again see him alive.

The next day when I came back from work I went to see him, but he was gone. I asked for him and they told me that he was taken away. I don't know whether he was alive or dead when they took him. No one seemed to know where they took him, no one cared.

I don't know to this day where they took him. I was orphaned, all alone. But somehow, I managed to survive by myself. Early one morning in January 1945, in the middle of winter, without any warning, all the inmates in our camp were taken on the infamous "Death March." We were all weak from hunger and being overworked. It was very cold and I didn't have any warm clothing, nor closed shoes. Those who had some paper, wrapped their feet and bodies in it. I was lucky to find some paper and did the same. It didn't take very long for us to prepare for the march. The guards ordered us to assemble and then gave us a lecture on the way we should behave during the march. After we heard their threats, the march began.

Soon, many of the marchers were falling behind from exhaustion, hunger and thirst. As soon as one fell, the German guards shot the fallen in the back of the head and left the body by the road. We spent a night at a new camp. The next day we marched on. At the end of the day, about half of us were still alive from the original group. That night we came to another camp, Blechhamer, and they sent us into the barracks. I was very exhausted; all I wanted was to lie down at any place. I was barely alive. I must have fallen asleep immediately. Next morning I woke up to the loud screams of the prisoners. They were shouting with excitement: "The German guards are gone! The Russian soldiers are here!" At first, I thought I was dreaming. I couldn't comprehend what I had just heard. I thought they were crazy.

I stood up and walked outside. To my amazement I saw Russian soldiers on tanks and trucks. Some were on foot, shaking hands with the survivors. This was the day of my liberation from Hitler's murderers. Finally, there were no more

German SS to make our lives miserable. We were free at last! Perhaps I may have a life again…Perhaps I will have a family…

The Russian soldiers gave us some food. I can't remember what we received but as hungry as I was, it really didn't matter. I began to realize that I was free at last. Now, after all these years, I can't understand how I was able to endure all that suffering.

How could people be so cruel and impose such hardships on others because of their religion? The Nazis blindly followed Hitler, a madman. Even now I wonder how the German people, highly educated in every field, scholars, professors, doctors, lawyers, bankers, and so on, could fall under the spell of that henchman, Hitler?

I often wonder how any of us, survivors of the Holocaust, still function physically and mentally? Where did we get the will to live through that hell? Why don't I have frozen feet and fingers? Why don't I have tuberculosis? Why am I still here?

People who hear my story ask me all the time how did I manage to survive? I really have no logical explanation, call it luck; call it being at the right place at the right time. Perhaps it was my strong will to live and survive—it's hard to say. I know that had that "Death March" lasted one more day, I probably would not have survived. I strongly believe that I was extremely lucky. My prisoner's number, 6+5+0+7 = Chai or 18, might have been my talisman.

After several days of eating well and resting at Blechhamer, I got much stronger. Soon, I was back on my feet. I finally had a bath, clean clothes and shoes; it felt good!

I soon began thinking about my family. I was sure that my father was gone, but I didn't know whether my mother was alive. Was anyone in my family lucky enough to have survived?

I got restless and didn't know what to do. I heard that there was a way to travel. I decided that it was time to get back to Lodz and see whether I could find any of the twenty-five members of my family who had been in the Lodz ghetto in August 1944. I had no money. I hopped on a train toward Lodz. It was risky, but somehow I made it to Lodz.

Someone told me about an office where survivors gathered. I found it and there was a list with the names of people who had returned from the concentration camps. I didn't find any names I knew. I went there every day to search, to no avail. One day I found Uncle Huna, my mother's brother, who was very sick. Sadly, soon he died. I was again alone and miserable. At that point I lost my memory.

I spent five months in Lodz. I don't recall where I lived, what I ate, what I did; it's all a complete blank. I must have felt very miserable and tried to forget everything. I remember going to the survivors' office in June, where I spoke to someone who had just come back from the American Zone. I remember asking him whether he had seen any Baigelmans, the musicians. He thought that he had seen a group of survivors, all musicians, in Cham, a small town in Bavaria, not far from the Czech border. He heard them play in a DP camp.[6] He also thought that he heard the name Baigelman. I had nothing to lose and decided to return to Germany and try my luck there. My memory began to function once again. Meeting that man was the first piece of good news I had received since liberation. I didn't waste much time. Without a penny to my name, I hopped on a train going toward Prague. I snuck across the border from Poland and stopped in Prague for a few days in a hotel for survivors. I took another train to Germany. That train passed by Cham. As the train got close to Cham, I jumped off while it slowed down near a curve. It wasn't easy, but I was determined to try it, and I did succeed. Luckily, I didn't get hurt; all was well! I walked to the town and found the office for survivors. I asked if anyone knew about a group of musicians from Lodz, specifically anyone by the name of Baigelman? They directed me to a building on the square. I dashed over there. You can't imagine my joy when I found Uncle Henry, my mother's brother, my cousin Sam Spais, and cousin Abe Mutzman. I also found several musicians, friends of our family.

My life restarted at that moment. Out of thirty-five close relatives before the war, only the four of us survived Hitler and his executioners. My newly found family had formed a jazz band; they called themselves "The Happy Boys." They played for American officers clubs, American troops and for DP camps, as many such camps were formed after liberation.

Life was again good for them and for me as well. I spent the rest of 1945 and half of 1946 there. That year America opened its doors to DPs like myself. I always dreamt of going to America. That was my opportunity! I heard that UNRRA[7] was registering Jewish orphans. They were preparing transports to send orphans to either America or England. Along with others, I went to register. After many inquiries, they found me eligible. It didn't take long before I was called to report to the railroad station in Cham, from where, along with other orphans, I was shipped to an orphans' home at Indersdorf, Germany, a gathering point for juvenile immigrants near Dachau.

---

6.   Displaced Persons' Camp.
7.   United Nations Relief and Rehabilitation Administration

It wasn't easy to leave my family and friends, but I was getting older and began to think about my own future. I felt I had to find a way to get the education that I was deprived of for the past six years; find a profession or trade to sustain myself. My Uncle Henry and my cousins were very good to me, but I felt that it was time for me to move on.

Finally, the day arrived for us to leave; we were a large group. At first we were scheduled to go to England, but that plan was changed a few days before our departure and we were sent to America instead. They put us on a train to Bremenhaven. The "Marine Perch," a troop transport ship, was ready to sail for the United States from that port. This was the first time for me on a large ship; it was very exciting! It was also the first time I had American chow. The ship took a week to reach the shores of the United States. When I saw the Statue of Liberty, tears of joy filled my eyes. This was the most wonderful sight to see, this magnificent statue representing "Freedom." I lost more than five years of my youth to Nazi persecution and the slave camps. My dream of coming to America finally materialized, I had arrived!

Social workers from the Jewish Children's Bureau took us from the ship to an orphans' home in the Bronx for a short stay. The staff at this home was trying to find foster homes for us in America. I only had to wait there for two weeks before I was sent to a foster home in Cleveland, Ohio. Mrs. Winifred Fryer, "Winnie," my foster mother was a teacher before her retirement. She was a socialite; very well known in Cleveland. Rabbi Aba Hillel Silver, a Reformed rabbi, was one of her best friends. The rabbi was once asked to be the first president of the State of Israel.

Mrs. Fryer was a wonderful person! The first day at her house she told me that from now on we speak only English even though she spoke German as I did. She gave me a good start in my new life. Shortly after my arrival, Mrs. Fryer with the help of Julia Starr, my social worker from the Jewish Children's Bureau, arranged for me to start school. When I came to the U.S., I didn't know more than two words of English, but I learned quickly. They decided to put me in the seventh grade in a junior high school. They knew that I was older than most of the students in my class. I was glad that the UNRRA workers in Germany made an error in my age when I registered. It made me younger and gave me an opportunity to attend school in the U.S.A. It was my luck that this could happen!

I tried very hard to do well in seventh grade. My love and appreciation for music prompted me to begin to study the clarinet and I advanced very quickly in music. As my English improved, the teachers promoted me to higher grades. I finished three grades in one year and graduated from the Patrick Henry Jr. High

School. I also took private clarinet lessons. I entered Glenville High School in 1947, taking a regular schedule and continued with my clarinet. With a few summer courses, I could graduate from high school in two years in 1949.

As my music was also improving very rapidly, I decided to go to college and continue my clarinet and music education. I applied to Oberlin College in Ohio, and asked to be auditioned at the Conservatory of Music. I passed all the scholastic tests and they invited me for an audition at the Conservatory of Music. Oberlin gave me a partial scholarship. My foster mother was very proud of my accomplishments and I also felt good about myself.

While attending junior and high school, Bernard Okin and I became good friends. Bernie also played clarinet and helped me play the instrument, as he started to play at a much younger age and knew a lot more than I did. We became lifelong friends. Bernie's parents and his brother also liked me very much.

When I began college, Mrs. Fryer moved to smaller quarters and I could not stay with her any longer. I needed a place to stay during summers and vacations. Bernie told his parents about that. Without hesitation, the Okins insisted that I stay with them. Joe and Gertie Okin were the most wonderful people; they took care of me as if I had been their own child; they didn't want any compensation. They ran a fruit stand at the Farmers' Market and I volunteered to help them there on weekends and on other busy days all through the summer. I was very grateful to them; they offered me money for my work, but I refused to take it. I felt obligated to them for the opportunity they gave me and for their love and kindness.

I attended college for two years and was a very good music student with average grades in other academic subjects. As I needed money, I washed dishes at the school's dining room. I wasn't ashamed to do an honest day's work, whatever it was.

During the summer of 1951 I met Rita Goodman, another survivor. Rita was born in Berlin, Germany. She lost her parents in Auschwitz, but survived with two sisters, Suzanne[8] and Sylvia. During the war her parents left Germany and escaped to Belgium. They lived there for about a year before they escaped to the south of France. After her parents were taken away to Auschwitz, Rita, the oldest, took care of her sisters as well as she could under the circumstances. At first they lived with a French family and later they went into hiding with the help of French nuns in a cloister in the south.

---

8.   Suzanne (Gutmann) Ringel's story is also part of this collection.

Rita told the nuns that the girls had family in Switzerland. The nuns eventually found her relatives and arranged for the French underground to smuggle them into Switzerland, where they spent the remainder of the war. In 1946, they immigrated to the U.S.A.

In the summer of 1951 Rita came to visit her relatives in Cleveland. Her aunt arranged for us to meet. We started dating and became very fond of each other. We fell in love.

Our romance continued after I went back to college, even though she lived in New York City.

At the beginning of my third year at Oberlin, during the Korean War, I received notice from the draft board in Cleveland to report for a medical examination. Young men under a certain age were getting drafted. My friend, Bernie, enlisted in the Air Force and after his basic training they sent him to play with an Air Force band in Michigan. He was supposed to be drafted into the Army but preferred the Air Force. He suggested that I should also enlist in the Air Force and could also play in the band. He would speak to his bandleader to audition me for his band. I received a notice from the bandleader to come to Michigan for the test. I passed it without any problem and the bandleader told me to enlist in the Air Force. He also assured me that after basic training I would have orders to report to his band. I quit college and enlisted as suggested. I did not like the idea, but I had no choice. Meanwhile, Rita and I were seriously thinking about getting married. Mrs. Fryer, who still was very much a part of my life, was happy about my meeting Rita and decided to give us a wedding. She knew that we couldn't afford one and it was her heartfelt desire to make that gift to us. She arranged everything, including the participation of Rabbi Abba Hillel Silver at his temple in Cleveland.

We had a wedding we never dreamed of, for which we were very grateful to her. It is very sad that she didn't live long enough to see our first son, as she died of cancer before our Sandy was born.

Rita and I spent two and a half years in the service living together in Michigan and Macon, Georgia. The Korean War ended and I was honorably discharged from the Air Force. We moved to Cleveland. Rita was expecting a child after aborting her first pregnancy in Macon. I felt that I had to make a living for my family. At first, I took a selling job, which I quit to go into my own hardware business. That was the biggest mistake of my life. I should have gone back to school to earn my degree in Music Education. I had the opportunity to use my G.I. Bill of Rights; the U.S. government would have paid for my education. I was preoccupied with earning a living, instead of pursuing my life's goal, a career in music. I didn't have anyone to advise me; I had to make all the decisions throughout my life by myself.

Thinking back now, I must have been afraid that I might not get as far in music as I wanted to go. It was wrong. I gave up and did the best I could in what I was doing, running successfully several retail operations and always making a good living. However, going into business was a good move for us, for my marriage to Rita. She was an excellent wife and a superb mother to our children. We were very happy together and had a good life. Sadly, she became very ill when she was about fifty. She was diagnosed with dementia with paraplegia, a neurological disease. She suffered for ten years; the last few years she spent in a nursing home and she passed away at the age of sixty. Our children, Samuel, Mark and Illana, and I miss her. She never knew her four grandchildren: Molly, Jordan, Nina and Reed. We were happily married for 42 years.

While living in Cleveland with my family, I became involved with my fellow survivors of the Holocaust. We formed an organization, the Kol-Israel Foundation. Our goal was to get together in remembrance and commemoration of our loved ones who were so brutally killed in the Holocaust. We were also interested in helping our beloved State of Israel. The Cleveland survivor organization was one of the first in the country to build a lasting monument to the Six Million, the men, women and children who perished in the Jewish Holocaust. We felt that since none of us had graves to visit to say a prayer for our loved ones, we would have a place to visit before the High Holy Days to remember our loved ones and commemorate them by engraving their names in the walls of this monument. I served as President of Kol-Israel for six years. I am still an honorary member of the Board of Directors. This organization later became involved in helping our beloved State of Israel and in other charitable endeavors, social functions for our people and the "Second Generation" of survivors, our children and grandchildren.

At the foot of our monument, bones, hair and ashes are buried, imported from the crematorium at Auschwitz in Poland.

There were several ambulances among our contributions to Israel. Our organization personally delivered one of those in June 1981 at a special dedication ceremony held in Jerusalem during the "Gathering of Holocaust Survivors." Some people wonder why after 36 years of silence such an event was conceived. It was partially caused by the outburst of anti-Semitism, the growth of Neo-Nazism, the constant denials of the Jewish Holocaust by noted academics at various universities. A variety of publications, as well as bad propaganda in many Moslem countries, prompted the survivor communities all over the world to guard the world's conscience about the Jewish Holocaust. During Hitler's reign the world stood by silently. Another factor was that the survivors were getting up in age and realized that it was time to pass on their legacy to the Second Generation, our children and beyond. Six thousand strong gathered in Jerusalem with their children and grandchildren from four continents, twenty-three countries and hundreds of cities to let the world know that we are living witnesses, united in freedom.

As we were enslaved, an indivisible bond was forged among us in the death camps of Nazi Germany. Originally this idea was conceived in the ghettos and concentration camps. While enslaved, we dreamed of freedom and hoped that if we survived, we should meet in Palestine. This Gathering was both a celebration of our survival despite our suffering, and the commemoration of the six million victims of Nazism's assault on European Jewry, the greatest crime against humanity in modern times.

Rita, our daughter, Illana, and I were among approximately one hundred survivors from Cleveland and its vicinity attending this unique Gathering. I had a special personal reason to attend. I was too young when the war broke out and for that reason I never had my Bar Mitzvah. I promised myself that someday, when I go to Israel, I will have my Bar Mitzvah at the *Kotel,* the Wailing Wall in Jerusalem, at the remains of the Temple built by King Solomon more than 2000 years ago. This is the holiest shrine for the Jewish people.

It was a great honor for me to celebrate my Bar Mitzvah there in the Holy Land. As I had dreamt of a Bar Mitzvah all my life, this place and time were perfect. In Cleveland I mentioned my idea to my family; word got around and I received a lot of publicity both in Cleveland and nationally. I must have been the only survivor who thought of going through with a Bar Mitzvah at that time. Public Television filmed my Bar Mitzvah at the Kotel and at Yad Vashem. Wherever I went in Israel, they followed me.

David Hartman's "Good Morning America" show interviewed me from Jerusalem on International Television; Rita and Illana were also interviewed.

A Cleveland television station and the Public TV channel aired my Bar Mitzvah. In a documentary of the entire Gathering, Public TV rebroadcasts it from time to time.

My Bar Mitzvah was one of the highlights of my life. My wife, my daughter and all my friends from Cleveland witnessed it. This event was forty years late, but my dream was fulfilled at last. The rabbi who performed the ceremony and his wife gave a party for me at his Yeshiva in the old city in Jerusalem. Rita, Illana and about thirty of my Cleveland friends were invited and participated.

My children, Samuel (Sandy), Mark, and Illana are my pride and joy. Sandy is an engineer in Coconut Creek, Florida. Mark is an attorney in New York City. Mark and Elaine, his wonderful wife, have two beautiful girls, Molly and Nina. Jordan and Reed are Illana's two wonderful sons.

I am still very active with the Kol-Israel in Cleveland; I am also a member of the board of the Florida Holocaust Survivors.

I have remarried. Rose[9] is also a survivor from Sosnowiec, Poland. She was widowed at about the same time as I was. Rita and I both knew Rose and Henry very well. Rose was the president of the Kol-Israel Sisterhood. She and I worked together for the same causes. Rita and I bought a condominium apartment in the same building where Henry and Rose lived in Sunny Isles, Florida. We spent our winters there and so did they. Henry and I had a very good relationship both in Florida and in Cleveland. Rita and Rose were close friends. My children and Rose's children also knew each other; they attended the same schools in Cleveland. My children love Rose and I hope it is the same the other way around. I do think it is. We both got lucky, we need each other and we are very compatible. Most importantly, our children are also happy for us. We now spend six months in Cleveland and six months in sunny Florida. We have many friends, both old and new. We both play tennis and we are also bridge partners. We hope that the Almighty will give us health for many years to come.

In conclusion, I must extend my gratitude to America for giving me a new chance in my life after the horrors I went through in my teens in Nazi concentration camps. I am very fortunate to be living in my seventies. With a few exceptions, life has been good to me here in the U.S.A. May God bless America and Israel! There should finally be lasting peace in Israel and on Earth!

---

9.   The story of Rose Kaplovitz is also included in this collection.

The Story of my Life

✦

Rose Kaplovitz (Zaks)

I was born in Sosnowiec, Poland. My beloved parents, Mendel and Hinda (Helen) Zaks, had seven children: six daughters, Regina, Cesia, Tola, Mania, Cyma and Rozia, and a son, Romek. My father owned a grocery store. We lived at Ostrogorska 6 in a middle-class neighborhood. I attended a public elementary school for Jewish girls. They taught us all the mandatory Polish subjects and, once a week, Jewish religion. We wore black uniforms with a white collar. For lunch, I would take along two rolls, one for me, and another for a poor student. During the break our teacher would place the roll under a poor student's desk. I never knew who that person was.

My parents always encouraged us to study hard and read a lot. I began to read at five, before I even started school. My school was on my street. There were many children of my age in the neighborhood and we played all kinds of games, volleyball and hide-and-seek, among others. In the winter, we enjoyed sledding and ice-skating. My sister Tola danced beautifully on ice and she taught me to ice skate. My brother Romek played soccer and I liked to watch him. During the summer, we either traveled to various resorts in Szczyrk, Ustron, Bystra, or visited my mother's sisters who lived out of town.

Our home was always filled with songs and laughter. I still remember most of the Polish songs we used to sing—those bring back warm memories.

My mother and my older sisters helped my father in the store. My mother was always busy, even though we had a maid living with us. From time to time she would go to the theatre or a movie with some of her friends. My father went to the synagogue every morning. On Fridays he often brought a guest for Shabbat dinner, an orphan or a poor man. One day he invited a small hunchback; when we stood up to say a prayer, some of my siblings began to laugh at his looks. My father immediately made them leave the dining room. Later, he had a talk with all of us. He taught us a lesson I will never forget: respect others as this misfortune could also happen to any one of you.

On Rosh Hashanah and Yom Kippur my father blew the *shofar* while I was standing next to him, proudly holding on to his *tallit*.[1]

Regina, my oldest sister, was married in 1935. It was a beautiful wedding and for the first time I saw my father dance with her gracefully. Regina gave birth to Lala, a lovely girl, whom we all adored. I played with her all the time.

In 1938, my sister Cesia married Bernard Kaiser and moved to Kielce. That summer they took Cyma and me along with them on their vacation. While playing ball, Cyma ran into the street and was hit by a car. We rushed her to a hospital; her leg was injured. I felt guilty, because I was playing with her in the street.

In the summer of 1939 rumors began to circulate about the coming war. Since we lived so close to the German border, my parents decided that we should go to Kielce where Cesia lived. We started out by train, but we never reached our destination, because on September 1 the German planes began the bombing raids. The train had to stop several times and we had to get off. At one of the stops Romek was missing. He didn't get back on the train at the last stop. He returned home with one of our neighbors, but we were all worried about him.

The German army occupied Sosnowiec immediately, and it was then, at the very beginning of the war, that I felt its terrible impact, when my only brother, Romek, was killed. As soon as the Germans entered our city, they began to terrorize us. They approached several buildings and hollered,

"Alle Juden Menne, Raus!" (All Jewish men, out!)

My uncle, his son and Romek, who was in their house, came forward along with thirty-eight men from that building. They were all shot and buried in a mass grave. Romek was still a teenager. He had done nothing wrong; he was shot only because he was a Jew. I am certain that he did not know why he was dying.

It was a terrible tragedy for my family and me. My parents were devastated and our previously happy home became a quiet and sad place. I knew then that life would never be the same, but little did I know that this was only the beginning. At first, our troubles began to evolve very slowly, very gradually, very systematically. We were being conditioned, but slowly, one at a time, our liberties were taken away. First, we were ordered to wear a white armband with a blue Star of David on it; soon this was changed to a yellow star with the word *"Jude,"* which we wore on the front and back of our clothes. Then we were forbidden to

---

1. Prayer shawl.

enter a theatre or movie, we could not travel by train or streetcar, and we were forbidden to enter certain streets of our hometown.

In December 1939 they proclaimed that no Jewish child could attend school. This ordinance was very difficult for me to accept, as I loved my school and my teacher.

What was I to do all day, every day? At first, my mother hired a tutor in her belief that this was a temporary ordinance. We were hoping that eventually we would be allowed to return to school. I couldn't imagine that for the next six years, the duration of the war, I would not be permitted to attend school. I often watched my Christian neighbors, my friends going to school, and there I was, left behind, not understanding why this was happening to me.

In 1940, the Nazi raids began. They were careful to keep the dates of the raids secret. Without any warning, they surrounded a section of our town and began rounding up our people. Other times they came in the middle of the night and forced their way into our homes.

By the time we realized what was happening, several members of our family had already been taken away. The Nazis knew the family structure of European Jews. They knew that it was part of our heritage and upbringing to feel deep responsibility for each other. They knew that by breaking up the family unit, they often broke our spirit and weakened all of us. By then we had also lost contact with our sister Cesia, who lived in Kielce. She gave birth to her son, Jurek, in January 1940.

It was during one of these raids that my sister Mania was taken away and sent to the Oberaltstadt concentration camp. Our family was growing smaller all the time.

One day, two German soldiers came to our house and took my father's identification card and ordered him to report at the center of our city. They were going to hang three Jewish men and wanted the head of each Jewish household to witness this action to instill more fear in all of us. The same day some of the kids were talking about the hanging. Not realizing what we were about to view, we decided to go and watch. While we were standing there, I began to hum the song "San Francisco…" to myself, when suddenly a scream rose from the crowd. As I looked up, I saw three bodies swaying in the air. Today, 62 years later, when I hear this melody I still see the three bodies in front of me.

In the summer of 1942 we were ordered to report to the *Umschlag Platz* (a gathering place). It was announced to be a routine check; we would have our I.D. stamped, without which we would not get our ration card. This place was a former sports field that held many pleasant memories for me; we used to ice skate there in the winter and watch my brother play soccer. As soon as we were gathered there, we were surrounded by SS troops and held there without food or water for two days and two nights. As long as I live, I will never forget the horrors of that place. I will never forget the cries of hungry and thirsty children. At night we cuddled, we were cold, hungry and filled with fear for the future, not knowing what the next morning would bring. Finally, on the third morning, the selection began. We were ordered to stand in single file. An SS man stood at the head of the line; by the turn of his thumb he decided who shall live and who shall die. The young and healthy were sent to the right, my sister Tola was among them. They were soon shipped by truck to a labor camp in Germany. My parents, my sisters Cyma and Regina, her husband, Srulek, their daughter, Lala, and I were sent to the left "to be resettled to a different town," the Nazi's lie to deceive us. We knew nothing of the existence of the death camp in Auschwitz, where most of the Jews were being shipped. While waiting for our turn, we managed to escape with the help of a Jewish militiaman and our family doctor, who was our neighbor, and we returned home. There were only four of the nine members of the family left.

In 1942 we were forced to leave our home; they allowed us to take only personal possessions, which we could carry in our hands. We were then settled in the "Srodula" ghetto, completely cut off from the outside world.

The ghetto provided the Nazis better control over the Jews and made it easier to deport us later to the death camps or labor camps.

Life in the ghetto was a nightmare: one room per family, no schools, libraries, or synagogues; hundreds of children drifting throughout the ghetto, whose parents had already been shipped to Auschwitz, with no one to care for them. I was ordered to work in a factory where we were making dominoes and checkers for the German army. On the way to work I often passed a school building and saw children playing ball, carrying books, laughing. I wondered why I was not allowed to attend school, what had I done, why were we in the ghetto?

As the Nazi raids became more frequent, some people began to build bunkers, hiding places. Our family also built one in the basement of our building. It was a dark, very narrow space between two walls; one had to enter it from the floor above. I hid there for only one night, terrified. Many times when we suspected a raid at night, someone from the building would watch from the attic to warn the rest and give them a chance to hide. Whenever my father was assigned to the watch, I would go with him. As terrifying as those nights were, those remain fond memories in my heart. Having seven children, my father seldom had time for me alone, but it was there, in the attic that I had my beloved father all to myself. It was there that he told me all about his childhood, about my grandparents. From time to time we would practice multiplication and division, or recite Polish poems, which were a vital part of Polish education. I believe he did this to help me forget for the moment where I was, or to instill hope in me that there was still a future for me. As long as I live I shall never forget those precious moments I spent with my father.

One day as I arrived home from work, no one was there. I found out that there was a raid and thought that my parents and Cyma, my youngest sister, were taken away. I was all alone. I cried and no longer cared what might happen to me. The next morning I did not report for work. That night, while lying awake, I heard a faint sound. I discovered that there were people hidden in the bunker. The Nazis took away only the person who covered the entrance to the bunker and there was no one to help me until I found it myself. I was so happy to be reunited with my parents; I could not stop crying from happiness.

By that time the population of the ghetto was reduced to a much smaller number; Regina, her husband and Lala were still living there and I went to see them as often as I could. My mother knew how much I missed reading, so she would practice spelling with me, or tell me stories of the First World War. She also sang Russian songs for Cyma and me.

One day, in July 1943, my father took me aside to convince me to volunteer for the Oberaltstadt concentration camp. I began to cry and ran to my mother. My first thought was my father had gone mad, but my mother calmed me down and urged me to listen to him. I didn't know that my father had learned that the liquidation of the ghetto was imminent and he thought if I volunteered, I might have a chance to survive. He told me that he found out that only families with a single child would be allowed to remain in the ghetto. I listened to him and having no alternative, finally agreed. I believe that by then my mother had given up on life. Of her seven children only two were left, and I was also leaving. She was holding on to me; my father had to tear me out of her arms. But it was my father who was ready to give his life for me, his child. He had to take me by my hand, knowing that he might never see me again, and deliver me to the Nazis. On the way there he tried to instill hope in me.

I remember his last words: "Be strong, you must live, for we will be waiting here for you. The war is coming to an end in a month or two." I believe that I am alive today only because of my beloved father's wisdom and foresight.

I arrived at Oberaltstadt Concentration Camp not knowing that only two weeks after I left, our ghetto "Srodula" was declared "Judenrein" (free of all Jews).

They were all shipped to Auschwitz, where they and the rest of my beloved family perished in the gas chambers and the crematoria. Had I known that I would never see them again, there would have been nothing to sustain me and I also would have perished. The belief that some day I would be reunited with my family helped me survive. I was fortunate to end up in the same camp with my sisters, Mania and Tola. We helped each other go on and survive together. The day I entered the concentration camp, all my belongings were taken away from me, even my last personal possession, my own name. They gave me a uniform with a number and a Star of David on it. By being reduced to just a number, you lose your personal identity.

Life in the camp was a nightmare; I worked twelve-hour shifts in a factory, making thread. Our food consisted of a slice of dark bread, a cup of black coffee and a small bowl of watered-down soup. Hunger was our most significant everyday problem. Starvation was a devastating weapon; it stripped us of our strength, pride, dignity and often our will to go on. But even though starvation depleted our meager bodies, the inmate's links with others in the same situation provided a life sustaining force; a feeling of solidarity developed among the girls who shared the same room.

We would help and comfort one another; we tried to maintain some kind of order and unity in our miserable life. We were forced to retreat to a very primitive mental life. Somehow we managed to preserve the spiritual freedom of mind. Years of discrimination have turned us inward towards our own people. Many times when our spirit sank low, someone in the room would break into a song. It was our only means of expressing our pain, sorrow, grief, but also our hope. Our religion was still a strong part of our lives.

Many times we would return from work, tired, hungry, cold, and be called to *appell* (roll call), where we were forced to stand outdoors in all sorts of weather. Our Nazi guards, both men and women, would think of ways to humiliate us, degrade us, and would squeeze out of us the last reserve of human dignity. When it snowed, they would make us lie flat in the snow and crawl. When it rained, we would have to use our drinking cup and scoop out water from the puddles. It was the worst when they ordered us to remove our uniforms and stand there in the nude. All the time they were laughing at us and calling us "untermensch"(subhuman). The brutalities and inhumane treatment left wounds and mental anguish that nothing could erase. Our passport to life was work. They allowed us to live as long as we were able to produce.

Once we became ill, we were done away with. Mania became very sick with typhoid fever; she was taken to the sickroom. There was no medication for her.

After three days, the nurse, a girl from our hometown, told Mania that she would have to go to work the next day.

In the morning the nurse helped her get dressed and sent her off to work. At first we were very angry with the nurse for being so cruel, but after we came home from work we realized that by sending Mania to work, she saved her life. The nurse suspected that on that day the Gestapo would come and take all the sick girls away. And that is exactly what happened. We never saw any of them again.

◆   ◆   ◆

In March 1945, they closed our factory. We didn't know that the Allies were advancing. The Germans could not deliver the supplies to our factory. We were forced to work outdoors, building trenches and tilling the fields. By that time all the girls in our concentration camp were very weak, sick and totally exhausted.

On May 8, 1945, the war was officially over. That night we went to sleep as usual. But we didn't know that the war was over. Next morning we woke up, there were no Nazi guards around. At first we didn't understand what was happening. The girls began moving about and pushed open the gate of the camp. We ran into the streets, where we met the oncoming Russian Army. We jumped on top of their tanks and trucks. We kissed and hugged our liberators. We were free!

Liberation came much too late, but it was the greatest day in my life! That night we celebrated our liberation in the assembly hall of the factory together with our liberators and Russian and British prisoners of war from the nearby prisoner camps.

As transportation in Europe was totally paralyzed, we had no immediate chance to return home; we had to remain in the camp for two more weeks. Finally, we were able to return home. The arrival was the worst day of my life! Our house was still there and so was our furniture, but strange people were living there. It was then that we found out that our father, mother, Cyma, Regina and her daughter, Lala, all perished in Auschwitz. As heartbroken as I was, I was fortunate that my sisters, Tola and Mania, were alive and we were together. Soon we learned that Cesia and her five-year-old son, Jurek, had survived and they were living in a small apartment in Sosnowiec. Bernard, her husband, was killed in one of the concentration camps, but Jurek survived because of two goodhearted Christian families, who hid him in their homes. We all moved into that small apartment with Cesia. Taking into account my situation and young age, my sisters decided that I should return to school. At first I was excited about going to school, but then I asked myself, what school? What grade?—After six years without schooling, there was no way I could enter regular school and also be the only Jewish child there. My sisters began to make inquiries and learned about a Jewish children's home in the nearby city of Chorzow. We all decided that this was the only place for me. I lived there happily and attended a special school with other children.

Some survived in the streets of Warsaw, some were hidden by gentiles, and others, like me, were survivors of concentration camps. I lived there for about eight months. Eventually we realized that there was not much future for Jews in Poland. With the help of Cesia, I joined a kibbutz formed by a youth group and soon left Poland for Germany.

◆   ◆   ◆

Ironically, Germany was the only country where survivors could settle after the war. The gates to all the free countries were still closed to us, even *Eretz Yisrael*, officially Palestine.

I lived at the kibbutz in Leipheim at the D.P. camp for eight months, preparing for immigration to Palestine, which later became the State of Israel. I was happy to be living there with young Jews. My sisters also arrived in Germany and settled in the Bergen-Belsen D.P. camp. They wanted me to live with them, but by that time I was so attached to kibbutz life that I refused to leave. I was learning Jewish history and Hebrew songs, which I loved. My only dream and desire was to leave for Palestine. At that time the British closed the gates to Palestine to Jews and the only way one could get there was with the *Bricha*, Jewish soldiers who smuggled Jews into the country. One day Reuven, the head of the Bricha, called me out of my room and began to talk to me. He told me that he learned that I had three older sisters who wished to go to America, where our maternal uncle was living, but they would not leave without me. He made me realize how lucky I was to have three sisters. Since I was the youngest, he believed that for my own benefit he would not permit me to separate myself from my siblings. He was a wise man!

In December 1946 the UNRRA[2] registered me as an orphan to immigrate to America. While I was at the kibbutz, the Bricha changed the year of my birth to make me younger to be eligible to go to Palestine legally as a child. I used that document to register with the UNRRA. They immediately transferred me to

---

2.   United Nations Relief and Rehabilitation Administration

Prien am Chimsey, a children's camp, from where I would eventually leave for the U.S.A. The camp was on a lake, it was beautiful! There were many children there from various countries. In September 1947, many of us left for America on the battleship Ernie Pile.

On September 21 we arrived at the shores of this wonderful land. I looked at the great Statue of Liberty with amazement and tears in my eyes. I questioned her: Where have you been all those years? Why didn't you help us sooner? I can't describe my deep emotions upon stepping on this land, "Home of the Free!" I too was free. Soon we were taken to a children's home at 22 Coldwell Avenue in the Bronx. We had to stay there until we were placed either in a foster home or with a relative. After six weeks there, they sent me to Cleveland. I was placed under the auspices of the Jewish Children's Bureau. Miss Julia Starr was my social worker, who placed me with my uncle, David Kleinman, aunt Mary and cousins, Sylvia and Eileen. They were the most wonderful people, kind and gentle; I loved them dearly. Miss Starr registered me at the Alexander Hamilton Junior High School, where they placed me in the ninth grade. I had not been in school for eight years and I can't describe the feeling of finally having that privilege.

It was very difficult at the beginning, because I did not know the English language, but I made a vow to myself to learn it, and I was going to be just like all my new American schoolmates. Three months into the school year I told my social worker that I would also like to attend Hebrew school. She was surprised; she looked at me with amazement and asked me why? How would I be able to do that? Hebrew school was held four times a week, after school. She felt that I had too much catching up to do in a language that I didn't know. I told her that I suffered a lot because I am a Jew, but I don't know much about my religion, my history and my heritage; I don't know Hebrew, I don't know how to pray, and I don't even know how to say a prayer for my parents. She agreed under the condition that I would keep up my grades in school.

I finished the ninth grade and went on to the John Adams High School. They gave me an aptitude test and told me that I excelled in mathematics and science. For these reasons I pursued college prep classes. I loved my teachers, who were kind and helpful, but it was Irma Schlager, my homeroom teacher, who helped me the most. She got me involved in many types of school activities: student council, intramural and class president. The students were very friendly and understanding. They knew that I was a refugee girl but knew nothing about my past because I never spoke about it in those days.

My aunt and uncle told me not to speak about my life during the Holocaust. They believed that with time I would forget my bad memories and move on toward a normal and happy life. Even my dear cousin, Sylvia, who was very close to me, knew very little about my past. We just went on and had a very good and happy time together. I graduated from high school with honors after two years. I was installed into the national honor society, and graduated fifth in my class. At the same time I also graduated from Hebrew high school. My uncle, aunt, cousins, along with my sisters, Tola and Mania, were all very proud of me. That was in January 1951. Case Western Reserve University offered me a scholarship and I was scheduled to start the first week in September 1951. Instead, on September 16, 1951, I married my Henry Kaplovitz, a survivor, with whom I was in love. We shared our desire for our own home and family. I chose marriage over furthering my education. Henry was in the jewelry business, which he had learned in a D.P camp. I started to work in an office as a bookkeeper. We were very happy together and enjoyed our life as we were helping each other to go on.

◆   ◆   ◆

On January 5, 1953, I gave birth to Hedy, our fist child, named after my mother. We were very happy and rejoiced at this event. Finally, we began to raise a family of our own! Marc was born on July 8, 1955; he was named after Henry's and my own father. We tried to keep the names of our families alive. Ronnie, our third child, was born on October 20, 1957; he was named after my only brother. The children were growing and Henry and I were enjoying the fruits of our marriage. We finally had a family after for so many years of loneliness.

◆   ◆   ◆

Raising my children became my first priority. I wanted them to have a normal and happy childhood. Now, that I am a grandmother and I love my grandchildren with all my heart, I realize what my own children had missed. They never had the unconditional love of a grandmother or grandfather.

◆   ◆   ◆

When Ronnie, our youngest, started school, I decided to enroll at the College of Jewish Studies, and eventually became a religious school teacher.

As the children were growing up, we took vacations with our friends and relatives. Most of our friends were survivors, so our children felt comfortable with all of them. We lived on Stonehaven, in South Euclid; their school was at the end of the street. The street was always filled with children and that always reminded me of my street in my hometown.

Education was a vital part of our family life; they also attended Sunday and Hebrew Schools. In 1968, our son Marc became Bar Mitzvah. This called for a great celebration! Ronnie became Bar Mitzvah in 1970. Henry and I were very proud of our children! We were happy to see our children growing up. My sisters were also married and had children; we were all living on the same street. All three of our children attended college: Hedy became a psychiatric social worker; Mark followed in his father's footsteps and became a successful businessman and eventually a private homebuilder; Ronnie became an attorney. I am grateful for their achievements and Henry, of course, was very proud of all of them. He taught them many practical lessons in life, including investments in business and finance. In time, all our children married and began to raise their own families. Jenna and Katie are Hedy's children. Marc and Elise have Joshua and Brie. David Henry is the son of Ronnie and Marla. They are my pride and joy!

In 1970 I began speaking in public about my life during the Holocaust. I have spoken in public schools and universities throughout Ohio, Florida, Pennsylvania, Kentucky and many other states. I believe that speaking and teaching about the Holocaust is my moral responsibility. It is a lesson in human relations, a lesson on hate, prejudice, and discrimination, but also a lesson on courage, tolerance, and the will to live. It is essential that this discussion should be at an academic level to bring the awareness of the catastrophe to all the students. I have also participated in many Holocaust conferences and teachers' seminars. Governor Richard Celeste appointed me to serve on the Ohio Holocaust Educational Council. I also serve on the American Holocaust Survivors' Committee and have been active with the "Holocaust Survivors Organization Thiokol Israel Foundation" in Cleveland. I had served as president of its sisterhood several times and served on the Community Relations Council of the Jewish Federation, and on the Board of the Jewish National Fund. The Kol Israel Sisterhood Greater Cleveland State of Israel Bond Organization honored me for my contributions to Holocaust education and I have received many honorary plaques. Youngstown University also honored me with its prestigious Janus Korchak Award. In 1981, I attended the first World Gathering of Holocaust Survivors in Jerusalem, Israel. This was our very first reunion. I was happy to be reunited with many former inmates of the Oberaltstadt concentration Camp, who are living all over the world. It was great to see them again! We rejoiced in our gathering and, along with our children and grandchildren, celebrated life.

Cleveland was well represented by survivors. We, the members of the Kol Israel Foundation, brought an ambulance as our gift to Mogen David Adom. In 1983 and 1985 I attended similar gatherings in Washington and Philadelphia.

Henry and I had a very happy life together, we raised three wonderful children and had five grandchildren, whom he loved dearly and enjoyed spending much time with them. They enjoyed playing all sorts of games with him and Henry was very good and generous with them. He was very proud of the grandchildren and had a lot of fun with them. We lived happily together for forty-two years, but sadly, he suddenly passed away in May 1993. This was heartbreaking! We all miss him very much and will never forget him. May he rest in peace!

◆   ◆   ◆

In 1999 I went on a Second Journey of Conscience through Eastern Europe and Israel with Leatrice Rabinsky leading our group. I felt that this was my only opportunity to take my two oldest grandchildren: Jenna Gelin and Joshua Kaplovitz with me. I wanted them to have a better understanding of the Holocaust Era and to trace their heritage. We traveled to Holland, Austria, Czechoslovakia and Poland. Along the way we stopped at the concentration camps in Teresienstadt, Mauthausen, Treblinka, Maidanek, and Auschwitz-Birkenau. At Mauthausen, Jenna and Josh paid tribute to the memory of their grandfather, Henry, in a special ceremony. Henry was an inmate there during the Holocaust. In Auschwitz, we held a memorial service for my parents, my family and for the Six Million Jews who perished in the Holocaust. Jenna and Joshua wrote a very moving recitation and read it to the assembled group. That was their way to honor their great-grandparents and the family they never knew. I hope these events provided them with a better understanding of the tragedy of the Holocaust and what we, their grandparents, lived through under the Nazi regime. I am certain that they will always remember this journey and hope they will pass on the memory to their children and grandchildren.

In January 1996 I married Jack Baigelman.[3] I had known Jack and his wife Rita for forty-five years. Rita passed away six months after Henry. We had been friends all along. Our children have known each other since childhood. They even went to school together and met at all Kol Israel functions. Ever since its creation, Jack and I had both been involved with the Kol Israel Foundation. Jack was its president for several years and I was president of the Sisterhood. We

---

3.   Jack Baigelman's story is also included in the collection.

worked hand-in-hand for Holocaust survivors and the State of Israel. We are happy to have each other and appreciate that neither of us is alone.

I love America with all my heart, and I am forever grateful to this country for giving me the opportunity for a better life and for my loving family. GOD BLESS AMERICA!

I am forever grateful to God, for giving me the strength to speak to young students today. I hope that they will have a better understanding of what prejudice and hate can do to others. I speak in the hope that history does not repeat itself.

Entombed

✦

Bernard Mayer

I was born in Drohobycz, Poland. As I recall, my early childhood was uneventful, but happy in Drohobycz. I was the youngest of four children. My mother and father were very attentive to me as were my sister and brothers. The population of Drohobycz was fifty thousand: about seventeen thousand Jews, eighteen thousand Poles and fifteen thousand Ukrainians. Everyone in town knew his place.—The Jews were businessmen, artisans and professionals. The Poles were government workers and professionals, and the Ukrainians were mostly peasants, who provided produce, grains and so on, for the population.

Most of my extended family lived in town including my grandfather, aunts, uncles, and cousins. I experienced a lot of joy in those early years, when my father was a successful businessman.

When I was eight years old, my father died. My mother opened a chocolate store and my brother Simon married. My brother Jacob, my sister Clara and my mother lived together in our apartment. I enjoyed school, reading, shows and concerts. My cousins attended college. Cousin Helen attended medical school in Lvov.

On June 29, 1941, the German army entered our town. I was 13 years old. It was the beginning of the tragedy for the Jews in Drohobycz. All the Jews became disenfranchised. We were required to register, wear white armbands to indicate our Jewish identity.

We had to surrender anything of value, including items of gold, silver, fur and art works. We were forced to work in camps, set up by the Germans, without pay. My sister worked in a nursery, my brother Jacob in a coffee factory, and I was making brushes in a small camp.

Many people died of starvation; others, who were younger, worked in the camps for meager amounts of food.

In August of 1942, the Germans and their collaborators started a weeklong hunt. They gathered up about 70 percent of the Jewish population, including my entire family except for my mother, sister and my brother Jacob. They were forced into railroad cars for cattle and transported to Bezec, a death camp, where, they were immediately gassed and cremated.

In October 1942 all Jews were driven out of their dwellings into the ghetto. A second hunt took place on November 19, 1942, when most of the rest of the Jews were taken away from the ghetto. Many were shot on the street, including a famous artist and writer, Bruno Schulz.[1][2]

By January 1943 only a handful of Jews were still in the ghetto. My sister Clara escaped to the forest, but she was caught and killed. My brother Simon and his family were also killed. My brother Jacob was still working in the coffee factory. I was in the camp, and my mother was hiding in a closet in a ghetto apartment.

One day she ventured out to the little grocery store. There she met Mrs. Schwarts, who knew a Ukrainian Catholic, Ivan Bor, who was willing to let some Jews build a bunker under his house. He was paid for each person who entered that bunker.

My brother organized the construction by hiring an expert named Aron. It took three months to build it, in complete secrecy. The bunker was 10 feet by 30 feet and 6 feet high. It had cisterns for water, gas and electricity, a toilet connected to the sewer, and a radio as well. The bunker was built for sixteen people, but eventually forty-five people lived there for up to eighteen months, never seeing daylight.

This bunker was the only one that had so many people and survived. Life in the bunker was described in my book: "Entombed: My True Story."[3]

Out of those seventeen thousand Jews in Drohobycz only one hundred and fifty survived, including two small four-year old girls—the only children out of four thousand.

---

1. "One of the most remarkable writers who ever lived...He wrote sometimes like Kafka, sometimes like Proust, and at times succeeded in reaching depths that neither of them reached."—I. B. Singer. From the dust jacket of "Letters and Drawings of Bruno Schulz" Ed. J. Ficowski, Harper & Row, 1987.

2. "Bruno Schulz was one of the great writers, one of the great transmogrifiers of the world into words...Schulz's verbal art strikes us—stuns us, even—with its overload of beauty."—John Updike; source: the same dust jacket.

3. Bernard Mayer: "Entombed—My True Story: How Forty-five Jews lived Underground and Survived the Holocaust." Aleric Press © 1994.

On August 5, 1944, the Soviet Army liberated Drohobycz and all forty-five souls emerged alive from the bunker.

We left the bunker without anything of tangible value, very weak and thin. We had to start anew. We sold potato knishes on the street, baked cookies, and opened small eateries.

Within a few months we had clothing on our backs and I went back to school. By May 1945 we left Drohobycz for Krakow; and eventually immigrated to Paris. It took three years before my brother, mother and I were reunited in the U.S.A.

We had to start anew once again, selling goods at flea markets and working in factories.

My mother got married to an American man, who was able to support her. After many menial jobs my brother Jacob eventually owned a successful gift store, married and had two daughters.

Eventually, I entered New York University, where I received a Bachelor of Science degree in Economics. Later, I was engaged in a successful business.

I married and have two sons. Both are professionals, married, and I have a grandson.

About twenty-five years ago I decided to change my profession. I earned a Master's degree in Social Work and practiced psychotherapy in Miami.

A few years ago I wrote and published the book: "Entombed: My True Story." Over 18 thousand copies have been sold. I also visit schools and talk about the Holocaust to the students in the hope that their generation will learn from our experience.

On a Wing and a Prayer

◆

David B. Zugman,
formerly Dow, Dov, Dave Zugman

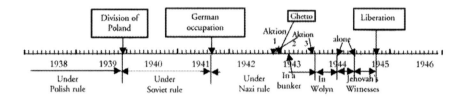

THE YEARS PRIOR TO GERMANY'S INVASION ON JUNE 23, 1941

Sokal, the town in Poland, where I was born, is about 90 km north of **Lvov**, formerly Lemberg. Today its name is **Lviv** and it is in the Ukraine.

The River Bug runs through the town. It earned its place in history when Nazi Germany and Soviet Russia invaded Poland in 1939 and divided the country with the Bug as the border. The west side of the river was occupied by the Germans, the east side by the Russians. We lived east of the River under the Soviets until June 23, 1941, when the Germans crossed the river and began the invasion of Russia.

I remember little about our life in Poland before 1939. I was an only child and very spoiled. I remember that each year mother and I went to the mountains, Zakopane, for more than a month;…that I was paid to eat;…that I broke the rabbi's *kanchik* (cat o'nine tails) and was thrown out of the *cheder* (the Hebrew school);…that my mother was a seamstress and had employees working for her;…and that I was told that my mother rejected a suitor for he lit a cigarette on Saturday.

In 1939 I was nine years old and I don't remember much about our life under communist Russia. I do remember that my father, a grain merchant, had to give up the business and work somewhere else; and the penalties were severe for being late for work.

JUNE 23, 1941 TO MID-JUNE 1943—UNDER THE NAZIS

A week after the Germans crossed the Bug, they issued an edict that all male Jews from 16 to 60 had to report under penalty of death in the center of town. Until the last minute my father was debating whether to go. After he consulted a Ukrainian neighbor, a "friend," who was already wearing a police uniform, he did report. This "friend" probably told him not to worry. The Ukrainian police chose 200 Jews, including my father, and killed them near a brick factory outside the town. However, we did not know that this happened. We were told that the men were taken to a work camp. The Ukrainians or Germans took personal items from the dead men and periodically managed to send something to the families from various parts of the country to create the impression that they were alive and working in camps.

Meanwhile, the Jews in town were subjected to forced labor, economic restrictions and physical attacks. On September 17, 1942 the first *"aktion"* took place in which approximately 2,000 Jews were deported to the death camp at Belsec. Our Jewish neighbor was part of the *Judenrat*, the Jewish police. He forewarned us, so we hid in the barn of our Ukrainian neighbor and survived that *aktion*.

On October 15, 1942 (I found out all the exact dates after the war), the ghetto was set up and more than 5,000 Jews, including some from other towns, were concentrated there. We had to leave our home, our furniture and most of our belongings, and move into the ghetto together with our cousins. The ghetto had only four wells and we suffered from severe shortages. As I said, there is a memory blockage. I don't recall much about my life in the ghetto but a few things. Thanks to mother's trade, we had food. Her Polish and Ukrainian customers kept coming to the ghetto to have dresses made and altered. We also received some packages from friends in Italy, including such delicacies as sardines, which we traded for bread and other necessities to exist.

I recall another episode: I was a stamp collector. Before the ghetto, I subscribed to receive new issues by mail. The German commander of the town somehow found out about the Jewish stamp collector. He probably did not know that I was a boy of 12; he ordered the Jewish police, the *Judenrat*, to find the stamp collector. They found me and brought me before him. He demanded my stamp collection. I told him that when we moved to the ghetto the stamp collection was lost. Looking at the small scrawny boy before him, perhaps he believed me. Nevertheless, he slapped me around a bit and ordered me into a cellar for three days, where the *Judenrat* continuously kept asking me where the stamp collection was. Then he ordered me released.

The second *aktion* took place between October 24 and 28, 1942. They awakened us early in the morning, screaming *"Raus!"* I saw people being shot on the spot. I cannot recall why; perhaps they tried to run. We were gathered at the center of the town near the railroad station and waited for the train. We numbered 2,500 men, women and children. While we were waiting, we saw a Ukrainian with an "SS" man coming toward us. Mother recognized the Ukrainian. She was in the process of making a dress for his wife. He knew us well. As he approached, we were hoping that he was coming to help us, but he only came to retrieve the cloth for the dress. Mother pushed me towards him, begging him to take just me, but all he wanted was the cloth for the dress.

They herded us into the cattle train, like sardines. After a while, we carved a small opening in the side of the car and some started to jump out. Mother didn't want to go, but I convinced her. At last, she jumped! I jumped right after her. The Germans had a machine gun on top of the train. Some jumpers were hit. I fell to the ground and was not hurt. I found my mother. She had a broken nose and was unconscious. With great effort, we succeeded in getting back to the ghetto. As the saying goes, ***"Wi ahyn soll ich gehn."*** (Where should I go?) There was nowhere else to go. I do believe that among the 2,500 Jews herded into that train, I am the only survivor today. The train went to Belzec, not a labor camp, but an extermination camp. I am not aware of anyone alive among those who jumped.

Returning to the ghetto, we found all our belongings gone. We were able to live by selling those belongings, which our former landlady, outside the ghetto, returned to us.

Eight months passed. Then the third and final *aktion* took place around the 27th of May 1943. It was named *"Judenrein;"* it meant that every Jew found would be killed so that the District of Lemberg would be free of Jews.

Our relatives dug a tunnel into a bunker. Thirty of us stayed in the bunker for 12 days. A young child was choked deliberately so that the Germans or Ukrainians would not hear the baby's cries. When we ran out of bread and water, we were forced to leave. Fifteen went to Wolyn, an area about 25 km north of Sokal. It was a relatively safe area as it was under the control of Ukrainian partisans. The Germans generally stayed away from that area. Thirteen of those were caught and killed. Mother and I went to our old landlord, who was afraid to hide us. We went into a corn stack. The Ukrainian police found us, took everything we had, but let us go. Mother was ready to surrender and be killed. I could barely dissuade her. We were also able to sneak through the border to Wolyn, where there were no Germans any more, only Ukrainians.

JUNE 1943 TO LIBERATION, EARLY AUGUST 1944

For about five months we lived together with a number of other Jews in a village in Wolyn. Mother was able to provide for us by sewing for the Ukrainian women.

When I said there were only Ukrainians in Wolyn, it was not quite true. There were Poles living among the Ukrainians in the village, just as there were Ukrainians living in Polish-controlled areas. The Ukrainians were preparing for an independent state and were doing some ethnic cleansing. One Sunday afternoon, the Ukrainian partisans surrounded a Polish church filled with people for Sunday services and killed every man, woman and child in the church. Fear descended on us and with good reason. When the Russians were only about 200 km from the village, the Ukrainian *"Bandrovtes"* started murdering the Jews in Wolyn. We hid in the straw. It was the end of December 1943; the weather was freezing. We had nothing to eat. Mother went to the villagers where she used to sew and asked for bread. Another Jewish woman and her son were with us. The villagers gave her bread, but later they betrayed us to the *Bandrovtes*.

I have blocked out of my memory most of the details of the horrors perpetrated against my family and me during the Holocaust. I only remember some peripheral episodes. I believe that this blockage has helped me function and live a somewhat normal life. Until recently, all I could recall about the events of that night at the end of December 1943 was that my mother was killed by the Ukrainians and thrown in a well;…my feet were frozen, and somehow I survived that horror.

In 1946 while the memories and the nightmares were still vivid, I wrote several letters in Polish and Ukrainian to my uncle in America and my aunt in Israel. Some of the letters were translated into Yiddish and published in a book about my town, Sokal. Today I am unable to read those letters in the language I used for writing. The blockage has deepened. My original letters were lost, but I arranged one letter with details of the events of that horrible night to be translated from Yiddish into English. It is quite unbearable for me to read the horrible details of my mother's murder.

…Zugman's letter starts to relate his memories from the moment when he and his mother are lying hidden in a haystack:

It's evening. It's dark outside. It's about 3:30 a.m. After so much thinking and clamoring during the entire day and night, they fell into a deep and snoring sleep. Only I cannot fall asleep…. something is choking me, biting at me…. My mind wanders…I don't know where…

*My mother woke up for a few minutes and told me about the dream she had. She told me that she dreamt about cookies and flour…and that afterwards, she left by train, after she had kissed me and said goodbye. **"That's not a good sign,"** my mother continued, **"because during the first and second "aktion" I had the same dream. But now, it's all the same to me, I don't want to be tortured anymore—all this time I struggled and suffered for your sake. While still in Sokal, I wanted to give up because I knew that we wouldn't be able to hide. I would only like to live to see the day when those who are torturing us will be avenged. But, that's impossible because even if they don't find us, we'll freeze to death and the lice will eat us.—When they took your father, I cried so much; but your father didn't suffer as much…. and now, after so much pain, I will die.—Your father was truly a saintly man."***

And with these words, my mother fell asleep again. But, I couldn't fall asleep. I wanted to catch at least a nap, but I tried in vain. Several different thoughts were going through my mind. I thought about each word that my mother had spoken. Finally, I lost control and started to cry.

*I calmed down and began to think again, but the frost and the lice disturbed my thinking. Because of the cold, the lice attached themselves to my body and sucked my warm blood. From time to time I had to reach into my clothes…. and never in vain. Each time I took out some lice…. never missed. My mother used to say, **"If God allows us to live, although that's impossible—and I will be free, I will ask the doctor, how lice can multiply, a thousand at a time."***

*While these thoughts were running through my head, I heard footsteps. The sound of footsteps became clearer, and someone was screaming, **"Who gave you permission to sit here?"***

*My heart felt as if it had stopped…. my breathing was irregular…. I became confused. A hand began to pull on the coat that I used to cover myself. Not knowing from fear what I was doing, I began to yell, **"Mother!"** But my mother was no longer sleeping. When they pulled me out of the hold, my mother was already near me…. she was the first to crawl out by herself.*

It became quiet. Suddenly, I heard terrible wailing. The other woman and the child, lying on the other side of the stack, in the hope to be forgotten, had not given any sign of life this whole time…. Only now, as they were pulling her out, did she start screaming and sobbing. The Ukrainian murderers paid no attention to her crying and pulled her by force. Her crying prompted one of the Ukrainians to speak with greed in his voice.

***"Whatever you have—give it to me!"**, he yelled. In a moment, a sparkling ring appeared in his hand.*

"You have nothing more?"

"I don't."

"And you", he spoke to my mother, *"Do you have anything?"*

"No, I don't."

"What if we find something on you?"

"You can do with me whatever you want!"

"Good!"

"Now, come behind the barn and we will talk."

We were all afraid that they would kill us behind the barn and began to cry and yell as loud as we could. Each of us was talking, crying and screaming at the same time.

The Ukrainian commandant, a short, fat **"Vlasovietz"** *(Vlasov, was a Soviet general who went over to the German side with his entire army) didn't want us to awaken the villagers and started to speak to us in Russian.*

"Why are you screaming and wailing? I am going to tell you...it's like this: the Jews are suspected of reporting on us to the Soviet partisans. That's why we're looking for you...We're not going to do anything to you...We're supposed to take you to the people in the village...What they will do to you, we don't know...I believe that they won't kill women and children...Men?—maybe...but you...they'll probably put you to work...and you will work! Now get in the wagon and we will take you to the leaders."

Hearing these words, our hearts lightened for a moment. We started to climb into the wagon. Only I—because I was barefoot and my feet were swollen from frostbite, couldn't make it to the wagon on my own. One of the assassins took me and carried me to the wagon. From the way he carried me, it became clear to me that they were taking us not to the leaders but to the well. Only when I was already on the wagon did I tell my mother what I thought. My mother answered, **"If you want to, run away! I can no longer run. It was only for your sake that I have forced myself for so long."**

"But...dear mother...I won't run away without you! Aside from that, I'm barefoot, my feet are swollen, and I wouldn't be able to walk three steps."

Our journey continued. The peasant who was driving the wagon was the same person whose place we used for hiding, and he must have given us away. Three Ukrainian bandits were walking behind the wagon.

"Where are you taking us?" *my mother asked the peasant.* **"Tell me!"**

"I don't know..."

We continue. Snow-covered fields surround us...everything is white around us. As luck would have it, it is a bitter cold night and we're all shivering. We're probably far from the village, because once or twice, I heard the crowing of a rooster from a distance.

Suddenly, the wagon stops. At first glance, I was wondering why we stopped in the middle of the white fields. But there was no time to wonder. Three Ukrainians approached the wagon.

"Down!...Down! What are you waiting for?...Down!..."—they were barking in Ukrainian.

Now we understood what was coming...we heard screams...and crying...but what good would screaming do in an open field?

"Are these the authorities?"—my mother asked.

"Down! Why are you waiting?...to death...finished!"...and waved the butt of his rifle.

We climbed down from the wagon and didn't stop screaming and crying...we knew that we were approaching our last moment.

"Get down on the ground...get down quickly!...Don't ask so many questions!..."

"Dear people, what have we done to you?...Why do you want to kill us?"....

"How do we trouble you.... have pity!...Don't kill us.... We came to you.... We want to live, too!..."

"Why are you wasting time?!"...one of them yelled and with his rifle butt lashed out at my mother.

"You'll die and it's over!...You, Jewish Muscovite partisans!...You have betrayed our country!"...

With aching heart, knowing what was going to happen, we lay down in the snow. But I couldn't lie still...even though I knew for sure that I wouldn't be able to run away. A Ukrainian beat me twice with his rifle butt and threw me to the ground...but I got up again. I stood and saw three coiled up bodies in the snow, like herring...awaiting death.

Suddenly I heard a command from the dark Vlasovietz.... His strong voice roared like thunder and tore into the stillness of the night.

"Konvodir!"—(the driver who drove the prisoners)—*"Shoot!"*—echoed the voice...

In that same moment, a shot was heard...There was a flash of light, and it lit up everything around me. I turned ice cold...I began to shiver as if I had a fever...I became confused.

Not a minute passed before we heard the second command...again a shot, which tore into the stillness of the night and lit up everything around me again. Now I could also see the bodies lying in the snow.... And then I heard a soft moan that escaped from the child's mouth...from the child that was lying in the snow near his mother...A bullet had probably gone through the child.

After a minute the same thing was repeated. I was standing there confused and looking at everything around me...One of the Ukrainians struck me and I fell to the ground.

I didn't even try to get up this time, because I knew it was my turn. Another sudden shot was heard...For an instant I was frozen and stuck to the ground...I curled up and remained still. In this pose, I was thinking...I don't feel anything...maybe my soul is already in heaven?...

But soon the Ukrainians started to scream again:

"Let's throw them in the well!...Tear off their things!"

I turned toward the direction of the yelling. Two murderers approached the Jewish woman, who was lying there, wounded right from the beginning, and as soon as they started to tear her clothes off her, she started screaming and shouting for high heavens.

*I also heard my mother's voice…And her voice will forever remain in my memory until the end of my life, because these were my mother's last words, **"In the name of God, aren't you afraid? While still alive, you are going to throw us into the well?…"***

But the Ukrainians wanted to be rid of us as quickly as possible. When the other woman wouldn't stop screaming, they surrounded her and one of them hit her on the head with his rifle butt. Blood spurted into my eyes…. After that I don't remember anything.

When it came to murdering Jews, the Ukrainians did not need any lessons from the Nazis. When I awoke the next morning, I was in a stable. My feet were tucked into the woolly coat of a little lamb. The stable belonged to religious Baptists. They found me and put a concoction of hot chickpeas on my feet that gradually reduced the swelling. After a while they became afraid, and I had to leave.

I wandered from house to house. I had to cry and asked for pity to be permitted to spend the night. Each day I had to run away. I roamed from village to village. Life had become horribly ugly and loathsome. Three Ukrainian partisans caught me and kept me for 24 hours while waiting for instructions, but again, I managed to run away. I believe they actually let me do it. I wandered around lost for a whole night and at 4 o'clock in the morning I went into a house where Jehovah's Witnesses lived. They let me stay in an attic for about five months until the Soviets arrived.

The family was very religious and was supported spiritually by their publication, the Watch Tower. Even in those days, they were receiving it periodically. They made a concerted effort to convert me, and for a 13 year old who saw his people being destroyed, it was not too difficult to believe that it was because of the "sins of thy fathers," and salvation lay in becoming a Jehovah's Witness. One has to remember that these were Ukrainian Jehovah's Witnesses who had been inculcated for centuries that the Jews were responsible for killing Christ, their savior. I read and quoted the New Testament as they interpreted it. I became a Jehovah Witness. I really was.

Early August 1944 to March 1948
From the Date of Liberation to the Date I Sailed for Canada

After liberation, I returned to my town, Sokal. There were less than 30 Jews who survived. Most wanted nothing to do with me when I told them I was a Jehovah Witness. However, among the survivors were Dr. Kindler and his family, a wife and two children. (A Polish woman hid and saved three Jewish families, a total of 12 people.) Dr. Kindler brought me into this world; I was a premature baby. He was a Zionist and a worldly and wise man. He said, "So, you are a Jehovah Witness. Come and live with us anyway." He treated me like his own. I registered and attended school.

A month later some Jehovah Witnesses came to see me and told me that I could not attend school because, in school, they teach Communism and extol Stalin, which was contrary to "our" religion. They would teach me all I needed to know. I answered that I was interested in learning other things. I didn't care about Stalin and Communism, and that I could still remain a Jehovah Witness. They disagreed and for a period of three months kept asking me to quit school. When I didn't, they dropped me. Dr. Kindler said, "So, you are no longer a Jehovah Witness. Good!"

Dr. Kindler was a Zionist and was planning to go to Israel. But, we were under the Russians. The River Bug again divided the town. Our side was Russia and the other Poland, controlled by Russia.

Dr. Kindler cured a Russian captain of syphilis when penicillin had just come to us and, in return, the Captain agreed to take us across the border all the way to Krakow. One day all of our belongings were put on a truck and off to Krakow we went. I remember very little about the trip or where and how long I stayed in Krakow. As if in a haze, I recall some shooting at the border, but nothing else. One more thing, I remember trading with a Russian woman soldier all the furniture we had left with our landlord at the time we were herded into the ghetto, for a pair of boots.

From Krakow I joined a group of Jews, and with a *Sheleach* from Israel, we crossed borders all the way to Rumania. I don't remember the details. I was later told by my friend, Moniek (Emanuel) Blatt, that when he saw this emaciated forlorn boy getting off the train, he said, "I am waiting for you." Moniek was five years older and at the time he wound up in Bucharest. He was there to watch for and help Jews. I believe the Jewish Brigade and UNRRA were involved.

I lived with him and another fellow in Bucharest for about three weeks, supported by UNRA. Then again, with a *Sheleach* we crossed borders. I have no memory as to details, except that we did a lot of walking. I know we crossed Hungary and passed through Graz in Austria on the way to Italy.

I wound up in a hospital in Italy. I don't know how or why, but I believe it had something to do with a skin disease.

From the hospital I was taken to the House of Sciesopoli in the village of Selvino, approximately 100 km from Milano, Italy. The house once served as a resort for the Elite Fascist Youth movement during Mussolini's reign. It was a beautiful place. It was taken over to be the Youth Aliyah House, a children's home and education center, which would prepare the children to go to Palestine. This was accomplished with the help of some prominent Italians and the Jewish Brigade, with Moshe Ze'Iri of the Brigade becoming the Director of the house. About 800 children who survived the Holocaust made *aliyah* through Selvino. We were divided into *kvutzas* and the members of each *kvutza* became like a family. The children themselves did all the work. I washed dishes and did all kinds of chores. Finally, I was assigned the job of postman. Every day I went to the village post office, collected the mail, and distributed it to the children. We were learning Hebrew, we played, and the children kept coming and leaving (illegally) for Israel. There was one rule, however, not to speak about our past, but to look toward a new future in *Eretz Israel*. Many years later, in 1984, at a reunion, Moshe Ze'Iri asked forgiveness of the children for not allowing them to speak about their experiences.

In the meantime, Emanuel Blatt, with whom I lived for about three weeks in Bucharest, Rumania, settled in *Kiryat Motzkin*, about 1 kilometer from *Kiryat Shmuel*, where my aunt and cousin lived. And so, it came to pass that they met and he told her about the boy, Dov Zugman from Sokal, who survived. A search began and soon I received a letter from my Uncle Henry from New York. Henry lived in Italy before the war, married an Italian Jewish girl, Daisy, and had to run when Mussolini started deporting Jews. Daisy's entire family survived and lived in Milano. Henry came to Italy and visited me in Selvino. When I became interested in going to America, Moshe Ze Iri told my uncle that I had to leave Selvino because, "One rotten apple (wanting to go to America) may spoil the whole barrel." As it turned out, quite a few from my *kvutza* eventually wound up in Canada and the USA, without my influence. Moshe Ze Iri would never talk to me, or anyone who did not make the *aliya*, he was such a strong Zionist.

I left Selvino on October 7, 1946 and was put into an Italian boarding school, where the children and teachers spoke no other language but Italian. I spoke very little Italian. It was like an *ulpan* in which I had to sink or swim. I graduated public school and was three quarters into the middle school when an opportunity arose to go to Canada.

MARCH, 1948—SAILING DATE TO CANADA TO THE PRESENT

I left for Canada before graduation.

The Canadian Jewish Congress sponsored immigration to Canada for 1,000 Jewish child survivors up to age 18. Uncle Henry was able to arrange that I became one of the 1,000. It was quite a feat. I sailed on the S.S. Nea Hellas and arrived in Halifax, Canada on March 21, 1948. I was seasick the entire time. Very seldom did I leave the cabin. Years later I found out that a friend from Selvino was on the same ship at the same time, and we never met. He was also seasick and seldom left his cabin.

I wound up in Montreal. I told the social workers from the Canadian Jewish Congress that I wished to go to school. After they gave me a number of tests, they agreed. They registered me in tenth grade at Stratheona Academy, a Protestant school in Outremont. But again, at that time I spoke Polish, Yiddish and Italian, but very little English. I had to have private tutoring in English. French I could muster on my own because of my knowledge of Italian.

The deal was as follows. The Canadian Jewish Congress paid room and board at a Jewish family, for whom I had to baby-sit four times a week, including most weekends. This did not bother me much because, in addition to attending classes, I had to catch up and had to study practically all my waking hours. My social life was zilch. I graduated high school in two years. I had to pass a graduation test for 10 out of 11 subjects at the same time, including oral and written French (which I soon forgot after passing the exam). My United States visa came through and I left without waiting for the ceremony. My high school graduation certificate is dated August 1, 1950, but I entered the United States on June 30, 1950. I hadn't even realized that I graduated with honors. Years later the honor medal was delivered to me personally by a mother of one of my classmates.

My uncle, aunt, cousins, and some of their children met me at the New York train station. There were hugs and kisses. They took me to my aunt who lived with her son in the old east side of Manhattan, 5th Street and Avenue B. My initial inertia probably arose from the warm reception at the train station. Somehow, I felt that someone would take care of me. Today, I realize how foolish it was to think that. Reality soon set in. Two weeks later I was asked to find a place to live and get a job. They might have been a little afraid of me. I was later told that I looked and acted like an animal. I also don't think my cousins were impressed with my ambition to go to college, with my accent and all. Anyhow, through their friends I got a job as a packer in the ladies' garment industry. I found a room to live in the Bronx, and with $100 to my name; I started life in the United States.

I registered for night classes at the City College of New York, Business Division (now called Baruch College). The Business Division was located at 23rd Street and Lexington Avenue, downtown New York. There were probably more than 40 students in each class, and no air conditioning. The temperature reached over 95 degrees at night. After work, I attended night classes till 10 P.M., four nights a week. My shirt was soaking wet every night.

Even though City College was supposed to be free, immigrants had to pay unless they maintained a B+ average grade. For the first year, until the grades came in, I had to pay $5 a credit. This may not seem to be much, but for me, who earned $26 per week gross, it appeared a fortune. Suffice to say that after the first year, my average was a B+ until the end, when I graduated Cum Laude.

I was let go from the packing job (it was seasonal) and my cousins advised me to get a messenger job so I could study in the subway while making deliveries. (I wonder if anyone ever succeeded to concentrate on a subway.) But then, I began to learn my way around a little.

I decided to become a CPA because it was the quickest path to a decent living. In New York, at that time, in addition to graduating from college and passing the State's CPA exam, three years of working experience at a CPA firm was required before the state would issue a license to practice.

Since I had to go to school at night and work during the day, I was able to get my working experience while going to school. After the first 12 college credits, I obtained a job as a bookkeeper at Saks Fifth Avenue. After 24 college credits, I left Sacks and obtained a job at my first CPA firm. By the time I graduated, I had my three years experience.

The main partner of my first CPA firm is probably responsible for my subsequent success in my profession. After working there for about two years, he took me aside and said, "David, you appear to be a very bright fellow, but with your thick Polish accent, few people will ever get to know it. Get yourself to a speech therapist to clear up your diction and people will hear what you can do." I did, and after six months the therapist felt I was okay. Today, if I advised one of my employees with an accent that is hard to understand, to go to a speech therapist, I would be sued for discrimination. What a pity!

I got my New York State CPA license. In 1960, I married Jean, who had previously lived in and loved Florida. We moved to Florida in 1962, after an offer of employment from Joel Hoch, of the firm of Hoch, Schriber and Frey. In 1966, I became a partner and the name of the firm changed to Hoch, Frey and Zugman and has remained that to this day.

With Polish Refugees in Russia

❖

Judy Berkowitz

The story of my immediate family's survival of the Holocaust is quite different from those who had stayed in the areas controlled by the Nazis. For this, I feel fortunate. Nevertheless, we were displaced from our home and lost most of our family.

Our home was in Wlodowa, a small Polish town near Lublin, where my parents lived with their two daughters, my sister Miriam and I.

My father owned fisheries and shipped fish in huge barrels all over Poland. Our mother was always involved in the business and we had a Polish girl—she helped at home.

I was supposed to start school in September 1939, but the war broke out, the bombs were falling—my sister and I were very frightened.

My parents decided to pack up and cross the border into the Ukraine. They thought it would last only a few weeks and we could then return home.

Our immediate family and my two uncles stayed in a room rented in the Ukraine. I do not know how long we were there, but one night the Russian NKVD knocked on the door, questioning whether we wanted to stay or go back to Poland? My parents said they wished to return. The Russians did not like that; they took many of our valuables and put us on a train to the Urals, deep in Russia.

My two uncles managed to escape and stayed behind. We never saw them again.

We were part of a large group of refugees from Poland, distraught as we did not know our destination—it was a secret.

After a whole month on the train, at last we arrived in Maikor, a large village near Sverdlovsk in Russia. Small living quarters were assigned for each family; we were very crowded. My parents were sent to work in a steel factory.

When my mother refused to work there, she was jailed, on and off, for about six months because Dad was bribing the guards.

My sister and I were placed in school, but because their schooling starts at the age of eight and I was only seven and petite, I was taken out of school and placed back in kindergarten. That was detrimental to my psyche, I cried all the time, especially during a Christmas party in which I could not participate, but only watch it sadly through a window.

We lived there until 1943. The winters were extremely severe, food was pretty scarce—typhoid, pneumonia and other contagious diseases were rampant.

One morning I woke up and could not move my legs. It seems that I had a form of polio. There was no medical help available. A woman witchdoctor helped me, who recommended hot salt compresses. Eventually these did help.

We lived under very primitive conditions. As I am writing this, I am amazed how we managed…

We were kept as prisoners without any rights and our keepers considered us spies against communism.

As part of an agreement with the U.S., all Polish refugees were freed in 1943. A whole group of us packed our things and moved towards central Russia, near Sacharov on the Volga.

The climate was milder and our living conditions were much improved. Father worked for the local government overseeing the wheat fields. Mother had two cows, chickens and a garden. She soon set up a business making cheese, butter and other dairy products. My sister and I helped her after school. Our big problem was that the entire area was prone to malaria from which we suffered terribly.

We went to school with all the other Russian children; there was no discrimination.

After the war ended, we were allowed to leave Russia and return to Poland in 1946. Sadly, among the survivors we found only two uncles on my mother's side, the rest of the family had all perished. They were both in Stetin. Shortly we all went to Berlin to the Schlachtensee camp for displaced persons, "D.P.s."

We went on to Landsberg, in 1948, and came to the U.S. in 1949 to my father's family who came here before the war.

It was not easy for my parents to begin a new life in a new country.

My sister and I finished our education and adjusted to a new language and new customs.

After graduating high school, I met my husband, Michael. We moved to New York where we started our family.

Regina, our only daughter, is Director of Development at Cambridge Community T.V. She has two daughters, Emily at Brown University, Hannah at Park School in Brookline, Mass. Their father is a law professor at Boston College.

Sam, our son, is a lawyer and has four children, Annie 14, Rich 12, Lisa 10 and Katie 8. Carly, their mom, is busy taking care of them.

We are extremely proud of all of them; they are our pride and joy.

Hallandale, Florida

Broken Glass, Shattered Lives

◆

as told by Arnold Geier,
Berlin, Germany—Miami, Florida

It was the spring of 1915. The battle was ferocious. One German soldier, preparing to sprint ahead, suddenly caught a bullet, screamed, and fell. About twenty yards behind him, another soldier crawled along the ground until he reached the wounded one, and slowly dragged him by the belt toward a trench at the rear. Medics were waiting with a canvas stretcher and carried the bleeding soldier away.

In wartime, this was not an unusual incident, and it was soon forgotten.

For Jews in Germany, 1938 was not a good year. Special laws, specifically aimed against them, had been passed in the last two years, limiting the social, political, and economic activities of their daily lives. The handwriting was on the wall, but not all Jews saw it clearly. Although some had left as soon as Hitler had come to power, others were convinced that the political winds would change and that persecution belonged to bygone days and would never be revived by a civilized nation in the 20th Century. Many had made contacts with relatives, friends, and organizations hoping to find someone to sponsor them for emigration to a specific country or to any country that would have them. So it was not unusual to hear of a Jew in Germany who was planning to emigrate to the U.S., Shanghai, Colombia, Cuba, England, Palestine, or South Africa. But most Jews had no friends or relatives abroad and simply faced their uncertain future with trepidation mixed with hope.

My family was lucky. Mama's sister and her husband had moved to New York in the 1920s, in search of the "good life." My uncle worked as a night-janitor in a skyscraper. The family lived in a low-rent state supported apartment project in Brooklyn. They had no money, but they had compassion, love, and courage. My aunt set out to help us by finding someone wealthy enough to qualify as a sponsor, as required by law. She called and searched all over New York. She pleaded, cajoled, and begged every prospect until she found one, an orthodox Jewish brassiere manufacturer, who was willing to sponsor our family and my grandparents and aunt for immigration to the U.S. This was no small task. It meant preparation of an "affidavit" consisting of disclosure of financial holdings, copies of tax returns, and a sworn guarantee that the sponsor would support the newcomers so they would not become a financial burden to the U.S. government.

In the fall of 1938, we received our affidavit on a Thursday, and Papa immediately brought it to the U.S. Embassy in Berlin to register it and to receive a number. My grandfather decided to hold his over the weekend and to have an attorney-friend verify that all was in order. When he brought it to the Embassy on Monday morning, the quota had closed. His affidavit was not accepted.

In a "Jewish area" of Berlin, Grandpa, Grandma, and Aunt Dora were in their apartment on the evening of November 8th, when they heard a firm knock on their door. Grandpa froze. In Germany, such knocks usually meant trouble. The knock sounded again. With fear and apprehension in his heart, Grandpa opened the door slightly. There stood a tall man with strong Germanic features, dressed in a gray suit. He seemed to crowd the door, casting furtive glances to each side, as if he did not want to be seen there. "May I come in, please?" It was not a question but a command. Grandpa stepped back and the man quickly entered, closing the door behind him. He remained standing as if frozen to the spot. "Herr Geier, I can only stay a minute." Grandpa held his breath. The man looked down, avoiding Grandpa's eyes. "Herr Geier, do you remember when you saved a soldier on the battlefield many years ago? I am that soldier." Like flood waters bursting a dam, almost forgotten memories overwhelmed Grandpa. At first, he had put the incident on the back shelf of his mind. After the Nazis came to power, he had forced himself to forget it altogether. "I work with the Chief of Police in Berlin and have kept track of you for a long time. Listen carefully now. Tomorrow night, police and S.S. will round up adult male Jews all over Germany. I have seen the list, and your name is on it. Do whatever you wish." He paused. Now his eyes met Grandpa's. "My debt to you is paid. *Auf Wiedersehen!*" And with that he turned, went through the door and disappeared into the darkness.

Grandpa was stunned. It took him several minutes to realize what had just happened. He trembled with fear and bewilderment, then quickly called my father and told him to come right over. He did not dare to say anything on the phone, so Papa was very concerned and took a taxi. Grandpa told him what happened, and both men knew they had to do something and quickly. After deliberating, they arrived at a plan. For the rest of that night and most of the following day, Grandpa and Papa were on their telephones spreading the news of the arrival in town that evening of Mr. *Malach Hamoves* (Hebrew for the angel of death). They suggested that he be greeted by all of our friends and their friends, and that news of his arrival be passed along to other interested parties. Those who were called presumably were warning their relatives and friends. Hundreds were probably contacted during those 12 hours. In late afternoon, Papa told us that he was going on a business trip for a while, kissed Mama, and left. To a 15-year old girl and her 12-year old brother, this didn't appear unusual. Actually, he took public transportation to the home of one of his customers, a self-professed anti-Nazi, who had offered to shelter him for a few days. So Papa spent the night there—to him it was the night of November 9th, 1938, and to history it would become *Kristallnacht.*

Early the next morning, I was suddenly shaken out of my sleep by a large hand on my shoulder. The shock forced my sleepy eyes open. There above me was a man. He looked like a giant, in a black uniform with silver emblems and decorations. He shouted: "Where is your father!" I was never so scared in my life. The words barely left my lips. "He's on a business trip somewhere." The giant let go of my shoulder. He looked under my bed, in the closet, grumbled, and left to search the other areas of the apartment. When he found nothing, he confronted Mama with anger.

I could hear her promise him, in a soft and pleasant voice, that she would have Papa call him as soon as he returned. Finally, the Nazi left. Mama quickly tried to calm us and assured us that everything would be all right. She rushed us to get dressed and have some breakfast.

While we were eating, the noise level from the street below seemed to swell. Suddenly, there were sounds of breaking glass, and a mixture of shouts, orders, and laughter, blending with screams of terror. We rushed to the window, three stories above the street, and saw hundreds of men, women, and children milling about, watching groups of storm-troopers in action. One was smashing the windows of nearby shops, destroying their displays, and painting their walls with Stars of David and anti-Semitic slogans. DIE JEW! DON'T BUY FROM JEWS! THE JEWS ARE OUR MISFORTUNE! Another group was beating a bearded elderly Jew with nightsticks and bare fists. When I saw the blood streaming from the old man's face as his beard was being pulled off, I went wild. "No, no, leave him alone" I screamed out the window in my 12-year old voice. Of course, my plea was promptly lost in the tumult below. The police stood nearby and watched. No one interfered. Mama pulled me away from the window and held my sister and me close to her bosom. I cried like I had never cried before. Where was Papa, I wondered?

My father had spent the night with his German customer, hoping that Grandpa's alarm was a false one. By early morning, the radio news reports of a "spontaneous citizens outburst" against Jews all over the city and throughout the country convinced Papa it was all true.

He had formulated a plan. He was afraid to remain with his German host. It was dangerous for both. He wasn't sure just how anti-Nazi this family would be if circumstances put them to the test. Papa had heard that the authorities did not bother Jews who had a visa to another country. As far as Germany was concerned, they were considered gone—good riddance. The American Embassy had our affidavits, and Papa had an official number with the embassy. That's where, he figured, he must go.

The American Embassy did not open until 9 A.M., so Papa had to use up at least two hours. He rode whatever trolleys and busses were operating, and changed from time to time so as to appear like a normal commuter and not to arouse suspicion. When it came closer to 9 o'clock, he took the bus, which went into the central area and past the American Embassy. As the bus approached, he was surprised to see hundreds of people, many still in their pajamas and robes, jammed against the front and garden gates, trying to push them open. On the other side, on American soil, several people stood around watching the events, but they did not open the gates. On the fringes of the mob, Gestapo and S.S. men were picking up screaming and struggling figures and dragged them to waiting trucks. It was 20 minutes before 9.

Papa continued on the bus for exactly ten more minutes. Then he got off, crossed the street, and boarded another bus going back toward the embassy. If his calculation was correct, he would arrive there at precisely 9 A.M. He did. As he stepped off the bus, the embassy gates were opened and a flood of people poured onto the grounds. There was no stopping them. The Gestapo and S.S. men were shoved aside and Papa joined in the mob and pushed his way through with the others. For the moment, he was on American soil, safe from German authority.

The embassy people were sympathetic and did what they could. They brought in food, allowed the pathetic crowd to stand and sit in the doorways, halls, and gardens, and tried to calm frightened adults and children. After several hours, Papa finally managed to get the attention of one of the embassy clerks. He told her that he had an official visa number and pleaded with her to arrange an appointment with an officer. The young woman reminded him that there was little work being accomplished under the circumstances, but she promised to do what she could. He never saw her again. He gave up hope. At 5 P.M., the embassy was ready to close. Hundreds of people still lingered on the grounds. They refused to leave. A high-ranking American embassy official rushed out of his protective office to plead with the crowd. Papa intercepted him in the hall, grabbed his sleeve, and held on. With tears in his eyes, he told him of his visa number and begged the official to have our number changed into an actual visa there and then. The bewildered man looked at Papa, at the crowd he was about to face, back at Papa, and motioned to an assistant. "See this man now," he directed, "and if he checks out, give him his visa."

Within an hour, Papa was the proud owner of a precious American visa. It was no more than a large rubber stamp on one page of his passport, with names and dates of birth inserted, but, in Germany on this day, it was life itself. Papa came home. On the way, he was stopped several times, showed his visa, and was left alone.

I never learned the fate of the others who had fled to the security of the American Embassy that day. Grandpa had hidden with a German family on the outskirts of the city and returned only after the pogrom had calmed down. He had an unused affidavit. He never obtained an official number for a visa, because the quota was never reopened. Grandpa, Grandma, and Aunt Dora did not survive. Thanks to Papa's determination and courage, we did.

December 25, 1938 was a glorious day. The world celebrated Christmas, and even the Germans we had encountered that morning seemed almost mellow. A small segment of humanity would celebrate the last day of Chanukah that evening, and our little family also celebrated a most important event—we were finally on our way out of Germany, headed toward a new life in the "Golden Land," the U.S.A.

We had survived every measure the Hitler regime had contrived against Jews, including the recent *Kristallnacht*, and finally had received our passport to freedom, an American visa. Now, on this sunny but chilly day, we sat quietly in a second-class compartment of the train that had left Berlin early that morning and was due to arrive in Holland later that night. Two stern Germans shared the compartment with my father, mother, my 15-year-old sister, and me. I was twelve. We children peered out the window and occupied ourselves with chatter about the sights racing by. Papa was deep in thought and Mama interrupted her reading from time to time to whisper to him. I overheard her reassuring my father, a Cantor and an Orthodox Jew, that, under these circumstances, God would surely forgive him for having to ignore the last day of Chanukah.

The journey was uneventful. We ate the sandwiches Mama had prepared, we dozed, we stretched our legs with occasional walks to adjoining cars, we chatted quietly so the Germans in our compartment would not be angered, and we watched the time drag by ever so slowly.

After darkness settled gently over the countryside, the train slowed and puffed its way into a special railway station at the German-Dutch border, its brakes squealing and hissing as it jerked to a stop. We braced ourselves for our final encounter with German police, Nazis and Gestapo. Freedom was close at hand. A bit more time and a few more miles and our old lives were over. No matter what was ahead, it surely would be better.

The train sat in the station for an almost-endless ten minutes while we watched teams of Border Police officers and Gestapo agents organizing themselves with typical German efficiency on the platform for the task of checking everyone's passport and travel papers. Finally, small groups began to climb aboard.

Papa looked tense and broke out in a sweat. I was afraid.

At that instant, without a flicker of warning, every light in the station and on the train went out. The area was pitch black. Noises of confusion and alarm cut through the blackness. Several people struck matches and their eerie and frightened faces suddenly sprang from the darkness, casting ghostly shadows, and quickly disappeared with the flame. I wanted to scream, but I didn't.

Papa suddenly stood up, groped around the luggage rack above him, pulled down his overcoat, reached into one of its pockets and pulled out a small packet. He gently pushed me away from the window, struck a match, lit a candle, and, using its flame, slowly and deliberately warmed the bottoms of eight other Chanukah candles and placed them neatly in a row on the window ledge. He then murmured the appropriate blessings as he lit each one carefully and finally planted the ninth candle slightly off to the side. He sank gently into his seat and, for the first time in a long time, I saw a smile on my Papa's face.

Someone on the platform shouted, "There's light over there!" Within a few minutes, different teams of Border Police and Gestapo agents came into our compartment to check passports and papers by the flickering Chanukah lights. The chief Border Police officer, seated at the light, complimented my father for being wise enough to take along "travel candles." We discreetly left the compartment and watched the amazing scene from the passageway near the door.

After about a half hour, the Chanukah candles seemed to have no more than a few minutes of life left in them. Suddenly, as unexpectedly as the lights had gone off, they came on again. There was momentary shock at the harsh glow of the instant brightness but there was also a sigh of relief. One officer curtly thanked my father, left our compartment, and joined the others who were spreading out to continue their work throughout the train.

Papa turned to me and smiled. "Remember this moment, son," he declared softly, "like in the days of the Maccabees, a great miracle happened here."

Miracle in the Pyrenees

✦

Faye Lazega Stern

About four years ago my son, Ronald F. Felton, was given an assignment in oral history. He chose to interview my mother, Lea, and me over several hours. Ronald's research paper[1] helped put many events in their proper sequence. I will use his work as the basis of my own story for this anthology.

These interviews provided the perspectives of a young mother and her child more than a half century after the events. My mother, Lea Lazega, was 85 when Ronald interviewed her in 1997. This is Ronald's characterization of his grandmother:

"Lea was born in Lodz, Poland in 1911. She was the youngest of three children who all left home at a relatively young age, probably due to the turmoil in their tumultuous family life. Interestingly, her older sister was born in the United States when her parents immigrated there in the early 1900's. Disenchanted with life in the United States, her parents returned to Poland, where her brother and Lea were born. Her sister, however, moved back to the United States as an adolescent. That her sister was a native born citizen of the United States did play a key, but not necessarily helpful role in the story. In 1928, at the age of 17, Lea left Poland and sneaked, illegally, into Brussels ostensibly to live with an aunt. She quickly settled there, married, and had two daughters. Her husband was also a native of Poland. Jacob was a tailor who produced men's suits for clothing stores in Brussels. Lea describes herself as the one who took charge of the family and the business. She describes her husband as an excellent tailor who was able to make finely crafted suits, but whose manner was very mild and non-assertive. Lea clearly gives the impression that she made the major decisions for the family."

---

1. Ronald K. Felton: Lea's Story: An Oral History of a Holocaust Survivor (Submitted in partial fulfillment of the requirements of EDF 6475 Qualitative Foundations of Educational Research—Instructor: Dr. Valery Janesick) April 9, 1997—unpublished.

My mother was a spirited and fiercely independent woman. These characteristics did not escape any of us.

On May 10 1940 our lives changed abruptly when Germany attacked Belgium and Holland. I was eight-years old and known as Fannie; and my sister Eva was five. The Belgians were hoping to remain neutral and had not joined forces with the British and French in preparation for the inevitable German invasion. The Jewish community in Brussels received some warnings about the treatment of Jews in case the Nazis took over Belgium. There were many German Jews who had escaped between 1933 and 1935 and were living in Belgium. They often spoke of their terrible experiences in Germany following Hitler's rise to power while visiting Jacob's tailoring shop. Based on her interview, my mother was determined to leave Belgium if the Germans invaded. My father was reluctant to leave. We did exactly what my mother wanted to do and very early in the morning on May 13, 1940, while bombs were falling on Brussels, the four of us gathered up our belongings and headed for the train station. According to my mother, before our departure, our parents delivered suits to their customers, collected their receivables and paid their employees. They left their apartment with a Polish-Jewish refugee whose husband was in jail. Taking only what we could carry in cloth sacks of the material used to line suits, we left for the railway station. Throngs of people were trying to get out of the city by train. The station was crowded and chaotic. Most people were trying to escape to France, as it had not yet been invaded. In the panic and confusion there was clearly no need to purchase a ticket. We headed for a train and boarded.

Ultimately the train left and after a few hours it stopped at the Belgian-French border. Border guards entered the packed train and announced that anyone who was neither French nor Belgian, in particular Polish citizens, should remain on the train. The others were to exit into a waiting room at the border station. This was important, as there were many Polish and other refugees among the passengers who had recently fled to Belgium to escape the Germans. This posed a problem for our family. Although both my parents had lived in Belgium for a number of years, and had children who were born there, they had not yet become Belgian citizens. My mother had one more year before she could apply for that status. Nonetheless, my mother had a sense that those who stayed on the train would be sent back, at best to Brussels, at worst to occupied Poland. I remember my mother's comments that the Belgians and the French were not likely to be hurt, but nothing good could happen to those from Poland, as they were not generally liked. My mother is convinced that those who stayed on the train were deported and ultimately found themselves in German concentration camps. She told us to get off the train and ignore the instructions from the border guards. It was also made clear that French was the only language to be spoken from this point forward. This was critical, although we were all fluent in French, we often spoke Yiddish at home.

Ronald, my son, observed "the tales of human triumph over external forces intent upon destruction show clearly that elements of shrewdness are usually mixed with nearly equal amounts of luck." Despite questionable documentation of our status as Belgians, the Lazega family boarded another train for Paris. In that chaos, we managed to proceed without anyone asking for our papers.

Once in Paris, my family headed for the Jewish section of the city and sought out some old friends from Poland and Belgium. My parents found a tiny apartment that was simply a small room. The communal bathroom was in the hallway.

Once we had settled in Paris, my mother reported to the local police to obtain a legal permit to stay in France. She made it clear that her ultimate intent was to leave Europe and join her sister, who lived in the United States. She had already contacted her sister for assistance to immigrate. However, immigration permits were a long way off due to the severe protectionist policies of the United States.

My mother was able to obtain a temporary resident permit in Paris, but it required weekly renewals at the governmental office. However, she could only make a few visits, as on June 14, 1940, about a month after we arrived in Paris, the Germans marched into the city. Our family was lucky that morning, as we went to *le prefecture* to renew our papers. My father came along reluctantly as he had little interest in the details of the paperwork or in his wife's ultimate goal of getting to the United States. My mother never allowed the papers and documents to be out of her personal possession, but the rest of our belongings were in the apartment. Shortly after we arrived at the government office, my parents learned that the Germans occupied the city and that the officials, along with their families, were planning to evacuate to the western part of the country. From the patio of *le prefecture* we could see German soldiers marching on the street. The officials began to board buses for Bretagne (Brittany). Mother made a quick decision. Leaving our belongings behind, we boarded a bus to leave Paris. After a long bus ride, we arrived in Lac Mariaquer, a resort area near Vannes in Brittany. French agencies had set up services to assist those who fled Paris. We were placed in a pension, a bed-and-breakfast lodge, where we were to stay for a while. At this point my mother earnestly began her struggle for immigration permits to the United States. After all, in Brittany we were very close to England, from where, it seemed, we could easily board a ship for America. This was not to be! The first German troops in Bretagne were part of the regular army rather than the SS or the Gestapo. For a short time our family felt fairly safe. I remember my parents conversing with some of the German soldiers. The Germans ultimately told my mother that we would have to return to Belgium and would not be permitted to stay any longer. She agreed and accepted a travel permit for our family to return to Belgium, but she had no intention of doing so. It became clear that we must travel further south in France, which was not yet under German occupation.

Our family boarded a train in Vannes and headed south. About halfway to its destination our train was bombed by German aircraft. The rear half of the train was demolished and there were many casualties. We were in a compartment with an American journalist, in the front of the train. The journalist suffered a minor injury to his nose when a suitcase fell on him after the explosion, but we were relatively unhurt, although I was unable to hear in one ear after the explosion. To this day I have a significant hearing loss in that ear. According to my mother, I stopped speaking for several days after the bombing attack. It took a couple of days to clear the bodies and the wreckage. The site around the train was horrifying. The surviving passengers were kept in an armory until the front part of the train was able to continue its journey. After an overnight stop in a small city where the passengers slept on straw mattresses in another armory, our family finally arrived in Albi, a picturesque small town about 350 kilometers from Marseilles. Once again, our family settled down. We were able to rent a small cottage in the back of a house, where we stayed for several months. Although the Vichy government did cooperate with the Germans, our family was reasonably safe for a period. The Vichy government was supportive of the Nazis and not particularly fond of Jews. Their measures against the Jews, at this time, were not as severe as if the Nazis had occupied the region. Each month my mother reported to the city government's office to renew our permit to stay in Albi. My sister and I entered school and our father took a job as a tailor. My mother spent all her time tending to the family and making frequent long trips to governmental offices in Marseilles in her continuing attempts to gain passage to the United States. She found a lawyer in Albi to assist her in this. As a payment, my father made some suits for the attorney. Despite affidavits from my aunt and other relatives in the United Slates, the visa was denied. Life in Albi was quite comfortable and my mother became pregnant with her third child. This added another dimension to our family's ordeal.

Despite any positive response from the American consulate in Marseilles, my mother persisted and repeatedly made the long trip to Marseilles from Albi. Eventually she concluded that we should be closer to the consular office where our persistent inquiries would produce the desired outcome. Our family moved to Marseilles.

The nations of the world were reluctant to accept refugees from occupied areas, particularly Jews. In 1939, the United States made immigration more difficult. By July 1941 the gates to the United States were effectively closed. This made it nearly impossible for Jews, trying to escape annihilation in Europe, to obtain entry into America, even if they had relatives there. Despite our move to Marseilles, our family was no closer to our goal to enter the United States than when we were in Paris. I remember my mother dealing with mounds of documents and correspondence. She would make trip after trip to the consulate. Despite letters from relatives, who were U.S. citizens, guaranteeing the care of our family upon our arrival, permission was denied. My mother would not give up! She was convinced that persistence would ultimately pay off.

In Marseilles, we shared a small apartment with two other families. The living arrangements were abysmal. My mother found the apartment through her contact with a local rabbi on one of her many visits to Marseilles from Albi. The authorities ordered my father to be placed in Camp Les Milles, a refugee camp operated by the Vichy government outside of Marseilles. Under Vichy French law foreign and stateless Jews were subject to internment. Some of these Jews were transported from occupied France into Vichy to camps such as Les Milles. These camps were built before the war to house Loyalist refugees from Spain and were recycled for this new use. Although the camp was gated and guarded, visitors were allowed, and occasionally even the inmates were permitted to leave for short periods. I visited the camp often and brought items for my father to sell. Then I would bring the money back to Marseilles to my mother. The only good news was that on account of her pregnancy, mother received a *carte prioritaire* for extra rations and it helped her avoid the food lines. However, the baby was due soon and she had to make arrangements for the delivery, and someone to care for her children in the interim. My sister and I were separated. Eva was placed in a convent, since she was younger and somewhat frail. I was sent to St. Raphael, a refuge operated by a Jewish agency in a seaside resort not far from Nice.

My mother was afraid to check into a hospital, as she did not want to call extra attention to her refugee status and risk deportation. Instead, she asked to be admitted to a convent with a facility for unwed mothers. This way she would be admitted to the hospital when she was ready, without any questions. She told the nuns that the father of her unborn child was a soldier and she was not married to him. On December 29, 1941 Max Pierre Lazega was born. From the hospital they returned to the one-room apartment that was now shared among 5 people, and arranged for the circumcision by a rabbi. When Max was almost 2 months old, my mother sent for my sister and me to return to Marseilles. The tiny apartment became even more cramped.

Mother continued her struggle for our passage to America, but to no avail. Meanwhile, the Germans tightened their grip on the entire country. There were rumors of imminent deportations from places such as Camp Les Milles. When she heard this, she met my father at the camp and urged him to leave as soon as possible. Deportation meant internment in a concentration camp and probably death. Father was able to leave the camp to visit his family. He did not return, but moved back with us. However, he had to live behind a fake brick wall in the cellar of the building. Deportations were increasing and it was far too risky for him to be in the apartment. I remember the nighttime raids when men were arrested and taken away. Our father would hide in the cellar with some gypsies who also lived in the building. My mother would pinch Max so he would cry, making it apparent that there was a family with young children living in the apartment. Women alone with infants were not deported at this point.

By November 1942, Vichy ceased to be a free zone. It became too dangerous to stay anywhere in France. Our family decided to leave as soon as possible. The reasons are now vague, but my father decided to stay behind and join the Resistance. There were two reasons for this decision. First, it was more dangerous to travel with a man; a lone woman with children had a better chance of getting past the authorities. Men were scrutinized much more thoroughly. Second, he was no longer interested in running and felt it best to remain and attempt to hide out. My mother helped her husband obtain false French identity papers, which were widely available in Marseilles and other large cities. The former Jacob Lazega, with his new identity as a Frenchman, set out on his own. As the Germans were tightening their control over southern France, my mother began to plan our escape from France.

The Jewish agency in Marseilles was assisting the refugees. They advised my mother to try to escape to Switzerland and they offered her some money for that. She accepted the money but had already decided that Switzerland was not where she wanted to go. She had heard from other Jewish refugees that the Swiss would turn away refugees who did not have significant funds available. She did not have that kind of money, and being turned away at the Swiss border would very likely lead to their capture and deportation. She felt that heading for Spain would get her closer to a port that would ultimately be a point of embarkation for her and the three children to the United States. We headed for Perpignon, a city near the Pyrenees; approximately 350 km from Marseilles. One could enter Spain through the mountains. It was a nerve-racking bus trip from Marseilles to Perpignon.

German soldiers were traveling on the buses and massive deportations were underway. In Perpignon, my mother went to a small cafe and asked the owner to speak to his wife. When she explained that she needed a safe place to stay for the night, the woman directed us to a small hotel with a restaurant. As we entered, we saw that the place was occupied largely by German soldiers. The owner assured my mother that we would not be bothered; these were soldiers on leave. Tired and famished, our family sat down to eat. As we ate, some of the German soldiers approached our table. Our mother had already reminded us to speak only French, not Yiddish. The soldiers played with Max and chatted. My mother and I both recall the soldiers talking about being homesick for their families in Germany. Except for 11-month old Max, we were gripped with fear as the dinner conversation progressed. Ultimately the owner of the cafe provided us a room for the night and agreed to wake us early so we could continue to Amelie-les-Bains, the small village south of Perpignon, the gateway to the Pyrenees.

It was the day before Christmas, December 24, 1942. The most difficult part of the entire ordeal lay ahead of us. It would take days to cross the mountains into Spain. Mother had no idea what would await us there. She had spoken to a number of refugees and was advised that this route was their best chance to avoid capture by the Germans. Alone with three children, including an infant to be carried throughout the trip, she set off on the long and strenuous trek across the mountains. Max was not a small infant and mother carried him the entire way, while Eva and I held hands and walked together. All our belongings were in one small bag, including our precious papers that, my mother hoped, would ultimately get all of us to the United States. Along the way we encountered a Frenchman who was traveling back from Spain with salt, apparently a scarce commodity.[2] When he saw us, he offered us some food and a chance to rest. While we sat, mother nursed Max. The Frenchman offered to guide us to a church that was still quite a distance away, but we would be able to rest there for the evening. It was the middle of the night when we arrived at the church, where the nuns let us in. Having walked for more than eight hours, we were happy with the food, shelter and rest. The nuns were hospitable and gave my mother directions for the next leg of our trip. We slept the night and then, in the early hours of the morning, set out to complete our journey.

After another full day of walking with the baby in her arms, my mother was exhausted. We were all hungry and tired. Although there were others traveling through the mountains, we never encountered anyone other than that salt merchant. We were on the lookout for a house that the nuns suggested as a rest stop for the second night of the trip. We finally spotted it. My sister and I were really frightened by its appearance. It reminded us of the house in "Hansel and Gretel." Our fear was aggravated when an old woman with long, stringy gray hair answered the door. Once inside, we knew that we had found a safe haven. There were others, mostly men, on their way across the mountains, sleeping in the house. At this point my mother's legs and stomach were swollen from the strain of two days of walking and carrying Max. We received some food and were given a room for the night, away from the others. This was the last stop before Spain. We headed out early in the morning, but mother now had trouble walking. I found a tree branch to serve as a walking stick for her.

After another whole day of walking, our family arrived in a small Spanish village at the base of the mountains. My mother knew that she had done significant damage to her body and could not walk any longer. She found the local police

---

2.   Excerpt from Lea's interview:

"...All of a sudden a man comes from Spain to go to France. A six-footer. He said...This was already Christmas night, December 24th. And he stopped and he said: 'Where are you going?' I said I am going to Barcelona, Spain. He said: 'first you have to go to Canda de la Mavella (Note: probably Andorra La Vella). Barcelona is far away. I'll show you.' He said: 'First of all, you are all tired, you came up so much with the kids. Sit down.' It was already dark. He took stones and there were branches. He said: 'Sit down everybody!" He opened up a sack and took out French bread, a bottle of wine, a salami. He took out a knife, cut pieces and gave everybody eat and drink. Even Maxie ate the bread and drank the wine. We all...at that time I didn't think anything! An angel...an angel on my shoulder...What can I tell you? We ate and he made a little fire. It was December. It was not cold anyhow. I told him not to do that...the Gestapo might come and...He said: 'Now is Christmas night. Everyone is in churches.' But he was not. You can figure out...whatever...Maybe it was an angel. Who knows? And he gave us food. And we were sitting there. And the *kinderlach umzech a mechia gerazen* (approx.: the children were having a good time). The wine and salami and bread...And then he got up. Maybe it was one (o'clock) already. At night! He said to me: 'Give me the boy!' I thank God he took him from me. My belly was swollen already from carrying him. He took the boy and left his bag. I asked him: 'What you've got there?' He said: 'Salt. We can't get salt in France. So, I bring it from Spain.' Something like that...And he said 'Let's walk!' He walked with me for maybe two hours. He said: 'Let me tell you! I'll go back now. Go for another hour maybe and you will see a church.' He showed me where to go. 'To the right you'll see a church.' I didn't see from where he comes from. And I didn't see where he went away. Nothing! He gave me the baby. I started walking. I didn't see where he went. So tell me, what is that? Not a miracle...? OK. So I walked an hour or two. The children had holes in their shoes from walking. And me...And sure enough, we come over and there is a church."

station and went inside. For fear of being deported back to France, she told the police that her husband was awaiting them in Barcelona. The police officer offered us some oranges and drove our family to the police station in Gerona, the nearest large town. In Gerona, we were arrested as illegal immigrants. Max spent his first birthday, December 29, 1942, in jail.

There were many illegal immigrants, men and women, in that jail. The children, including Eva and me, were taken to a convent by the local church, but Max remained in jail with our mother. After a few days without any information about their future, my mother demanded to see a priest. She was feeling more and more ill from the trip across the mountains and felt that a priest might be sympathetic to her plight and of the other refugees. Her body was swollen and she was exhausted. When the priest arrived she demanded that the Jewish agency be contacted in Barcelona and notified that there were so many refugees being held. Within a few days, representatives of the Jewish agency arrived to assess the situation. The refugee children and the parents were reunited and given temporary living arrangements in Gerona. Ultimately we were taken to Barcelona by train.

Without delay, our mother restarted her campaign for admittance to the United States. Her health was failing and she needed surgery for the injuries caused by the trek over the mountains.

There were some positive developments in the United States relative to immigration. Eleanor Roosevelt, the First Lady, applied some pressure to allow Jewish children trapped in France to enter the country. When it was determined that many of these children were now in Spain, there was an effort to get them to the United States. At first the U. S. State Department was going to allow mothers to come with their children, but that decision was rescinded. The children would have to come by themselves. Heartbroken, our mother gave up her three children to the Jewish agency, including Max. She allowed us to be taken to Lisbon, Portugal and eventually to the United States, without her. She did not want to lose the opportunity for us; and she needed surgery that she was not sure to survive. Whatever might happen, her children would be with her sister. We took our baby brother, left our mother in Barcelona and set off with the other children for Lisbon. From there, we traveled by boat to America. Almost immediately after our departure our mother was taken to a hospital for surgery. She survived.

With her children now in America, she settled down in Barcelona and waited for permission to join them. This took nearly a year, because the United States continued its rigid policies of immigration quotas. In May 1944 my mother boarded the *Serpa Pinta*, a Portuguese ship, and headed for the United States to be reunited with us. This should have been the end of the long arduous journey, but there was one more terrible event to occur. At 12:05 am on a Friday morning, the *Serpa Pinta* was stopped in open seas by a German submarine. Two passengers were taken prisoner aboard the German U-Boat. The passengers and crew of the *Serpa Pinta* were then told that the ship would be torpedoed, despite the fact that it was sailing under a neutral Portuguese flag. The captain ordered the passengers to abandon the ship in lifeboats.

Despite the well-known custom of "women and children first," my mother chose to remain on-board with the crew until the passengers were all in lifeboats. She assisted the crew with the boarding and lowering of the boats. There was much panic among the passengers. During the evacuation three people, including a 16-month-old baby girl were killed.[3] Finally, she was lowered into the sea in a lifeboat filled with sailors. After a tense wait that lasted almost nine hours, the captain of the German submarine announced that Berlin ordered him to allow the ship to continue to its destination. At first, the passengers were reluctant to re-board the ship, fearing it was a ploy to have them on board when the ship was torpedoed. Ultimately the passengers and crew re-boarded and were allowed to continue to the United States.

On June 2, 1944, four years after she left Belgium, our mother arrived in Philadelphia and was greeted by her sister, who had been waiting for her at the port for days.[4] The ordeal was over and our mother was reunited with her three children.

---

3.   Philadelphia Inquirer June 1, 1941, p. 1.:
       "U-Boat Radios Berlin, Frees Refugee Ship—2 Americans Seized, 3 Lives Are Lost; Vessel Safe Here—The Nazi persecution from which they were fleeing caught up with more than 300 European refugees in mid-ocean early last Friday morning, when a Portuguese passenger vessel bound for this city was halted by a German submarine and two of its passengers taken prisoners.
       …It was not until 5 A.M. that definite word was received not to sink the ship…"
4.   Philadelphia Inquirer, June 3, 1941:
       "Refugee Children Thrive in Paterson Home After Hazardous Flight From Nazis—Forced to Leave Their Mother Behind—Fannie, Eva and Max Lazega have begun the task of readjusting themselves to a new life after an arduous journey through Europe with their mother and alone across the Atlantic in their flight from Nazi horrors…Their mother, Leah Lazega, although still in Lisbon is awaiting the completion of the details, which concern her visa, and is expected to obtain passage here within the near future…Fanny, who is 12 years old had cared for the baby and her sister, Eva, now nine, throughout the entire trip and had carried the baby during the time her family was eluding the Gestapo, because, as she explained, her mother's arms were full of bundles…"

Fanny

✦

Frances Cutler

For many years I was running away from Fanny, a lonely, angry and confused little girl. I wanted to forget her. Many times I buried Fanny, but she had a way of returning, unexpectedly, painfully.

My protection was distance: a new country, a new language, new parents, a new family, a new culture, and the passage of time. When I think about Fanny now, I realize, I have been successful. I no longer remember as well as Fanny could when she was ten years old. Of course, I thought I would always remember.

Why do I attempt to tell my story again, now? Throughout the years, I have occasionally written about myself, in English classes, for Spielberg's *Shoah* project, for some oral presentations, and now for this book by the Child Survivors of the Holocaust of South Florida. Primarily I write so my story will be added to the history of child Holocaust survivors. Often in the retelling, there is also healing. Nevertheless, it is always difficult to return to the past to scratch the scab again.

A few years ago, while studying for my Master's degree at the University of Miami, I researched what had happened in Paris before, during and after World War II concerning anti-Semitism and the Nazis. I was an older student. As a child, of course, I was not aware of the horrendous situation that led to the deportation of about 76,000 Jews from France, about a quarter of its Jewish population of 300,000. Thirty percent of the deportees were French born and the rest had come from such places as Poland.

This is what I gathered: I was born in the 11th arrondissement of Paris on March 16, 1938. My parents, Cyla Lindenberg and Shlomo Zalman Kahane, had immigrated from Ciechanow, Poland about 1936. Because my father entered illegally, my birth name was Fanny (Feigele) Lindenberg. My mother was born on May 15, 1914. At 10:30 a.m. on July 27, 1942, the Nazis with the cooperation of the French police deported my mother from Camp Drancy in Paris to the Concentration Camp Auschwitz. Of the 1,000 Jews on Convoy 11, only 13 were alive in 1945, one of those was a woman. She was not my mother. (Information from the American Red Cross, 1997)

I was about three years old when my mother took me to a government children's home, *Maison des Petits,* to save me from the Nazis. For a long time I had thought that I never saw her after that day. But in a postcard to her family in Ciechanow, Poland, my mother wrote that she was allowed to visit me frequently. As I always wanted to go home with her, the frequency of her visits slowed to once a week. She wrote how painful it was for her to leave me each time and how she missed her mother and family. She understood that things were bad in Poland; and before too long it would be the same in Paris. Even those who had lived in Paris for more than 15 years had lost their right to work, and my father was having problems getting his papers extended. "This is our life, but this must end…. We are only waiting for something better to happen. It would be nice if it would finally happen." (Paris, 6 September 1941)

A group photo at *Maison des Petits* shows 29 small children, mostly toddlers. I am very obedient, standing at attention and seem amazed at a defiant little girl arguing with the uniformed attendant.

The first evening there, the children gathered at the back of the room in front of a statue of the Virgin Mary; they said their prayers and crossed themselves. They giggled when I did not know what to do. I'm sure that I was quickly taught to pray properly, but I do not remember those prayers.

M. Halbery of the *Societé de Charité Maternelle de Paris, Maison des Petits,* Montlignon, wrote to my father, warning him to make arrangements to have me moved, because I would be taken away on the next convoy. I was taken to a Catholic farm with a private family that cared for many children in addition to their own. In another photo, I am about five years old, dressed shabbily. I do remember eating at a long table with about ten children. The farm family sat separately. They had a cake with a hidden prize, but we were not included in that. I felt so jealous at this exclusion and resented that I was not part of a family.

Living on a farm, we probably ate better than others during the war. Sausage was a favorite food, but I found it incredible that it was made from pigs. The slaughter of the pig was always a wild topic of discussion.—I was a bed-wetter and they tried everything to stop that. One morning I feigned illness but to no avail—the wet bed was discovered. After being lectured, the caretaker marched me to a gated area, bared my buttocks so the geese could bite me. I was petrified,

I shrieked and howled, though the geese did not bite me. I saw nothing wrong with being punished; I thought it was my fault.

One morning, I saw soldiers marching outside and the caretakers warned me to be quiet. I probably knew that France was at war with Germany, but I did not know that I was Jewish. This might have been the time when I began to have nightmares of German soldiers lining people up against a wall, including children, and shooting them. I never actually witnessed such a scene, but must have heard others speaking about this.

There were trenches on the farm, and we were taught to get into those during bombing raids. One evening, we were told to rush to the bomb shelter. My group of children left, but somehow I stayed behind. I'm not sure why. The caretaker was perplexed about what to do, but I assured her that I knew where to go. So I went directly to the outdoor trenches and was surprised that no one else was there. Bewildered, I wondered what to do. Someone eventually found me and took me to the bomb shelter in the cellar, where we spent the night. It was frightening, of course, but the singing and the stories calmed us a bit.

When the War was over, I was thrilled to leave that grim and frightening farm, and swore never to return. My next stop was in an orphanage in Andresy. I remember a lovely girl whose blonde hair I loved to comb, and my telling her how much I wanted a little sister like her. I started public school here. Girls and boys were segregated. The children were seated according to their scholastic achievements: the smartest in front. I sat in the back. At this school, I sensed that Jews were different. They did not attend class on Saturdays. The other kids did not accept them. At the orphanage, we discussed Jews. Did we just learn then that we were Jewish?

Because I was so far behind the others as a student, I was allowed to walk by myself to a tutor's home, just outside the orphanage. There was always a cookie jar; the tutor was generous and patient. We received presents for Christmas. I received this most beautiful doll, dressed in a black cape lined in pink satin. She was the most beautiful doll; I was thrilled! I thought that the tutor was the anonymous donor and that the doll was mine. But in the summer, we were told to pack our clothes but not the toys..."those would be here when we return in the fall...there are toys at our summer destination." But I never returned and never saw my beautiful doll again, although I kept on writing and pleading to get her back.

Before my father died, I saw him twice in the hospital. He was wounded while fighting with the resistance and was recuperating from tuberculosis in a sanitarium in Limel-Brevannes. At the first visit, I found him sitting on a bench with a cane in his hand. I was very happy and excited to see him and very optimistic about his recovery. However, the next time I saw him, he was lying in bed. My father told me that he was dying and that his aunt would bring me to America and take care of me. He was not going to be with me. He must have also told me that my mother was dead, but I do not remember that.

My father, Shlomo Zalman Kahane, son of Samuel Kahane and Leja Dzlegel, was born in Ciechanow, Poland on September 3, 1910 and died on July 24, 1946, at age 36. He left Poland to join my mother, her two sisters and a brother-in-law in Paris. He worked as a tailor, a common occupation for many Jewish immigrants. The pictures and letters that I have were mostly his.

My mind blocked out my father's death. One evening we were discussing our future in the dormitory, feelings about adoption, and who would take us out of the orphanage. I stated that I would never be adopted, because my father would come for me as soon as he felt better. Another child said that my father was dead. I denied it. She insisted. I got hysterical.

I was painfully shy. At a train station with a caretaker, either on my way to another orphanage or to Paris for my passport, I spotted a fellow orphan. I was too shy to speak to her. On another journey, there were American soldiers on the train. I stared at a tall African American. He was the first black man I ever saw. When we got off, he offered me some Life Savers. I refused, but the caretaker said it was O.K.—I was a big hit at the next orphanage when I shared the Life Savers with the other children.—After a night or two, we were off again on another journey.

Aix-les-Bains was my last orphanage. The dormitory had two long rows of single beds. Mine was the first to the left of the door. Pleasantly, each morning a man played beautiful violin music to awaken us. Cousins and friends of my parents came to visit and sometimes took me to their homes during holidays. These included Mr. & Mrs. Pazdor, Leon and Gegne Shway, and Mr. and Mrs. Rosenbaum along with their children. Once I returned to the orphanage with hard-boiled eggs and tomatoes that Gegne gave me as a special treat. I put those goodies outside the window to keep them cool, but when a counselor found my stash, I was scolded, and the food was confiscated. Food was to be shared with everyone!—Before my departure for the United States, Gegne and Leon, along with a friend, took many pictures of us at the orphanage. It was a very happy day. We went to a park where there were swings.—Another time, I went to a fair with the Rosenbaums; I went on some rides and won a child's tea set. They bought me a beautiful doll; I named her Juliette. I was incredibly happy to have her.

During naptime, I let the other children play with Juliette. When I asked for her, they wanted to play more. The noise brought the counselor who scolded us and took away the doll. I was devastated, fearing I would never get the doll back. While waiting in the counselor's office, I became so distraught that I cried uncontrollably. When she finally arrived, I explained what had happened and apologized. She kindly promised to return my doll. When I left for the United States, she gave me a handkerchief holder and her picture.

It was at Aix-les-Bains that I realized that I was Jewish and learned a few Yiddish words. The orphanage was progressive, with communal showers that were very embarrassing. We tried to cover ourselves, but received a lecture about the beauty of our bodies. We learned about God and evolution. I spoke to the all-seeing, all-knowing God each night, reviewing the day's events and promising to make every effort to be good. We exercised outdoors, played in the snow in the winter, but I could not understand why anyone wanted to be out in the freezing cold. We went on hikes and swimming, ate bread with chocolate—a delicious snack, but the people in Philadelphia later thought it was weird.

There were visitors coming to Aix-les-Bains all the time. Some were either benefactors or potentials ones; others were looking to adopt. We were on our best behavior, of course, as they often brought chocolates or other treats. I visited the office of the head mistress twice: once when she translated a letter in Yiddish from my two aunts who had survived; the second time my great aunt in the United States had sent a package. I received one piece of candy, the rest went to the communal kitchen.

My childhood was chaotic and disconcerting. I did not understand what was happening. Nothing made sense. Except my father, I don't remember any adult taking the time to explain to me what was going on and was ahead to happen, to allay my fears and confusion. Life was a bit more normal at Aix-les-Bains, but I was still befuddled and anxious.

My father had told me that my great aunt would bring me to the United States. But as nothing had happened, I pretty much forgot about it until preparations for my voyage began. Some photos were sent to the relatives abroad; I traveled to Paris to obtain the necessary papers, such as my birth certificate and passport, and stayed with Mr. and Mrs. Pazdor. I imagined America as a wild jungle with crocodiles, but soon discovered my error when I arrived in New York.

Many years later, I discovered that Miami better matched my early preconceptions.

On May 24, 1948, I left for the U.S.A. from Cannes on the **Sobieski** and arrived in New York on June 7, 1948. I was the youngest in a group of about 20 traveling under the auspices of the HIAS (Hebrew Immigration Aid Society). I tried to learn a few words of English with no success. My picture, with a big smile and my doll, Juliette, appeared in some newspapers, but there were many errors in some of the stories.

I was welcomed in the port by my great aunt, Rose Kahane Schlessinger, by Blanche Moak, her future daughter-in-law, and a cousin, Matthew Goldshlag. We had lunch in the home of our cousins, the Greenhuts and the Kameroffs, an old brownstone in the Bronx. That same evening, my great aunt and I took the train to Philadelphia. She could not speak any French. I used my few Yiddish words, but she did not understand them. We arrived late at the Schlessingers' home in Strawberry Mansion. Except for the children, the whole family was there to greet me: Freda and Seymour Roberts, whose baby, Larry, was a few months old; Shirley and Harry Pein, parents of 6-year old Carol and Steven, who was four; and Albert who was engaged to Blanche.

That night I woke up hungry and walked down the stairs. I startled my great aunt who was writing a letter. I got out the French-English dictionary, but the print was too small for her to read. I gestured by rubbing my stomach and pointing to my mouth. She made some hot tea with toast and jam for me. It was delicious!

We overcame the language barrier quickly. They hired a tutor, but he returned to France after a month. Albert continued my lessons, but he could not speak French and wanted to teach me only in English. Learning English was quite hard. French has no "h" or "th" sounds. In French, each syllable is pronounced. Words such as "knife" and "Arkansas" were difficult. But in a year, I began to forget French. Years later, I lost most of my accent, and people thought I was British. I spoke precisely, not using slang, but sometimes I twisted some idiomatic expressions. By high school, I had so completely forgotten French that I was placed in a beginners' class. My pronunciation was good, and I had no difficulty with the concepts of masculine and feminine words, but some American students got better grades than I. French has never again become my primary language.

When school started in the fall, I was very fortunate to have Mrs. Sharpe as my teacher. She was very sensitive to my situation, and she encouraged me to interrupt the class any time if I did not understand something. She waived my homework until my language skills improved. With her encouragement, I felt very comfortable and special in class. When it came to math, I was more advanced than the other students and could do long divisions at the blackboard, but could not explain those in English. They put me in a lower grade and then I skipped a class when I learned to speak English more fluently.

My great aunt and uncle owned a kosher butcher store, and we lived behind the store. One of my chores was the delivery of meat orders. First, I accompanied Albert, sitting on the back of his bicycle as he darted through traffic, passing narrowly between parked cars and the moving trolley car. Then I went with my great aunt who often got involved in long social chats with the customers, mostly in Yiddish. Eventually, I did deliver the orders myself. I walked down York Street, imagining that I was speaking to my father, letting him know where I was so that he would be able to find me.

My great aunt was a vital working partner of the business. As there was no telephone in the store, she had to run in and out to answer the telephone to take meat orders and placate customers. She also cleaned and *kashered* the chickens, delivered orders, and so on, while keeping up with all the responsibilities of a homemaker in a traditional household, where the man did not help, but was served. She was extremely frugal and understood my reluctance to throw away any food. For many years, she schlepped sacks of food and clothing to the main post office in Center City to send to relatives in Israel and Australia. This stopped when she finally visited Israel and saw the relatives living as well, if not better, than she did in Philadelphia. After that trip she became more willing to buy herself a new dress.

Because I came from France, the boys expected me to be "hot stuff." I did not fit this image, but my accent and the beret that my aunts sent me from Canada gave me a French allure. But I did not feel French. I was not even sure whether I was French. My parents were born in Poland. Many people were surprised when I said that I was Jewish. They expected me to be Catholic. All this made me question my Frenchness. I felt that I belonged neither to the French, nor the American culture. I made every effort to become Americanized. In 1953, at age 15, I became a U.S. citizen. Because of my adoption, I did not have to wait until I became an adult. But I never felt that I belonged either to the culture or to my adopted family. My childhood experiences and memories made me feel different, apart.

In France my dream was to live in a home with my mother and father, as ordinary people do. After coming to America, my dream was partially fulfilled. Everyone, including myself, expected me to be happy and forget my past. But a home with adopted parents was not sufficient. No one understood it, and I could not express my pain. It was never discussed in the same way as the Holocaust was never discussed for many years. It took me years to understand the extent of the anger that was coupled with my pain.

My birth name was Fanny Lindenberg. My father had entered France illegally, so I had my mother's maiden name. I learned of my new name, Kahane, after the War. My American family began to call me Frances. I thought it was because I came from France, and I sometimes called them American, but soon I understood that they wanted me to have a more American name. For two years, I was known as Frances Kahane. In Hebrew school, my teacher often used the expression, "for instance." The way he said it, I thought he was calling on me. I was not used to the sound of my new name. After the adoption, I became Frances Schlessinger. The adoption was very difficult for me. I still thought my father might come back and would not be able to find me with a different last name. I also felt disloyal, and thought that I had had enough name changes already. Once I became a Schlessinger, I stopped the habit of speaking to my first father. The adoption process required me to acknowledge that my parents were dead and no one else had a claim on me. I remember that they asked me for proof of my mother's death, which I did not have at that time.

I have had other names: my Jewish name is "Feigele" that no one uses. The French version of my American name is "Françoise" that I used in French classes and when I lived at International House in my senior year at college, where I did identify again with my frenchness. My best friend, Sophia from junior high school, also called me by "Little Napoleon."

Referring to my adopted mother, Rose, as my great aunt seems awkward. That was her blood relationship to me, but that is not the way I think or feel about her. She is my mother! My first mother, Cyla, is also my mother. I sometimes refer to her as my real or birth mother. These semantic differences were most uncomfortable. I preferred referring to both Cyla and Rose as mother. I have called my great aunt "mother" almost immediately since my arrival, but I called her husband "Uncle Jake" for the first two years. I did remember my father and did not want to call anybody else "father." I saw nothing wrong with this and was not aware that I was hurting his feelings. After the adoption, I called him "Deddy," the same as his other children.

My mother, Cyla, was one of twelve children; she was somewhere in the middle. Only two of her sisters, Helen and Rachel, survived the Holocaust, and my cousin Jack (Jean). When I was 12 years old, my adopted mother, Rose and I took the train to visit my two aunts and their families in Toronto. In Buffalo, the

U.S. immigration officer checked our papers and told my mom that we could continue to Toronto, but they could not guarantee that I would be allowed to reenter the U.S.A. because I was not an American citizen. My mother's lawyer had told her that my adoption papers would be sufficient. We immediately got off the train. We called the relatives in Toronto and they were devastated. Aunt Helen and her family came to visit us in Philadelphia. I saw them again in Toronto when I was 16 and spent the summer with both my aunts and their families. I stayed up all night with Aunt Helen listening to her stories and going over pictures. I was hungry for information about my parents, and she gave me some photos that I treasure. As my Aunt Rachel was the youngest, she barely remembered my parents. I do love her dearly as an older sister and admire her greatly. Sadly, she is now suffering from Alzheimer's disease. The Lindenberg family in Toronto was warm and loving, and I felt that I belonged with them. Other Lindenbergs were also supportive. Cousins Annie and Hymie acted as my godparents, they bought me a typewriter, sent money for college, and were there for me at both difficult and happy times.

During my sophomore year at Temple University, suddenly and unexpectedly, my parents sold the house and moved to Atlantic City. I stayed with Albert and Blanche, my brother and sister-in-law, and their two children. This was my first long-term separation from my adopted parents, and once again I felt abandoned. That same year, on March 3, 1957, a drunk driver killed my Aunt Helen as she was crossing a busy street. I was devastated and could not understand how God could let that happen. It took me years to deal with this anguish.

When I met my cousin Jack, my identification with France returned. My mother, Cyla, had come to Paris to join her sister, Jack's mother. Jack's parents were killed in the Holocaust. He survived in his nurse's home and felt very French and loved France. His paternal aunt in Chicago brought him to the United States when he was 14 years old, but he did not like American culture. After receiving a master's degree in biochemistry and serving in the American army, he returned to France, married and has three children and a grandchild. When we first met at my Aunt Helen's funeral in Toronto, I was 19. His discontent echoed some of my difficulties in adjusting to American life. However, my memories of France were not positive and I did not want to return there. But I began to discover and appreciate the part of me that was French, while I was also becoming more and more devoted to the United States and its democratic ways.

There were times when my past caught up with me and I would get depressed. The pain was too much to handle. These bouts sometimes surprised me as I thought that I should be over them by now. It took many years to overcome the grief. Therapy was very helpful. By the time I got married, I understood and acknowledged Fanny's feelings of anger and rage at being abandoned by her mother at age three. This had festered until I was finally able to admit it. Rationally, Frances understood Cyla's courage, but Fanny did not.

I had serious doubts about raising a child, but the love I shared with my husband, Kenny, deepened, and I felt ready. When my daughter, Cynthia, was born, I was overjoyed. I was able to experience vicariously her normal and happy childhood. There were times when I was a difficult mother. I had managed with so little that I had little tolerance when Cynthia showed dissatisfaction with all she had. On the whole, I am a devoted mother and encourage open lines of communication and a trusting relationship. I have made every effort to keep her enlightened. I am proud of and thankful for my wonderful daughter.

My healing continued when with Kenny and six-year old Cynthia I returned to France in 1978. I visited the Pazdor family. I walked the streets in Aix-les-Bain and saw the outside of the orphanage, which was now a doctor's private residence. I saw the hill where we once tumbled down, and the little stores where we would gawk at jewelry, candies and pastry. I had been anxious about returning, but it did satisfy my soul and brought me peace. It validated my memories to be real and I began to let go. Joining the Child Survivors Group also helped, a group of people with similar experiences and feelings who do understand.

Now, I am coping with another grief, widowhood. Kenny died suddenly on January 10, 2001, only nine months ago, as I write this. I am in the midst of this struggle of constructing yet another new life, learning to live alone and remember Ken without feeling the pain of his loss. Everyone says this will eventually happen. My past has probably prepared me to deal with one more loss, but each loss is different. This one is not like the confusion and bewilderment of a three-year old separated from her mother, or the hysterical seven-year old whose father died, or the anguished nineteen-year old searching for answers when her Aunt Helen died, or the agony of the forty-year old when her adopted mother died and unresolved deaths of the past descended on her. This is coping with the loss of a partner of 32 years. There is greater understanding, maturity and thankfulness for the many happy years we shared. Though nothing can fill the void of Kenny's loss, I try to focus on what I have—a wonderful, loving, supportive daughter, who is my friend, and caring and loving friends and family who stand by me. That is still a lot to have.

Fanny Lindenberg—Fanny Kahane—Frances Kahane—Frances Schlessinger—Frances Cutler

Frances retired from the University of Miami in 2003 and moved to Nashville, TN, to be able to spend more time with her daughter, Cynthia, who practices law there. Frances asked the following remembrance of her father to be added to her story. She found this in a book about the Jews of Ciechanow.

"I knew Shlomo Zalman Kahane before the war; I knew him by his nickname as Yuzhek. He was the son of very poor parents, a tailor. He worked in Ciechanow. He dreamt of a more free and just world from the time he was very young, a world without exploitation of one person by another, where work would be a healing force of life rather than one that terminates it. He became a member of the illegal young Communist party to fight for his ideals and principles. He knew that he chose difficult work for himself and had a long and hard road ahead to travel. His belief in a better tomorrow was so strong that he was not afraid of any kind of hardship.

He gave up the best years of his life in the fight against the fascist Polish government. He was jailed and suffered all the time, but he still would not break. He was always filled with the joy of life and his belief.

The local police never gave him a moment of rest and he finally left Poland and went to Paris.

Even there he did not have an easy life. He had problems with working permits. Residence permits were not easy to obtain. In addition, he had worries about finding work. Shlomo Zalman worked late into the night and still found time for (others?), especially to better the lives of other workers.

When the Germans occupied France, without considering his poor health that was the result of his imprisonment in Poland, joining his French friends he threw himself into the underground fight.

After the Holocaust everyone was able to breathe freely, but he was very ill. He had to enter a sanatorium and his life that was fighting for the right and belief in a better tomorrow ended in July 1946.

His fellow Ciechanowans felt the loss of this idealistic fighter against Nazism and fascism and they moved his remains to the Ciechanow plot in Paris.

The organization of the friends of Ciechanow and the neighboring areas call all its members to honor two citizens of Ciechanow, Kahane Shlomo Zalman, a former fighter in the Resistance, and Menachem Kalenberg, a former fighter in the Red Army, whose remains will be transferred to the Brothers' Grave of Ciechanow and the neighboring areas at 9 a.m. on the 25th of February. The grave is located by the main entrance of the cemetery.

Everyone is invited!

The remains of Shlomo Zalman Kahane and Menachem Kalenberg were transferred to the Brothers' Common Grave. Two of our people were reburied at 9 a.m. on February 25. Shlomo Zalman Kahane was widely known by his nickname, Yuzhek. Ignoring his poor health, he took an active role in the Resistance until he fell ill. A year after our liberation he left us."

There is also a photograph in the book of the funeral of Shlomo Zalman Kahane in Paris. My Aunt Helen and Uncle Harry attended the ceremony, but I was already in the U.S.

"If you are not good, I will call the Gestapo"

◆

Louise Oberlender

My name is Louise Oberlender. My maiden name was Trojanowski. I was born in Paris, France on December 31, 1932. My parents, Abraham and Esther, came to Paris from Poland in 1928, and soon got married. My mother was a housewife and my father a tailor. My brother lives in Vancouver and my sister in Mexico City. My middle class family lived in a nice neighborhood and had a nice home. My parents spoke to each other in Yiddish and Polish. Our home was not religious. We were quite assimilated but observed the Jewish holidays, going to temple on *Rosh Hashana* and *Yom Kippur*. I remember feeling uncomfortable when my parents spoke Yiddish or when my father read the Jewish newspaper in public. I used to tell him to put it away. I also felt very uncomfortable when I had to tell the teacher that I would be absent from school because of the Jewish High Holy Days. This is a little of my background, and I believe that many Jewish families in Paris felt the same way.

In 1939, just before the Germans invaded Paris, many of our friends and family fled. It was called the exodus. We took a train that was packed with people, and traveled for many hours until we all came to a small town, found an empty house with no furniture and slept on top of hay. My father left to join the French army. He returned after a few days as he was rejected because of his flat feet. A few weeks later, we returned to Paris and resumed our routine.

On May 14, 1941, my father received notice to present himself to the prefecture of police. I was up at dawn when he came over and told me that he had to go out and would be back later. He kissed me, said goodbye, and told me not to wake up my mother. That was the last time I saw my father.

This was the first roundup when men were taken to work camps in France, and my father was taken to Beaune la Rolande. My mother visited him once.

When I was taken to the hospital for a hernia operation, I was hoping that the Germans would permit my father to visit me, but they did not.

Starting in 1941, every Jew had to wear a Jewish star, and it was not to be covered or hidden in any way. I must have looked very Jewish, because every time I passed a policeman or a German they looked to see whether I was wearing my star. I was always afraid of them.

Then the big day came—July 16, 1942, a date I will never forget. It was the first roundup of women and children. The Gestapo and the French police took 1500 people in Paris alone. I was 9 years old, my brother 11, and my sister 2. Before dawn, between 2 and 3 a.m., we heard loud knocking at our door. My mother signaled to us to be very quiet. She made me hold my sister's mouth so she would not cry. This continued for a long time. I cannot understand why they did not break the door. They kept on ringing and knocking hard. We heard the concierge, with whom we were on good terms, yelling to the Germans:

"I know they are there."

My mother did not open the door. They left and went to other tenants, but kept coming back without breaking down our door. Around 5:30 a.m., they left. We heard a slight knock from our neighbor who said that she had heard all the knocking during the night, and offered to buy some food for us. She promised to be right back. A little later we heard a knock. Thinking that the neighbor had returned, my mother opened the door, and there were two men from the Gestapo and a French policeman. The policeman told my mother she had ten minutes to take only a few things and come with them. I remember my mother standing there without saying a word. Then she approached the French policeman, looked in his eyes and said:

"Take my two oldest children and me but keep my little girl. She is only two years old and will bring you good luck."

The policeman became pale and said,

"I am sorry. My orders are to bring in Mme Abraham Trojanowski and her family."

My mother looked at the French policeman and said,

"Abraham Trojanowski—you already took him over a year ago."

The policeman didn't know what to say. He turned around and told the Gestapo,

"My orders are for Abraham Trojanowski, not for Esther. Those are my orders."

The Gestapo replied to let them come anyway. The papers would be corrected at the prefecture. The policeman said,

"No. We will go correct the papers first and then come back."

He turned to my mother and told her to get ready; they would be back in 20 minutes. When they left, we got dressed quickly. My mother dressed my little sister, gave me money for the metro, and told me to hold on tightly to my sister and not to let her go. On the other side of Paris, my father had a cousin who was a French citizen. At that time, French citizens were left alone. She told me to go there, and they would take care of us. My brother went to another cousin. I took the metro with my sister. My whole body was trembling. I was scared, because the train was full of Germans, and I was sure I looked so Jewish that they were going to grab us. We arrived at our cousins. They only wanted to take my sister. I started to cry and pleaded:

"Where am I supposed to go? I promised my mother I would take care of my sister."

They agreed to let me stay for one night. The next day, a young woman came and took us out of Paris to a small village, St. Cyr sur Dourdan, about two hours from Paris.

All three of us were placed with different families. I stayed with an older family who had no children. The lady's first husband was killed in World War I, and she didn't like the Germans. She was very strict. I probably was not a good child, because she would scare me by saying:

"If you are not good, I will call the Gestapo."

I was very lonely and lived in fear. I was only happy when we went to church. I loved to sing and pray. I used to look at Jesus and the Virgin Mary and asked to become Catholic. I did not want to be Jewish and promised to be a good Catholic. I wanted to have my communion.

Then I found out what happened to my mother. After we left on July 16, the neighbor, who had knocked on our door, saved my mother. This lady knew where we were and came to see us. She told me that my mother was alive.

I was lonely and scared. At night I used to hear the Germans parading and singing, and I always thought they were coming to get me. Sometimes I went to school. My brother was placed with a family next door to mine. My sister was also placed with a childless couple. They fell in love with her and thought my mother would not survive and planned to adopt her. They were nice people, but they did not want me to have anything to do with her. Every time I came, they said she was sleeping and I could not see her. They thought in time I would forget her.

In 1944, the French army was marching toward Paris and passed through our village. I decided to run away and look for my mother. I hitchhiked from one truck to another until I came to the city. Paris was still under siege and fighting, and the Germans were shooting everywhere. I walked many kilometers from one side of the city to the other. I knew where my mother was hiding. When I found her, she could not believe her eyes! I pleaded with her not to send me away. I promised that I would not eat a lot, as she said there was no place or food for me. She did not send me back, but we could not stay there.

Our apartment was taken by the Gestapo and given to French collaborators. They did not want to give it back, and my mother had no money. A distant relative was in a hospital and told us to stay in her place until she recovered. Once a week, on Sundays, we went to a soup kitchen with our pots and pans, where a Jewish organization provided food. In return, we were to stay and sing Jewish songs. I was eleven years old by then. I went to the police chief in our neighborhood and asked if he could help us get our place back. After many months, he took pity on us, and we got the apartment back. We struggled a lot. My brother returned, but my sister stayed with the couple that took care of her, because my mother could not. I finished elementary school and went to ORT for a year. I also joined *Hanoar Hatzioni*, a Zionist organization, and could not wait to go to Israel. At 16, I left my mother, brother and sister in Paris and went to a kibbutz, where I met my husband. We have been married for 51 years. When I left Paris, my sister returned to live with my mother. Later they immigrated to Mexico City.

My husband and I left the kibbutz and came to Paris where my first child was born. Then we immigrated to New York where my husband's parents lived. It was not easy at the beginning, but we were young. We were blessed with three children, two boys and a girl, and we now have eight grandchildren. First, I helped my husband in a business of stuffed toys. Then I worked for Metropolitan Life Insurance for seven years. We decided to move to Miami and bought a candy store, which we ran very successfully for 25 years. We sold hand-dipped chocolates, gifts and cards; we were well known. My husband and I retired and we are trying to enjoy life. I am a lifetime member of Hadassah and very involved as the treasurer and fundraiser of our chapter. I received the Woman of the Year honor last March.

Children of the Holocaust

◆

Suzanne Ringel

My happiest memories stem from the first five years of my life. I was born in Berlin, Germany, in 1933, the same year that Hitler and his Nazi party rose to power. My parents were also born in Germany as well as their many siblings. They all went to school, grew up, married, had children, and were able to lead comfortable, typical middle class lives. All my grandparents had settled in Germany from Poland at the end of 19th century to escape the pogroms and to have better lives for themselves and their families in a modern, enlightened country like Germany. I remember large, happy family gatherings on the birthdays of our many cousins, but best of all were my own and my sister Rita's birthdays. We would be dressed in our starched organdy dresses with matching bows in our hair; and everyone would bring us beautifully wrapped presents and toys. I also remember the Jewish holidays celebrated at our grandparents' house. My grandfather, with his long white beard, sat at the head of the long table laden with food, surrounded by our boisterous family. My mother was a vivacious, pretty redhead. My father was more serious, with a love for the opera. As a young married couple they loved to go dancing on Sunday afternoons at the coffee houses in Berlin. They always took along my sister and me. We watched them dancing to the beautiful waltzes played by the orchestra. Of course, at that young age I was oblivious to the evil doings already perpetrated against the Jews of Germany and Europe, and to the brutality and turmoil that lay ahead.

I do not remember the infamous *Kristallnacht* (Night of the Broken Glass) in November 1938, when Jewish stores and synagogues were set afire. German thugs viciously beat many Jews while other Jewish males, from the age of 13, were arrested and deported. It must have been soon after my fifth birthday when we somehow escaped from Germany and arrived in Antwerp, Belgium. We lived there in a small apartment in an area with many Jewish refugees, all desperate.

Even though our future was so uncertain, our parents always tried to maintain a semblance of normal life. Rita and I attended public school and participated in the youth programs of those Jewish organizations that were still able to function. Again, life for my sister and me became routine and quite pleasant. One day our parents told us that since we were such good little girls they would soon give us a wonderful present. On May 5, 1939, the present arrived: my baby sister, Ruth Sylvie Gutmann. We were ecstatic to have a little baby girl to play with. It was great fun when mama let us push Sylvie's baby carriage.

On May 20, 1940 we woke up to the sound of heavy bombardment. The German army invaded Belgium and a frantic rush to escape began. We dressed in haste, grabbed a few suitcases and arrived at the train station, hoping to get on any train that would take us out of the country. Everyone had the same idea. The station was crowded with thousands of people trying to get on a train. It took us a few days, but we finally landed in a crowded, dirty cattle car with little food or water, but lucky to be able to leave. A few days passed and the train could go no further.[1] We walked and slept in the woods. We finally arrived at the French border, tired, hungry and dirty. France did not welcome these thousands of desperate refugees with very limited resources; it was almost impossible to enter. I remember my parents desperately pleading with the armed border guards to have pity on the children and let us enter. Their pleading evidently worked and we managed to arrive in Paris, where we contacted the Jewish committee. They gave us the address of a wealthy French Jewish family that let us stay with them in their very large and luxurious apartment until we could decide what to do next. We had been there only a few weeks when the sickening announcement came on the radio that the German army had invaded France. With very little resistance, France capitulated.

While father was desperately trying to make contact with people who might help us either to get into neutral Spain or get far away from Paris, we were holed up in the apartment. Children tend to get restless or agitated, so on this beautiful

---

1.   Belgium is one of the smallest countries in Europe. How could a train travel for days and still be in Belgium?—There is a story about a G.I. bragging about his home state, Texas, in an English bar during WW II. He said:

"If you get on a train at one end of Texas in the morning, travel all day, that evening you are still in Texas. You travel all night and in the morning you are still in Texas. You travel another day and in the evening you are still in Texas."—A quiet Englishman from the other end of the bar responds:

"Hey, chap! Don't brag so much! We've got trains like that in England too." (P.T.)

summer afternoon, with the trees in full bloom, my mother decided to take my sisters and me to the neighborhood park. The park was crowded with children playing, nurses pushing baby carriages, and even young lovers smooching on park benches—a very pleasant scene.

While we were happily running around and playing, suddenly a dark cloud gathered over the park: police vans with screaming sirens were coming to a screeching halt and encircled the entire park. Gendarmes, despite the summer heat, were all dressed in black hats and overcoats. They left their vans and blocked all the gates of the park to arrest any Jews or others without proper papers. Panicked, we ran to our mother who was sitting on a bench with baby Sylvia peacefully sleeping beside her in the carriage. My mother, sensing the sudden grave danger, smacked Rita and me quite hard, which made us howl loudly with indignation, including baby Sylvia who was awakened by all the noise. She screamed at us to hold on to the carriage. Almost running, she wheeled the carriage toward the exit while scolding us in her rather poor French that she would put us into bed for not obeying her. This made us howl even louder. She gave an exasperated look to the gendarme at the exit and he stepped aside and let us out of the park with a rather amused smile. Perhaps he was the father of young children. Once we were safely back in the apartment, mother took us in her arms and apologized to us for what she had to do. We did not realize at that time that her amazing presence of mind actually saved our lives. On that day thousands of Jews were arrested, incarcerated and deported. Badly shaken by this close encounter, the next day we left Paris in a rush. Again, after many days of wandering, we arrived in the southern part of France, in Nay, a tiny village in the Basse Pyrenee region, near Spain. The Germans had not yet arrived in this region, but the danger of being Jewish in occupied France was very grave. Somehow we rented a small apartment and Rita and I started to attend the public school. My father's plan was to smuggle all of us into neutral Spain.

To get to Spain meant crossing long, treacherous mountain passes for 10-12 hours or more. This was very difficult even for able-bodied adults, but almost impossible for children of age 2, 8 and 9 years. Even though we were willing to pay, the guides refused to take us. We stayed in Nay until 1942. One summer morning, two gendarmes appeared at our door and told us that the Germans ordered them to take us to the town square. My father was sick in bed with asthma. The gendarmes allowed him to stay only until he got better. He insisted on coming with us, but my mother was able to persuade him to stay behind. They marched us to the square, where buses were being filled with all the Jewish families from the area. This scenario was replayed all over France on that day; 80,000 Jews were deported.

We were driven to a place where a train was waiting for us. Its windows were covered and sealed so that no one could see us within. French police, dressed in black, accompanied us. After several days of traveling during the night, we finally arrived at Rivesalte, the French internment camp, surrounded by barbed wire. There were gates and sentry huts manned by armed soldiers. Railroad tracks passed close to the walls. They pushed us into long barracks with straw on the cement floor. The straw was infested with lice and bedbugs. It was virtually impossible to sleep. A bowl of thin soup made from spoiled tomatoes was our daily lunch and supper. After about a week, they placed us in the children's barracks where the food and sleeping arrangements were slightly improved. My mother had to stay with the adults, but was able to care for us during the day. She was constantly encouraging us with stories that our father was working to get us out of this awful place.

One early morning, while it was still dark outside, they ordered everyone to get dressed and assemble by the railroad tracks. A locomotive was waiting with many cattle cars attached. These cars only had small air slits for openings on top. Sylvia, who was 3 years old by this time, was still in her stroller. I was nine and Rita was 10 and a half. We huddled together, terrorized, not knowing what to expect.

Over the loudspeakers the French guards announced that the adults assembled were to be sent to German camps to work. They could either take their children with them, or leave them behind. We were horrified when our mother ordered us to return to the children's barracks and wait there until our father would come for us. We cried, begged and clung to her. We pleaded with her to take us with her and not leave us alone in this awful place. She insisted on our return to the barracks while she quickly climbed onto the train and disappeared. With tears, the three frightened little girls walked back to the barracks while many of the other children were boarding the train with their parents. We did not know it, but they were doomed. Once again our brave and sharp-witted mother saved our lives.

It seemed like a miracle when a young dark-haired woman appeared a few days later and took us out of the camp. She brought us to our father who was living in Eau Bonne, a small town further south. He was still planning to go to Spain, but he first contacted the French resistance who were smuggling Jewish children into Switzerland. We stayed with our father for about a week. One morning, the same dark-haired young woman who had rescued us from the barracks appeared at our apartment. She explained to us, the three girls, that she was taking us to a safer place. Again, in tears, we said our goodbyes to our father. He promised us that soon we would all be together again.

This time we traveled in a comfortable limousine and train compartment. The young dark-haired mademoiselle always had a bag of goodies for us to eat. We arrived in Annecy, about 60 miles from the Swiss border. She delivered us to an orphanage run by Catholic nuns. We lived there for three months, attended church three times daily, and learned Catholic prayers. Early one morning we were startled when the stern and very old Mother Superior awakened us. She helped us dress, gave us a blessing and then took us downstairs where the same young dark-haired lady greeted us. It seemed that during the night the Germans came to search the orphanage. They accused the Mother Superior of hiding Jewish children. This courageous tiny woman stood up to them. She refused to allow the Germans to search the orphanage, as she did not want her children to be frightened needlessly. The Germans left but vowed to return soon.

In a few minutes we left the orphanage in a hurry with the young lady. We went to Annemasse, a nearby town, very close to the Swiss border. She took us to a small house in a deserted area in town. The young lady bade us goodbye and was gone. The people in the house were all working for the French underground. They told us that the young lady was actually Mademoiselle Rothschild, of the famous banking family.

Our final flight, the last chance to save our lives, had just begun. While waiting for nightfall, Sylvia became listless and feverish. Everyone was very concerned; this was a very bad time to get sick. When night fell, three men in their late 20s or 30s appeared, dressed as farmers. Large, empty milk cans were strapped to their backs. Each had a bicycle with an extra seat attached. It was dark and cold outside. Each of us children was told to climb up on the back seat of a bicycle and remain completely silent. If we had to address the men, we were instructed to call them "papa." Little Sylvia, only 3 years old, was still feverish and whimpering. They told her that this was a very dangerous trip and that the very bad Germans would surely shoot her if she made any noise. Not another sound was heard from her.

We rode silently through dark woods for quite some time. However, we could not avoid passing by a well-lit, large building that housed the Gestapo! The three farmers began to whistle cheerfully, pretending to be on their way home from work with their children. The armed German guards hardly glanced at us as we rode by. Soon we came upon some deserted railroad tracks and disembarked from the bicycles. They told us to take Sylvia by the hand and quickly run across the tracks to a large building on the other side. The three men then promptly disappeared into the night.

Rita and I each grabbed one of Sylvia's hands and quickly made our way to the building. As we entered, a startled Swiss border guard, who must have been dozing, looked at us in complete bewilderment, wondering how we got there. Soon after we were given some food. A doctor arrived to look at Sylvia. Her temperature was 105 degrees! Without so much as a goodbye, she was whisked by ambulance to a hospital in Geneva. The diagnosis was diphtheria.

Thanks to our parents, we arrived safely in Switzerland. Although we never saw our parents again, I know in my heart that before they died, they knew that the German beasts failed to take their beloved children.

In 1991, in response to my letter of inquiry, I received an answer from the international tracing service of the Red Cross. Their records revealed that my mother, Malka Gutmann, age 34, was committed to Camp Drancy on September 13, 1942 from Camp Rivesalte. She was transported to concentration camp Auschwitz on September 16, 1942. My father, Nathan Gutmann, age 42, was transferred on the 29th of January 1943 from Prison Fresne to Camp Drancy. On February 13, 1943, he was transferred to Auschwitz. My maternal and paternal grandparents were sent to Poland and killed. Most of my many aunts, uncles and cousins perished in various concentration camps.

My two sisters and I, at age 7, 13, and 14 and a half, came to this country as displaced orphan refugees in September 1946. What kept me going during these dark and scary days was my childish innocence in believing that when this was all over, I would be reunited with my family and return to the life I cherished and longed for.—That day never came!

After some time in an internment camp near Geneva, we were sent to Zurich by a Swiss Jewish organization and were again separated in different foster homes. We were still hoping to be reunited with our parents. We lived in Switzerland until the end of the war, when the Swiss government ordered all refugees to leave the country. Relatives in America sent us an affidavit and on September 6, 1946, we arrived in New York harbor after a long sea voyage on a ship named Athos #2. Rita and Sylvia went to live with an uncle and aunt who had two young children of their own. I went to live with a widowed aunt. We finally understood that our parents were never coming back. Our grandparents, our many aunts, uncles and cousins all had perished in the death camps.

At first, life in America was not very easy for us. They encouraged us to suppress our feelings, forget about the Holocaust and go on with our lives. When I was only 16, I impulsively married an American born man, and at 17, I had my first-born son, Stephen. At 21, my marriage ended in divorce. With my son, I joined my sister Rita, who had settled in Cleveland, Ohio with her husband, a fellow survivor, and their three children.[2] Rita has passed on, but I feel her smiling down at me, with my parents and all the other members of our martyred family by her side.

Eventually I married a fellow survivor and together we had two sons, Nathan and Michael, who made their older brother very happy. They all grew up to be fine, understanding and loving men, who made me the proud grandma of Hannah (11), Benjamin (9), and Eli (7).

Sylvia was only 7 years old when she arrived in this country. She completely obliterated her painful childhood. She had many problems growing up as she desperately tried to recall the parents whom she felt were the only ones who ever truly loved her. Today, she travels worldwide for the Jewish Federation as a speaker about the Holocaust and teaches that we must never allow this to happen again. Her son, David, a computer genius, lives in Texas.

At times when we are all fortunate to be together at family gatherings, my thoughts return to the past. The intuition and courage of my parents along with many brave people who risked their lives saved three little Jewish children from the forces of evil bent on the destruction of the Jewish people. It gives me personal joy to know that those evil forces did not and never will succeed.

North Miami Beach, FL

---

2. Until her death, Rita had been married to Jack Baigelman, whose story is also in this collection.

"My name is Barbara"

◆

Dena Axelrod

Miles of orange groves paint the windows of my train green, a very peaceful color. My train is full of people going north. I am on my way to sunny Orlando, the home of EPCOT and Disney World, where my daughter and her son Josh live. I am going to spend a few days visiting them. I love traveling by train, but it was not always that way.

The first time I traveled by train, it was scary. I stood on the platform at the train station in Skarzysko-Kamienna, in Poland. My brother Witold went to buy tickets to Warsaw for the two of us. I sat and waited patiently on the bench. I was six, looking forward to this exciting journey.

The train, pulling into the station, looked dark and monstrous, making rhythmic sounds: "Here I come, here I come, here I come!" I watched the people disembark with their luggage. Then I heard the conductor in the blue uniform announce: "All aboard!"

Fear spread through my body.

—"Where is my brother? Why are we not boarding?"

Then I understood: while others were boarding, my brother Witold was led away by two German police officers. He was only 14, wearing his navy blue high school jacket and matching hat with a visor. The German officers had a tight grip on his neck. My first instinct was to run to him, but having lived under German rule for the past three years had made me fear uniforms, especially German uniforms.

—"What am I to do now?"

—"What will happen to me?"

—"How will I find my way back home to my mother?"

Someone flying toward me in a blue jacket and hat interrupted my reverie. He grabbed my hand and ran with me toward the train that was just leaving the station. He lifted me on the first step of the train shouting:

—"Hold on to the rail!"

Once I was inside the car, like a ghost, my brother was gone. I passed through many compartments until I found a seat. My brother was nowhere to be seen. The lady next to me took out some sandwiches and offered one to her son. She asked,

—"Little girl, what's your name?"

—"My name is Barbara."—I answered. She gave me a cheese sandwich. It tasted very good—I was famished.

That day, January 3, 1942, was the first time I ever said, "My name is Barbara." Since 1936, when I was born, my Polish name was Danuta. They all called me Danusia, but my Jewish names were Rachel—Michal—Dena after my grandmothers—one of my grandmothers had two names. Until March 1941, I was the fourth and youngest child of loving parents, Eva and Moshe Wajnman. My sister and two brothers also nurtured me. We lived in a mixed neighborhood of Christians and Jews. My best friend, who lived in my building, and was my age, was a Christian girl, Irene. I remember playing with her in our large front yard. I used to tag along with my brother Janusz when he went to play with his friends.

My brother, Henry, was born in March 1941. We all helped to care for our doll—I mean my baby brother. Henry was a peaceful and cuddly child. I loved watching him smile or sleep peacefully. All I wanted was to be his caretaker, his older sister. Although World War II had already been raging for a year and a half, and we had a lot to fear, the joy of having a sweet baby brother compensated for all our troubles.

Then suddenly we lost him. To save his life, my brother Witold took him to a large city—Krakow. Henry was dressed in warm clothes, wrapped tightly in a blanket, and left in front of the city's orphanage. Witold hid across the street until he saw someone notice the bundle and pick it up.—I missed my baby brother, my doll, and my playmate.

The train rolls to a stop in Orlando; the town that has tripled since Disney World arrived here. This is not my station yet. I pick up my cell phone and call my daughter. Josh, my 14-year-old grandson answers:

—"Hi Savta, where are you?"

—"Tell your mom we are in Orlando. In twenty minutes, I will be in Winter Park."

—"Okay, we'll see you soon, Savta!"

Savta is one of my many names. It is Hebrew for grandma. Only my grand-children can use this name. Between my husband's two sons and my two daughters, I have seven grandchildren. I love all children, but I love most my grandchildren. Starting with the oldest: Benjamin, Jonathan, Joshua, Brian, Daniel, Rebecca, and Melissa.—What does it mean to be a grandma? I don't know. I never knew my grandparents; they were all, along with my parents, aunts, uncles, and brother Janusz, slaughtered by the Nazi criminals of World War II.

The psychologists say that we learn from our parents how to be parents to our children. Also, we learn from our grandparents how to nurture our grandchildren. What about us, the children of the Holocaust, who lost our teachers, our guides and our mentors? How are we to do a good job at nurturing the second and third generations of survivors? We often spoil them and provide them with everything that we did not have.

I didn't have family; I didn't have enough food; I didn't have enough clothes. However, I had many names. I liked my name Irena Kornacka. My adopted father, Stanislaw Kornacki, was a wonderful, nurturing person. He was my care-taker, my social worker and my savior. I don't know whether I would have survived in Warsaw if not for Stanislaw Kornacki. He had six sisters, who became my aunts. Here are some of their names: Aunt Zofia, Aunt Jadzia, Aunt Julia and Aunt Janin. I also had an Uncle Stephen, Mr. Kornacki's brother. They were all wonderful, loving and caring people. I was lucky to be a part of their family.

On Sundays, Mr. Kornacki would pick me up from the orphanage on the out-skirts of Warsaw. We would take the city bus or the electric train and visit one of his siblings. Mr. Kornacki was very proud of me and liked to show me off to his family. I loved all the attention showered on me. Mr. Kornacki was a widower. His wife had died some six years before. Often we would go to the cemetery on Sundays to visit her grave and put flowers on it. This was sad, but then we would visit one of his sisters and that was fun. These Sunday visits were the high points of my week. In the orphanage we didn't have much food: oatmeal for breakfast, some soup for lunch, a small sandwich for supper. But when Mr. Kornacki took me to visit his family, there was plenty of very tasty food.

This was before the Kornacki family officially adopted me, before he became my father, and his siblings my aunts and uncles. Until then I was still Barbara

Slozak, the lost girl from Mielce. That was what my brother Witold told me to say when anyone asked about me.

—"My name is Barbara Slozak. I come from Mielce. I came to visit my grandma in Warsaw, and while I was playing with some kids from the building, I hid in a church. Now I can't find my grandma's house."

Yes, this was play-acting, and it was supposed to be fun. So why was I so scared and shaking all over, when the church servant asked me who I was? Was it because I hated to lie, or because of the deep loneliness that fell upon me when my brother walked away from Saint Jacob church, letting me go up to its door all by myself?

Suddenly, the play-acting became kind of scary. Witold lifted his hat as he passed the church. That was the cue for me to enter the church without a steeple. It was not easy to walk in the snow, following my brother from the train to the church. It was hard for me to keep up with his long stride. He never looked behind him to see whether I was still close to him. As an adult, I understand that it was for my safety, in case he got caught. Back then, it was scary to be in a strange big city, full of tall buildings, that made me feel so much smaller and more vulnerable. Before entering the church, I looked back and saw Witold disappear from view, acting as if he didn't care what happened to me.

It was not the first time that I entered a church. My friend, Irene, invited me to join her family to church. Also the priest, Father Garbala, a friend of our family, taught us the Catholic prayers in the hope that it might save us children. However, this time I was alone in a much larger edifice, without the kindly priest or the friendly face of my friend, Irene. I looked at the picture of Mary holding the baby Jesus, and she looked back at me with a warm smile. She seemed to be saying

—"Do not worry my child, all will be okay."

I smiled back at her and her baby that looked just like my baby brother, Henry. I stopped worrying and began to pray.

A few hours passed, while I sat in a pew praying and wondering what would happen next, how the play would continue?

—"When will my brother Witold come for me?"

—"When will I go back to my parents, my home?"

The old church keeper approached me.

—"Little girl, I have to close the church doors. Please go home now."

—"I can't find my grandma's home."

—"Where is her home?"—asked the keeper.

—"Somewhere on the big street."

—"Which street?"

—"This one…"—I whispered.

The keeper took me by my hand and walked with me down the street. He asked again and again:

—"Do you recognize your grandma's place?"

—"No"—I said, over and over. Finally he gave up and took me to the apartment of the priest, who asked me many questions. I passed his test. I was a good actress. That night and the next few nights I slept in the apartment of the priest's housekeeper. Every day he worked on finding my lost grandma, while also searching for a temporary home for me.

—"What's your name?…Where are you from?…How old are you?"

—It was simple. I knew all the answers. A childless couple took me home with them. They wanted a child, any child, but not one that was responsible for crucifying their God. Many times each day I was asked:

—"Do you love Jesus?…Do you love Mary?"

—"Yes, yes!" was my answer.

—"Are you Jewish?"

—"No, no!"—I answered emphatically.

The questions continued. They were not sure. I was treated well by them. I had food and some toys, but they did not trust me. They promised me bigger and better toys if I only would tell the truth. They tried to bribe me, and my childhood weakness, my one and only weakness, won. I wanted the new toys. I finally responded:

—"Yes, I am Jewish, and I love Mary, mother of Jesus."

That day my caretaker brought me to the police station to get proper papers, she had told me. I sat on a bench for hours. She never returned.

In Winter Park, Florida, the train comes to a stop. Outside I can see my daughter and grandson waiting for me. Hugs and kisses, then a short drive to my daughter's house. They live in north Orlando, close to Winter Park. I love their small, two-story hundred-year-old house.—I belong to an antique club. Every month I go to educational lectures dealing with furniture, jewelry, pictures and irons (my husband's collection—he gave a lecture on it). I love the monthly lecture and lunch. My daughter's house is decorated in 19th century colors and furniture. Josh loves to show me his new computer that he uses for his homework. Living four hours' drive away prevents us from seeing each other very often. I appreciate the short visit with him. The next day my daughter and I travel to

Cocoa Beach, where my Toastmasters' District is having its conference. Three years ago I joined the Toastmasters Club to improve my communication skills. I have worked hard and I am proud of my achievements. My daughter and I enjoy our time together at this conference. We attend a humorous speech contest. It is fun.

I count my lucky stars: I have been married for the past 30 years to a wonderful, caring, educated man, who has provided us with a spacious, two-story house on a lake. He and I traveled and cruised many countries in Europe, South America, Australia, and New Zealand. We are having a wonderful time together. Yet, I can't help thinking that it was almost over for me on the day I was taken to that Police Station in Warsaw. I was very scared as I sat on a bench at the station, waiting for my caretaker to arrange some ID papers for me. The Polish police officers were questioning some people, filling out applications, and responding to other people's questions. When my turn came, an officer took me to another room that had a large desk in the middle. He sat behind the desk, and began questioning me:

—"Name?…City of birth?…Where are your parents?…Their names?…"

In a shaky voice I answered all the questions. I looked for some pity or compassion in those cold, blue eyes of my interrogator. There was none. He did not trust me as he got up and walked toward me. He was very tall in his knee-high black leather boots. They looked menacing. Under his belt was a rubber club.

—"Little girl, are you Jewish?"—he asked.

—"No."—I responded.

He quoted some Yiddish expressions—I had never heard them before. And then:

—"What is a bubale?"—This I knew. Victoriously, and eager to please, I said:

—"That is my baby brother!"

The police officer also felt victorious. A big smile appeared on his face. He pulled the rubber truncheon from his belt and exclaimed:

—"You lied to me, and you will be punished."

An angel of mercy suddenly appeared and saved me from those brutal high leather boots. The angel simply said:

—"Leave her alone. She is only a child."

My angel was another officer with a kind face and gentle blue eyes. He led me to his desk and shared his sandwich with me. Then he took me by the hand and walked me to a bus station. He watched over me on the bus. He shared a secret with me: his little girl died last year. We walked to a large building that housed an office of social services for the city of Warsaw. He said he would come back for me, after he spoke with his wife.

I did not have to wait very long. A slim, partly bald man asked me to sit at his desk. He was a kind looking man with a gentle smile, dressed in a brown suit. He took a large pad and filled out all the important information about me. He promised to find my lost grandma in Warsaw, or my parents in Mielce. I knew that he could not and would not find them. He knew that he would try hard. That day I learned to trust God's creation: a human being. A person, who does not have to know you well, yet be kind and gentle with you. This kind man, Mr. Kornacki, took me to the orphanage on the outskirts of Warsaw. He provided a secure home, while he was looking for my parents. Yet he did more than look for my family. He picked me up on days when he knew that the Germans or the Polish police would come to the orphanage for inspections. I always looked forward to Sunday mornings with Mr. Kornacki and his family.

After a few months, in response to his questions, I divulged to him my full true story. As he had promised, nothing changed in his attitude toward me. The opposite of what might have been expected happened: I spent even more time with him and his family. The German soldiers marching and singing no longer scared me. I had Mr. Kornacki, who would protect me…He said so himself!

One day in early 1945, Mr. Kornacki said that he would not see me for a few weeks, but would return soon. I did not know then, but learned later, that he was part of the Warsaw Uprising. While the Russian forces were closing in on the Germans, the people of the city rose up against the occupiers.

What did the approaching end of the war mean to me and the other children at the orphanage? Daily bombing of the city. Dead soldiers everywhere. The sirens would sound many short whistles: "Hurry-hurry-hurry-run-run-run!" We dropped whatever we were doing and ran for shelter; more than thirty children, from three to nine years old, running from the building into our cellar. We heard the shattering noise of bombs falling on the city. The teachers told us to keep our mouths open so that our eardrums would not break. Those were terrifying sounds, as if the whole world were falling apart. After an hour or two of bombing, a long sound of the siren would send us back to the house, to continue whatever was interrupted. Who could continue living a normal life? Fear was everywhere, in the eyes of the three year old, who could not stop crying, as well as in the eyes of our teachers who sat motionless, staring into space. The daily bombings made all of us feel insecure and filled with fear.

Then one day, part of our own building that held the orphanage was destroyed. Our teachers led us out of the wrecked building's cellar up to the street to look for another shelter. The street was full of Polish soldiers and civilians shooting at the bombers. Dead soldiers everywhere. Horses, lost without their riders, ran wild through the streets. Horses lay dying in the middle of the road. We were led into the soldiers' barracks and spent a night there. Gregory, our youngest, lost his life there. A piece of shrapnel tore his body apart. They told us not to look as a military medic carried him away. We prayed for his recovery for the next two days, but Gregory died.

The military officer directed us, the orphans, to stronger quarters, a well-built house. They promised that to be very safe. It was the cellar of a four-story office building; indeed, we did feel safer there. The people of this building provided us with food and blankets. All the residents came to stay in that cellar when the bombings started. Then the long siren would sound and they would return to their apartments. We stayed there; we had no other home. Then one day after a long period of bombing there came a knock on our cellar door. A German soldier stood at the door, commanding us to come out with our hands up. Children and adults, with our hands up in the air, walked up the cellar's steps into the fresh air. We looked at the German soldier with fear, who just stood there laughing. We made a funny picture: children with fear in their eyes, faces blackened with dust and smoke.

Around us, the whole city of Warsaw was in flames. The buildings were destroyed and burning. The flames were shooting high into the sky. Were we alive, or was this that burning Hell? We followed the soldier to a large square in the middle of the city. When all the surviving people of Warsaw assembled, a German high officer spoke to us, while another soldier translated:

—"Because the Polish people of Warsaw took up arms to fight the armies of the Führer, the city will pay for it by being burned to the ground. All of you will go to a camp in Prushkov."

The German soldiers lined up on the one and only street that was not burning. They directed the remnants of the people of Warsaw out of the burning capital. Inferno...fire on the right, left, and behind us. It was evening, but the sky was bright from the flames of the burning city. We began our journey out of Warsaw.

The picture of the burning city, the screams around me, the heat of the fires, will always stay in my mind. I lived in that inferno and survived it. It is a miracle!

You cannot live only within those terrifying memories. A person has to live now and find peace and perhaps happiness after such turmoil. One must try to create new and happy memories.

The Toastmasters' conference I attend with my daughter produces new, fond memories. The humorous contest is exciting! Eighty contestants from cities in Florida and one from the Bahamas deliver five-minute humorous speeches. They are delightful! A speaker, dressed as an angel with wings and a halo, describes how he should have stayed in bed that morning, rather than go on the road with his friends and get into a car accident. This is delivered like a play and makes us laugh without end. All the speeches are great!—The old memories of fire and fear of that long-ago night in Warsaw are relieved for the moment by pure fun.

The next afternoon I take a train back to Ft. Lauderdale. It is a pleasant and restful trip. My memories take me back to the train ride out of burning Warsaw.—German soldiers drove the majority of the people at gunpoint to the camp. It was a long and tiring walk, without food or water. The fires were behind us, thousands of people in front of us. When we could not walk any longer, we would sit on the ground on the side of the road. Some of us fell asleep. The smaller children had to be carried by the older ones. By that evening, we reached the end of the road. We were tired, so we sat again on the side of the road to rest. Our senior teacher went to speak to the German commander. She told him that he should have pity on us, since we were orphans. She asked him not to send us to the German camp. She touched his soul. The officer gave her instructions how to get us out on the midnight train. Tired and hungry, but alive, we climbed aboard the freight train and fell asleep. Early in the morning we arrived in Krakow, the second largest city in Poland. Buildings in Krakow stood proudly. Those were neither bombed, nor burned. I thought the whole world had been destroyed, yet Krakow looked whole, just the way Warsaw used to be. There were no Germans in Krakow by then, but I don't remember when we were liberated.

Within an hour of our arrival, we were led to a school building whose empty classrooms became our temporary home. The parents of the school's real students brought us three meals a day. On Sundays, each parent chose one of us to take home for a day. It was fun, but in the evening, when they returned us to our makeshift home, we were all very sad. We exchanged information about our "families for the day." After a couple of months in this temporary shelter, someone found a home for us in the mountains, in the town of Poronin. It was a private home with many bedrooms on three floors. The boys were on the third floor, the girls on the second, and the adults took the first floor. The semester was just beginning, so we were all enrolled in public school. Life began to feel normal. The people from the town knitted sweaters for us. Others from the next town bought skis for us and we learned to ski in the deep snow. A month later we had a party; we invited all our benefactors, including the town officials. We sang and danced for them, and one of us read a poem written by one of the teachers, in which we thanked all the good people for helping us.

But one thing made me sad. I knew that I was far away from Warsaw and Mr. Kornacki would never find me…Never!—I often cried thinking that I would spend my life in this orphanage. I often thought of my sister and brothers, especially my baby brother. I never missed an opportunity to play with, or at least look at the babies. In my mind Henry always stayed the same age, sweet and cuddly.

One day, when I returned from school with the other children, the orphanage teacher asked me to come to the office. When I entered, I could not believe my eyes! Sitting in the large chair at the desk was Mr. Kornacki, my angel, my protector. I could not believe my eyes! I jumped into his lap. I kissed him, hugged him, and bombarded him with a million questions:

—"What did you do all those months?…How did you find us?…How are Aunt Julia, Janin, Jadzia, Zofia?"—On and on my questions kept pouring out. Instead of answering me, he said:

—"Let's go for a walk."

I held onto his hand, and we walked outside. One by one he responded to all my questions. Then he had questions for me. I told him about the bombings; how we lost Gregory; about moving to the strong building in Warsaw; about the German and Polish soldiers fighting right in front of our building; how Warsaw was bombed and burned, and our walk with thousands of others to the German camp; our miraculous escape by train and, finally, our arrival in Poronin where we were now living. He did not interrupt me, but I saw tears in his eyes, and his hand held mine a little tighter as if to say: "I will take care of you. Fear no more!"—I understood, and then I asked:

—"Are you taking me home with you?"

He hesitated a while and then responded in his slow, logical manner:

—"I have no home. Warsaw is not a place to live. All my life it has been my city; now it is in ruins. But I promise you, as soon as I find an apartment, I will come for you."

The wait seemed endless. Sadness overtook my life. The war was over, but we, the children, were not aware of it. I did not see German soldiers on the streets of Poronin. I thought the soldiers were only in Warsaw. A few months later, after I had written many letters to Mr. Kornacki asking him to come get me, at last, he came. We left the orphanage early in the morning without any sadness. We took the train all the way to Warsaw. The city was still in ruins. Very few buildings were intact. On our street, the front of each building was bombed out. Five-story buildings had no floors, just hollow centers; the façade had no windows, but when you entered the main gate, there it was, the back of a building, all five floors, including the stairs, in very good condition. Our apartment was on the fifth floor with three bedrooms and a kitchen. Within a few months this apartment filled up with people: Aunt Zofia and her husband Roman, who returned from a German labor camp; Aunt Julie, alone; a couple with a small child; and a great aunt, who had no other place to stay; nine people in one apartment.

My new name, Barbara Irene Kornacka, was my treasure, and the new apartment, a kingdom. I started school with my new name on my school ID card. After school I would go to Mr. Kornacki's office. We would have lunch together, and then I did my homework. I had beautiful clothes, a large and loving family, and a good school. Life could not be better! After my fourth and fifth grades, I was sent to summer camp for a month. We swam in the river, picked blueberries and mushrooms, and played interesting games. I could plan my life, hoping to stay Barbara Irene Kornacka forever.

In 1947, Warsaw was being rebuilt, yet I was always told that there were many sick people on the street. I was not to talk to strangers. Just go to school, and return directly to the office, without stopping anywhere.—I followed those directives.—School was fun and so was visiting my father's office, where I helped with the office work. Whenever I had a school project, the whole family helped. Once our class planned a puppet show. Each child planned a part of the show. I took Pinocchio. My job was to make clothes for him. Two of my aunts helped me make Pinocchio's outfit: pants, shirt, hat, and jacket. It took a month of hard work. On a Monday morning I dressed warmly and walked to school, carrying my newly dressed Pinocchio with me. I sensed someone was following me. Stopping in front of a store window, I saw the reflection of a young man. I turned around: it was a young man in his late teens, wearing a blue hat. My heart stopped beating. Was I about to be kidnapped by some traumatized war survivor? The man said,

—"Is your name Barbara Slozak?"

—"No, my name is Barbara Irene Kornacka, and I have to go to school now."

—"Did you have a brother Henry?"—the man asked. Shocked, I looked at him, and wondered how he knew.

—"Yes, where is he?"

—"I'll take you to him; come with me!"—said the man. The fear of being kidnapped returned. I walked faster, trying to get away from this stranger. Then he said,

—"I am your brother, Witold. I found Henry, and he is living with me."—He held my arm, urging me to walk with him. I started to run away from him, but he caught me. He said that it took him two years to search for me, and he was not going to give up now that he found me. A police officer came and ushered us to the police station. Each of us was questioned in separate rooms. My brother was more persuasive than I. I was told to bring my father to the police station. I ran to his office, and exclaimed:

—"My brother stopped me! He wants to take me away, but I don't want to go! Please, don't make me!"

We went to the police station together. That day changed my life forever…It was very stressful, but Mr. Kornacki had to let me go when my brother, Witold, told him that he would rather not take Mr. Kornacki to court.

I went with my brother, Witold, to Czestochowa. He lived in the orphanage there with our little brother, Henry. I learned that my birth parents, as well as Janusz, my middle brother, were dead. My sister Ruth survived the labor camps and was living in the USA. Witold was twenty when he took care of us: Henry, who was six and I was eleven.

I hated to leave my adopted family. I hated living in an orphanage. But I was happy to see my baby brother and Witold. In 1949 we immigrated to Israel and lived in a kibbutz. My name changed from Barbara to Batya. Later, I remembered my first name, Danuta, and I changed it to the Hebrew name Dena. Our lives in Israel were difficult. Israel had just become a country. Our Arab neighbors did not like the idea of having a Jewish state among the Arab nations. Attacks and the killing of civilians were common. Both Henry and I went to school. Witold, who took the Hebrew name Ze'ev, worked on the farm. At the age of 18, I got married. A year later my first child was born. I named her Irene.

When Irene was a year old, we immigrated to the United States to be with my sister, Ruth, in Ft. Lauderdale. A year later my second child was born. We named her Barbara. I studied and became a Hebrew school teacher. Working with children gave me much joy; I enjoyed this kind of work. For 25 years I taught

Hebrew school. Many things happened during those years. I moved from Ft. Lauderdale to Hollywood, then to Miami, and for the past 15 years I have lived in Ft. Lauderdale. My first marriage broke up, and then I lived alone with my children. Later I remarried.

Mr. Kornacki passed away in 1967. His family is scattered around Poland in various cities. My husband and I have visited them three times.

My sister Ruth lives in Florida; she has four children and 4 grandchildren. Witold also lives in Florida; he has three children and ten grandchildren. Our brother, Henry, has never married. He has lived in many countries, including England, Israel, India and Germany, but he has never found a home.

My daughter, Barbara, graduated from college with a degree in psychology. She lives in Stuart, Florida. Barbara never married, but she has a boyfriend. She earns her living by playing the piano.

My daughter, Irene studied art in college. She is divorced and lives near Orlando with her sixteen-year-old son. Irene is a very private person and does not like me to talk about her.

When I arrive in Ft. Lauderdale after visiting Irene and Josh, my husband is waiting for me. He is never late. I can always depend on him. I am happy to see him and share my travel adventures.

Now that I am in the twilight of my life, I joined the organization of the Child Survivors of the Holocaust. Our goal is to share our stories in a safe environment. We are the children who survived the Holocaust in camps or ghettoes, or were saved by kind Gentiles. Some of us were saved by partisans in the forests, others managed to flee the Nazi persecution. What unites us is our age. We were 13 or younger when the war started. The stories of our lives as children during the war are unique, yet we find in our stories similarities. We can understand each other, and care for each other, as no others can. When I tell my story of abandonment and later finding a loving family, others in the group feel my pain and my joy. The war left a mark on my psyche, yet Mr. Kornacki and his family provided me with love and caring that filled my emotional life with warmth, when I needed it most.

To grow emotionally healthy, a child needs not only food and clothing, but also love. Orphanages do not provide love. I feel lucky because, as the song says,—"Love has been good to me."

Black Roots in the Hair of a Blond Cherub

◆

Elizabeth Zielinski de Mundlak

My maiden name that I have used for as long as I can remember is Elzbieta Zielinska. But when I was born, my name was Aliza Ash. All my life I thought that my mother's name was Justa, but at the time of her birth she was named Ruth. What has not changed since the day I was born? Only the date and place of my birth: Czestochowa, the town where my ancestors had lived. But this is a lot to start with! Recently, it allowed me to find documents about my true identity. The procedure was long.—How can you prove that a certain sixty-year old woman exists, if there is no birth certificate in her name, Elzbieta Zielinska? The nuns, who sheltered me after I was taken in a garbage sack from the Ghetto of Czestochowa, gave me my first name. That was before almost the entire Jewish population of that ghetto was taken to Treblinka, the infamous death camp.

Tadeusz Ferens was a gentile doctor who arranged my escape from certain death. My mother was also able escape. With her newly acquired identity as Jozefa Zielinska, she was able to reach Austria, where she was a slave laborer, a cleaning woman at the Hotel Post in Bludenz, in Vorarlberg province. All the rest of my immediate family, including my father, Shimon Asz, perished in the Holocaust.

The doctor brought me to the Orphanage of the Sisters of Nazareth in Czestochowa, as a child whom he found at the train station. There were many, many displaced and orphaned gentile children as a result of the steady bombing of certain parts of Poland. It was easy for the good doctor to convince the nuns that I was one of those children. No one wanted to hear the truth! Poland was the only country during the war, where the penalty for helping Jews was nothing less than death.

It was my good fortune that a Polish family came to the orphanage to adopt a little girl. They already had a 10-year old son, but his mother, Victoria, could not have any more children. She had lost her first child as an infant, but her heart was full of love that she wanted to give to a little orphan girl. I was lucky: my new parents were very loving people. My big brother used to carry me up the stairs on his shoulders after I had been running around the yard with my little friends. We were a weird couple. He was tall, strong and blond, and I was a tiny little girl with dark curls...

Dark hair...I had curly blond hair when my adopted parents took me from the orphanage. With my blue eyes I must have looked like a cherub. They fell in love with that little beauty. However, a big surprise was awaiting them after a few days.

One day, my new mother was washing my hair when she discovered some "dirt" on my skull that would not go away. She was surprised, but ignored it for the moment. A couple of days later the answer became obvious. Black hair began to grow fast on my little head. It was a big shock when my parents understood that they were sheltering a Jewish child. They became terribly scared. Their only child, their precious son was as much in danger as themselves in case the Germans would find out about me.

Victoria and Marian summoned their son, Andrew, for a family meeting. Jointly they decided that no matter what, they would not return me to the orphanage. The years ahead were not easy for my new family. Some neighbors insinuated that I must be a Jewish child. Once a man showed up to blackmail them: unless they gave him a substantial amount of money, he would denounce them. My adoptive father was in charge of an underground cell. At the next visit someone shot the man even before he entered our building to get the money that he tried to extort.

We lived through many instances of high drama during those long years of German occupation in Czestochowa. My parents and their son were living with continuous fear and anxiety from the fall of 1942 until January 1945, when the Russian Army liberated the city.

The war finally ended. There was a new and happy life ahead! What a relief, what a joy that was!

And then, at the end of 1945, a lady showed up at our apartment. She wore a black coat and a black hat. She asked to talk to my mother, Victoria. I suddenly became curious and came in, dragging my precious doll on the floor. The woman fell on her knees; she embraced me and began to cry. She called me by a strange name. I was confused and scared.

Our drama was unfolding: What to do? She was Ruth, my beautiful mother, who returned from forced labor. She had suffered for all those years thinking that her beloved family had perished, and she prayed for her little girl. She was detained by the Gestapo in Bludenz, when she was denounced to be Jewish. This pretty, blond, blue eyed woman endured terrible harassment, while the Germans were deciding whether she was Jewish or not. They performed all sorts of measurements on her head and her face. After several days of her terrible anxiety, they decided that she was a perfect Aryan specimen. So much for the racist theories of the Nazis...!

For some reason they did not return her documents and she could not go back to her work.

She had a good friend, also hiding under false identity. Through his connections some documents were arranged for her. By that time the war was almost over.

Ruth escaped to Switzerland with some friends, where she had spent several months and then she took the first available train back to Poland, and here she was! What to do, my God, what to do in this situation?

This is the moment when I wish to praise human goodness and intelligence. At first, Marian and Victoria had offered my mother, who used the name Jozefa, to live with them and be part of the family. She had no family, no roof over her head. She had nothing to offer me for the moment, while I had been pampered, sheltered and protected by this wonderful adoptive family.

When I was already an adult, my mother confessed to me that for a very short moment she was tempted to leave me there for my sake. But she soon recognized that her reaction was not realistic. It would not be acceptable to anybody! In the end; everyone would pay a very high price for this sacrifice.

Everyone around me was wonderful. For several months my mother was visiting me as an aunt, so I could get used to her. I hated those visits, and I was scared. I had a certain premonition that my precious world would all of a sudden fall apart.

Days, weeks and months passed by. It was time to make the big move. My mother was offered a job that would take her abroad for a certain time. This was her opportunity to establish closer contact with me. On the day we left, I did not want to be separated from my wartime mother, Victoria. At first I was trying to convince her that I would be a good girl and would never misbehave. This didn't work, so with tears in my eyes I tried to convince her that she should give away my big brother, since he would be able to manage more easily without her...

We all cried. Even today, whenever my older brother, Andrew, and I recall this moment, tears appear in our eyes. We remain the sole survivors of this drama.

I was told, that when my adopted family came home, they cried and cried for several days. I was told that Victoria had never recovered from this loss. She loved her little daughter, her inseparable companion, very much.

At times, when I look at my precious, pretty grandchild, Alexandra, another little girl appears all of a sudden. She is as sweet as her, but with sad eyes, insecure and confused. When I shake this nightmare and return to our pleasant reality, I find a happy child among loving parents, Simon, my only child and my daughter-in-law, Diana.

My childhood had a happy ending. I was lucky to get a wonderful stepfather, Julian Ritterman, who adopted the second name of my mother, Zielinski, so the three of us would have this same family name. We became an instant family without any official adoption papers and complications. The post-war era allowed these sorts of arrangements.

My little sister, Daniela, was born in 1949. She is nine years younger than me, just as I was nine years younger than my adoptive brother Andrew. She is a highly celebrated physician and scientist in Venezuela.

Both sets of my parents have already passed on to a better life. They joined my biological father, Shimon Ash, whom I do not have the privilege to remember, but I know that he loved me dearly. They joined all their relatives whose lives ended in Treblinka.

After the war, life in Poland was not easy for anyone and much worse for Jews. In 1957 we were able to immigrate to Venezuela, where my stepfather's family had settled. We became part of the Jewish community there. I married a wonderful man, Alexander Mundlak, when I was very young, only 19. He was also a Holocaust survivor from Poland. His parents were much like my own; we were a tight family. The Mundlaks lost everyone in their immediate family, as we did. The family consisted of three: Dora, Mayer and Alexander, who was three when the war broke out.

My husband was a mechanical engineer. I graduated as a chemical engineer and became a lecturer in the faculty of engineering at the Universidad Central de Venezuela in Caracas. While in that position, I was awarded a scholarship to work on the PhD degree in Environmental Engineering at the Polytechnic Institute of New York. We have one child, Simon, our pride and joy. Alex died at the age of 47 from a heart attack. At the age of 43 I was left with an 18-year old son and two aging survivors, whose worst experience in life was the loss of their only child. With love and mutual support we were somehow able to continue.

After my parents' and my in-laws' deaths, I retired from my position of Professor of Engineering at the Universidad Central in Caracas in 1993. As my son was living in the USA, my only family in Venezuela consisted of my sister, her husband and their two wonderful sons.

Having been active in our Jewish community for many years, I was invited to join the Board of Governors of Tel Aviv University in 1985. This required my assistance each May at the annual meeting in Israel.

While I was in Israel in 1996, I decided to visit my wartime brother in Poland after almost 40 years. I had corresponded with mother Victoria until 1973, when we stopped writing to each other. I sensed from her last letter that it was inconvenient for them to be in touch with anyone in the West.

I called my wartime brother Andrew from Tel Aviv. He was very excited and invited me to visit him. Our encounter, in 1996, was very emotional.

This became a big turning point in my life. Through my brother I met a wonderful lady, Bieta Ficowska, an active member of a Polish group of child survivors of the Holocaust. Bietka's husband, Jerzy Fisowski, is a great poet and writer, who dedicated a large part of his work to the minorities, the Jews and the Gypsies. While I was in Poland, Renata Zaidman of the group of Child Survivors in Montreal was also there. Under the influence of Bieta and Renata, I became an active member of our organization. I joined the Miami group, since my family lives here and I spend a couple of months here every year. This has changed my life drastically. From a retired person without any idea about how to dedicate my time and energy, I have become a quite successful movie producer. To honor Venezuela, my adoptive country, where being a Jew never caused me any anxiety, I produced a wonderful documentary film "Caribia and Koenigstein, Ships of Hope."

The beauty of this accomplishment is that the director of this film was my 20-year old nephew, Jonathan Jakubowicz, a student in the School of Communication at the same university where I was a professor. He managed to assemble a wonderful crew of very talented people, so the film could be produced on a really low budget. The film won many awards and was presented in many countries as well as on Spanish television for 10 million people through HBO.

The documentary tells the story of the arrival in Venezuela of two ships filled with Jewish refugees from Austria, trying to escape the Nazi terror just before the outbreak of World War II. Both ships were denied permission to put their passengers ashore at various ports in the Caribbean. It was Venezuela that gave them a safe haven.

Since that time Jonathan has become an accomplished student at the film academy in Austin, Texas. I have also followed my own passion, this time making a documentary in Poland. In 2001, I returned to the city, where I was born and saved, to film the dramatic story of my survival.

The director of my movie this time is Marek Maldis, a very talented and well-known Polish journalist and the director of several documentaries. It makes me feel very good that his grandmother is a Righteous Gentile. She had saved the brother of my dear friend, Renata Zaidman. He already has produced almost two hundred movies, some with Jewish themes. We worked very hard, trying to find Jewish remnants of the city that once had a vibrant Jewish community, where my great-grandfather served as Grand Rabbi and spiritual leader of Czestochowa for almost 50 years.

As one project leads to another, I am promoting an exhibition about Jewish Czestochowa at the Town Hall of that city that happens to be its Central Museum. It is to take place in October 2002. I have found many survivors and their children from Czestochowa, who kindly provided me with pictures from the time when life was beautiful there. Despite all the hardships, that was the place that my family and many others called "home" for many generations. In the holiest of all the cities in Poland, where there is the shrine of the Black Madonna, Jews had led an intense life with all sorts of institutions, organizations, newspapers, representatives to the city council, and so on…

I took up the mission spontaneously to rescue a part of the completely forgotten history of this city. It is a unique place in Poland because of its holy nature.

In the same way as I honored my adopted country, Venezuela, for the goodness of its people, while the rest of the world had taken an extremely egoistic attitude, I want my documentary film to be made in Poland to honor the good and brave people, thanks to whom I am alive today. I also want to encourage responsible educators to return to the Polish youth part of their own history that has been hidden from them. During the Communist period it was taboo to talk about the Jews before the war. It is time for a more honest period!

I feel more enthusiastic than ever, and very committed to contribute to better understanding between Christian Poles and Jews through dialog and education. It is also my goal to take my movies to many countries, so that young people can learn how terrible the consequences are when evilness is allowed to spread. I have already been invited with two of my dear friends from the Federation to teach in the schools of Boros, Sweden, where they annually hold a "Week of Fight Against Fascism."

I hope to receive more and more such invitations, as the young need to be exposed to this kind of experience. Once again I lead a meaningful and very exciting life!

Humanity in the Midst of Death

◆

Bianca Lerner

Fate was against my father's plans. Even though we had visas and tickets to come to the United States on the Queen Mary for October 1, 1939, the Germans attacked and occupied Poland one month earlier on September 1. There was no way for us to leave Europe and come to America, as planned. My father, Arnold Perlmutter, was a reserve officer in the Polish army; he left immediately for the front. My mother, Dr. Stefania Kranz Perlmutter, and I spent a month running from house to house while the Germans were bombing Warsaw with incendiary bombs. An artillery shell destroyed our apartment. At first we stayed with my aunt. Every night, my mother would drag me to the basement. One night my aunt's apartment was hit, but we were not in it, so that night we were not harmed.

One month later it was all over. The Germans overran the entire country of Poland.

The Germans came with detailed plans for making life difficult for the Jews and to exterminate them as efficiently as possible. Immediately, we were denied many things we had taken for granted, such as education; we had to wear a Jewish star to identify us; we could not change much money for the new occupation currency, and so on…Within a couple of months, the Jewish population of Warsaw was ordered to move into an old section of the city, which became the Warsaw Ghetto. My family was very lucky to share an apartment with four other families, as the first apartment that my father found was excluded from the ghetto. Many people didn't have any shelter. We shared a bathroom and a kitchen with four other families.

As soon as we moved into the ghetto, I became aware of small children roaming the streets without shelter or food; these children had been separated from their families. I became a little social worker at the age of ten and decided to get some food for them every day. I collected potato peels from the inhabitants of the apartment building, which I exchanged for milk with a farmer who owned a cow. At least once a day they were sure to get some food. I am amazed that as a ten-year-old child I conceived and executed this by myself.

As a pediatrician, my mother was required to examine people every day and write reports about rampant diseases and epidemics in the ghetto. She would burn all her clothes upon returning home each night.

At the beginning, the Nazis were randomly grabbing people off the street. Whenever my parents left the apartment, I had this sinking feeling, as I was not sure whether I would see them again. My father realized that education was the only thing I would be able to salvage from this time and place. He hired teachers for me for all the school subjects, including Latin, French and English. So that's where I learned my English, in the Warsaw Ghetto. My father tried very hard to inject something positive and happy into my life. He even managed to give me a rabbit. He was unbelievable! He was asked to join the Judenrat, but flatly refused, because it was only a puppet Jewish government to deliver the orders of the Germans to the residents of the ghetto.

As time passed, the Nazis perfected their plan for eliminating all the Jewish people. After three years, the Nazis were completely organized in this effort; there was a train running from the railroad depot within the ghetto to the nearest death camp, Treblinka. One day, they grabbed my mother from the bedside of a sick child and put her on the train with the rest of that family. That was the last time I saw my mother or learned anything more of her fate. As a physician she had obtained a capsule of potassium cyanide, a fast-acting poison that she always carried with her. I have always hoped that she took the capsule rather than die in a gas chamber. My maternal grandmother had died at the beginning of the war from dysentery, despite all my mother's efforts to save her. Her only sibling, her sister Ada, was also taken on the same transport. I don't know whether my mother took that capsule if she didn't have one for her sister. I will never know. My father and I were the only ones left.

Only a few Jewish people were left in the Warsaw Ghetto by this time. Before the war, Hanka Popowska was my closest friend. We spent a lot of time in each other's homes. Neither of us had any siblings. We went to a private school. I was the only Jewish student in a school for 500 girls. I took part in all kinds of sports and had opportunities to travel with my parents. I came from a very close and loving family; the first ten years of my life were idyllic. My father spoke English perfectly and he was a director of an import/export firm with many branches all over Europe. He was on the verge of opening his newest branch in New York

City and already had rented office space there. I was a lucky little girl until the Nazi takeover.

As soon as the ghetto was created, my friend's parents offered to have me stay with them, but I was only a child and I wanted to be with my parents. We did not believe the rumors about the horrible things happening in other cities and villages. We thought it impossible for any humans to carry out those acts against others. After my mother was taken away, my father got in touch with Hanka's father, Dr. Popowski, who immediately repeated his offer, which my father accepted. He managed to bribe the German guards at the gate—they were not SS, only Wehrmacht, regular German Army soldiers—and I walked out of the ghetto by myself. It was like a miracle! Dr. Popowski also encouraged my father to save himself and leave the ghetto. It was obvious what would happen to the rest of the Jewish population.

I met the doctor in a prearranged location and went home with him. They were wonderful! They gave me as much love and attention as anyone could, except my own parents. Since I had spent a lot of time visiting in their home before the war, a lot of their relatives and neighbors knew me. Whenever anyone rang the bell, I had to hide in a closet for the duration of the visit. After several months, Dr. Popowski felt it was psychologically detrimental for me to be hiding in the closet, and he thought it would be better for me to live openly with false papers. That's how I ended up in a Catholic orphanage run by nuns. Dr. Popowski provided me with forged papers under the name of Janina Marzec and created a false history to go with the name. He drilled me with the story: we had lived in a small village at the other end of the country; my father was a carpenter and my mother a housewife; I didn't speak any other language but Polish and had never traveled outside of the country. He also told me that my Polish was too refined and I had to learn some slang, because the other girls in the orphanage came from different socioeconomic strata and had little education. I had to blend in with the others.

In reality, I became a little actress. The only sisters who knew my true identity were the Mother Superior, Matylda Getter, and her secretary, Sister Teresa. Life in the orphanage was very Spartan; we slept on straw mattresses without heat in the room. One morning, I saw a rat on my bed. He was cold and hungry, too. I became well versed in the Catholic catechism and religion. We prayed many times a day and I had dents in my knees for seven years afterwards from all the kneeling. We were to be quiet during meals. Shortly after my arrival, a situation arose for which I was not prepared: confession and communion. I didn't know what to say and there was no one to ask. The Mother Superior was in charge of several orphanages and was traveling, so she was not accessible. Anti-Semitism was so prevalent that even the nuns and priests could not be trusted. There was no one to trust at that time in Poland; the country was terribly anti-Semitic. Even in the ghetto, some Jews would turn in their families to survive one more day. If I traveled by trolley, I was told to carry either flowers or a book to hide my face, so no one would recognize me. All this added up to a hard nut for me to crack. I thought long and hard and decided that everything about sex was taboo, so in confession I told the priest I had thoughts about boys, and that was okay. I was told to say some Hail Mary's for repentance.

My first meal at the convent was oatmeal cooked with water, but without salt or sugar. This symbolized to me how my life had been completely turned around. Before the war, I was sheltered and somewhat spoiled, and I gave my mother a lot of problems by not wanting to eat at all. But that changed quickly as I became quite hungry.

Shortly after I left the ghetto, those few who remained, mostly students, decided to put up resistance and kill as many Germans as possible.

They knew that they were going to perish anyway. With few weapons, without food or medical supplies, they put up a valiant fight, sometimes fighting in hand-to-hand combat.

It took a whole month for the Germans to overcome the ghetto resistance fighters. They had to smoke them out building by building and burn each building in the end. In contrast, the French, who did have food and weapons, gave up and capitulated with hardly any resistance. In one month, the Germans overran the entire country of France.

I was in the convent for a year and a half, and only saw my father a couple of times. Before the war, my parents had a lot of Christian and Jewish friends, but the Christian friends were all afraid to hide him. Finally, an old woman was persuaded to hide my father for money. This was a very difficult adjustment for my father, who had been a very active person. He resigned to having to stay alone day after day. The old lady would padlock the door and leave for the day.

One time, while I was visiting him, he had a cold and he had to muffle his sneezes and coughs with a pillow because the walls were very thin. It was known in the neighborhood that she lived alone. It was a ramshackle building. My father could only go as far as the middle of the room for fear that someone in the factory, across the street, might see him. I could only visit him a few times, and had to arrive at night and leave before daylight so I would not be seen. Every couple of weeks the old woman would demand more money or threaten to denounce him. He was alone, tortured by his doubts and anguish about what else he should have done to save his family, especially my mother.

In 1944 the Soviet army was on the other side of the Wisla River and encouraged the people of Warsaw to rebel against the Germans. I joined the underground immediately, with the blessings of the nuns. We built barricades on the streets and dug tunnels through the basements of houses to join them. I was 14-years old; at first, I was a messenger. The Russians, true to form, backed away. Then I found a gun. My only wish was to kill Nazis. We fought for an entire month with little ammunition, medical supplies or food. We were counting on the Allies or hoped that someone in the world would help us, drop us supplies, but the whole world stood still. Nobody helped. We had no choice but to capitulate. The Nazis were furious because we were the first city that dared to revolt. As punishment, they razed Warsaw to the ground. I was terribly disappointed and frustrated; I didn't care whether I lived or died.

Meanwhile my father had also joined the partisans, and he was struck in the lung by a stray bullet. It was a debilitating wound, but not fatal. He was placed on a cot in a makeshift field hospital and managed to send a note to let me know where he was. I still have that note. He signed it "Grandma," because I was supposed to be an orphan. All the people in Warsaw were going to be evacuated at the end of the month. I told my father that I did not want to be separated from him any longer, but he told me there was no way I could be part of the hospital and I should give myself up with the members of the underground. So with a heavy heart I left him, never to see him again.

After the end of the war Dr. Popowski immediately began to look for him. He told me that he learned that just before the war was over, a Polish nurse saw that my father was circumcised and told the first German she saw, who came and shot my father. At that time, only Jewish men were circumcised in Europe. It's so mind-boggling to lose my father because he was a Jew. There is no rational explanation. He had survived almost six years of hell to lose his life during the final hours.

As it was their custom, we expected the Germans to line us up against a wall to shoot and kill us. However, this did not happen. Because of our participation with the underground, we were treated as prisoners of war. I was in eight different prisoner of war camps. The conditions were horrendous. We slept in barracks, 200 women on the ground. When one turned, the other 199 also had to turn. Our food was a cup of broth made with rotten turnips and a small slice of bread. I had not taken any warm clothing with me, because when I left Warsaw it was still summer, and I had not expected to survive until winter. Twice a day at

Appel, we were counted hour after hour. There I was, during a cold, German winter, with my shoes stuffed with newspapers and without any warm clothes. My parents had thought I was so fragile and delicate…One of the camps was in Altenburg, where the German people would come and look at us like animals in a zoo.

We were shuttled in cattle cars from one camp to another, for days on end. Every 24 hours the train would stop and we had to relieve ourselves while the guards were watching. That was just one way to dehumanize us. In one of the camps I had to work in a factory to make bullets. I tried to sabotage everything I could.

One of the camps had English and American prisoners of war. They were far away, but we could see their silhouettes. When these men heard that there were women in the same camp, they began to write notes on pieces of paper and threw those, with little rocks inside, over the fence. It was quite a distance and not that easy to do. I was the only person who knew any English, so I was busy translating these notes and writing replies. We called this "rock mail." I personally corresponded with a couple of English and American POWs. I knew that one of my uncles, my father's youngest brother, had escaped to England from Vienna, but I didn't know his address. I told this to one of the English soldiers. He suggested I write a letter to my uncle, and he would send it to his sister, who would then try to locate him. When the war was over, I found out that the letter did actually reach my uncle.

My Viennese grandmother also escaped to England, but having no news from her other children, she died on her birthday with a broken heart.

After six long years of war, we finally heard planes overhead on their way to bomb specific sites. We could not understand why they would not drop a few bombs on the crematoriums, but they never did. In spring of 1945, we finally heard some artillery, and allied forces soon liberated our camp. They gave us uniforms and treated us as part of the allied forces.

After a while, we became displaced persons, DPs. I had no news about my parents or other members of my family who had been scattered all over Europe. But I was sure if they had survived, they would not want to stay in Poland, Germany or Austria. I did not know my uncle's address in England, because I was very young and no one expected me to survive alone. But the other members of my family all knew his address. I decided to put all my efforts into locating my uncle and I wrote many letters with fake addresses that I got from various books. After a while, the English Post Office was kind enough to put an ad in the newspaper, and my uncle was found. It took a while to get permission to go to England and then only with the provision that I was on my way to the US.

As soon as I arrived in England, a policeman came to the door to check me out. I was very afraid of anyone in uniform and did not answer the door, so he came another time. I was very happy to be with a member of my family. We hoped to hear from others, but apparently no one else survived. I spent a year in England waiting to leave for the US, and when the papers finally came, I hated to leave the only relatives I still had. However, they promised to come to the US, because they were not happy in England. With a very heavy heart I left and arrived in New York. The crossing of the Atlantic was quite unpleasant. The waters were very rough, so I became nauseated and seasick for the duration of the voyage. Also, I kept wondering what fate might await me in this new country?

The war was over, but not for me. My new relatives were not very welcoming. I could not understand why they brought me over, until I realized that my uncle had his own purposes, like claiming in his synagogue that he saved me from the clutches of the nuns. He also pocketed the monthly monetary aid sent to me by a Jewish organization to help me resettle. When the money stopped coming, after a few months, the uncle threw me out.

I was so naïve that I could not comprehend what was happening. At the time, I did not know that there were scholarships available to me at various colleges. I stayed with a great uncle who was a brother of my grandfather, but he was anything but great.

I got married very young and had two children, Arnold, who lives in the State of Washington, and Susan, who lives close by in Miami. My only granddaughter's name is Marissa. I am now retired, and my husband died three years ago. The most important thing I do now, in addition to some other volunteering, is talking to students about the Holocaust and educating them about hate and prejudice, and how to prevent those.

A Vignette

❖

Eugenia Schulz Rosen

The following is a small part of my story to be included in our book of the Child Survivors of the Holocaust of South Florida.

My name is Eugenia Rosen. For many years I had refused to speak about my childhood. My sadness repressed my memories and I never even told my own daughters about my experiences during the Holocaust.

I was born in 1936 to an affluent family. We lived in Warsaw, Poland: my mother, father, a nanny, various household help and of course I, an only child. My parents were not religious but traditional. My maternal grandparents also lived in Warsaw as well as my uncles, aunts and cousins.

My father had three clothing stores and my mom, like all mothers, was busy.

My parents used to go to the theatre in the evenings or see their friends. It was a good life. I recall my nanny taking me to play in the snow and for walks. I loved to dress up in my mom's high heels, gloves and beautiful hats with veils and loved to smell her perfume.

Slowly, the political atmosphere began to change.

I was three years old when the German army invaded Poland in September 1939. The mood became somber in our home; the nanny was gone!

As a decree was issued to reduce the Jews' living space, we had to accommodate two other families into our beautiful apartment in Warsaw.

As the bombs were falling, people were running in the streets, carrying bundles. We had to go to a shelter that was crowded and dingy. We put on several layers of clothing, as we never knew whether we could return to our home.

Many people were poor, most of them sad, hungry; some were crying. There was little air in the shelter. It was all very frightening!

A new ordinance was proclaimed. All furs were to be collected and I also had to part with the fur collar and pompom from my beautiful blue hat and coat.

My father was told to sign over his stores to the new German owners. Not too far, soldiers were standing with guns to make sure that the transfer was carried out smoothly.

The Warsaw ghetto was formed in November 1940 and we were sealed inside! Food was scarce and difficult to obtain; my parents looked worried and very sad. They whispered much among themselves.

I used to attend a kindergarten not far from our home.—I am alive today only because on a particular day I stayed home from the kindergarten with a cold. On that day the German Nazis drove up in an army truck and took all the little children with them.

Every Jew was to wear an armband with a yellow star. We lived in perpetual fear, listening for footsteps on the staircase, expecting those to be of Nazi soldiers.

The Nazis were rounding up people from the street; they even pulled them from their homes onto trucks to take them to the Umschlagplatz, a place where the Jews were gathered to be sent by train to Treblinka.

My parents and I were already at the *Umschlagplatz,* but somehow we escaped as my parents bribed a guard! I remember being held by both parents and running home through the empty streets of Warsaw.

By then I understood the seriousness of our life and the worries about survival—our situation was gravely serious.

At all times I obeyed my parents. Slowly my parents began to prepare me to be separated from them; they taught me Catholic prayers, and—most importantly—they instilled in me never to admit that I was Jewish. I was only six years old and suddenly I had to grow up.

On a cloudy, dreary day, we left the ghetto with a work detail to go to the Aryan side. I remember vividly the big fat German soldier in a gray uniform counting the people, with a German shepherd dog at his side. I was standing in front of my mom holding my breath, I don't know whether he saw me or not. In the evening the same number of people returned to the Ghetto, but others took our place in the group.

Once on the Aryan side of Warsaw, my name became Drzidzia Jankowska and my mother turned into Aunt Zofia.

Aunt Zofia brought me to a convent outside of Warsaw—but I did not stay there very long, because the Gestapo came to search for Jewish children.

I was hiding in a toilet. The fear I sensed at that time is beyond my ability to describe.

Meanwhile, my grandparents died of natural death in the ghetto; my aunts and uncles were taken away and, while I was looking out the window, my favorite cousin was shot by an SS man.

My mom, or aunt Zofia, was looking for another place for me. She also brought me to see my father where he was hiding. Once again my parents instilled independence in me and gave me an address where we would meet after the war.

I will never forget that address!

I assumed the identity of Mr. and Mrs. Umerski's niece, who lived in Berlin, Germany. The Umerskis had no children; they were of German descent and were willing to have me live with them. They were very nice to me but I was sad and lonesome. I had to keep out of sight in order not to attract attention, so I stayed mostly indoors.

As the Russians were approaching, Mr. and Mrs. Umerski had to leave Warsaw. As they were unable to reach my mother, who was in the "underground," they brought me to Mrs. Umerski's sister.

I was only eight years old, but Mrs. Stasia made me clean her house, take care of her daughter and go with them to church. She was very mean to me and my memories of her are not pleasant!

I received a letter from Mrs. Umerski who told me to study my multiplication table and be obedient. They would adopt me at the end of the war if my parents did not survive.

But Hitler did not succeed in his objective to kill all Jewish children and eliminate all future generations of our people.

My parents did survive the war—and I am the proud wife and mother of two wonderful daughters, Naomi and Monica. I am also the proud grandmother of four little boys: Moshe, 13; Aryeh, 11; Elie, 9 and Noam, 5 years old. They are taught about their heritage both at school and at home. They follow the traditions of our forefathers; but their parents strongly emphasize to the boys to respect all people, to be tolerant of all human beings and never to discriminate. They bring me much joy!

From Bratislava to the Budapest Ghetto

◆

Yosi Lazzar

Our family lived in Bratislava, where I was born in 1934. Bratislava is an old city on the Danube; it is closer to Vienna, the capital of Austria, than to Hungary's capital, Budapest. Pressburg is the German name of the city; the Hungarians call it Pozsony. Probably because of its proximity to Vienna, the city served as the seat of the Hungarian parliament until 1848. A lot of people used to speak all three languages fluently. At the time I was born, Bratislava was the capital of Slovakia, a province of Czechoslovakia, an independent country that was created in 1918, at the end of World War I. Before 1918, it was part of the Austro-Hungarian Empire. The Czechs and the Slovaks speak almost the same language and together they prized their independent and democratic country. My father was born in Komarno, a smaller town on the Danube, east of Bratislava. Slovakia is an independent country today. One side of Komarno is in Slovakia, the other side is in Hungary, it is called Komárom. My mother, Cecilia, was a homemaker and my father a chemical engineer. I was the third of four sons. Ernõ was my oldest brother, born in 1929. Sanyi was born in 1931. As a boy, my name was Józsi, and Jenõ, our little brother, was six years younger than I. We strongly identified as Jews, although we were not religiously observant.

In anticipation of the probable consequences of the Nazi propaganda and the rapid arming of Germany, the Czech army was preparing to defend the country against Germany. Thus, my father was drafted into the Czech army in 1938. At the time we owned an ice cream parlor concession during the summer.

Hitler's bullying brought on the Munich conference at the end of September 1938, with the participation of Great Britain, France, Germany and Italy, where they decided that certain western parts of Czechoslovakia with its German population be ceded to Germany. This decision was made without the participation of the government of Czechoslovakia. Five months after the Munich conference, Czechoslovakia ceased to exist as a state; Germany rapidly seized power and became the most powerful force in Europe. With this event the continent began to move rapidly toward the war that eventually involved countries from all five continents. Czechoslovakia had been the strongest and most viable buffer state between Germany and the Soviet Union. It had mutual defense treaties with France and the Soviet Union, which were disregarded by its partners.[1] Czechoslovakia's tragic fall into the German bloc was the first major step in the annihilation of the peace treaties following World War I in 1918.

On October 6, 1938, the second Czechoslovak republic was born that included Slovakia as an autonomous area. World War II began with the conquest of Czechoslovakia by Germany in March 1939. Slovakia soon became a National Socialist state and a satellite of Germany. On November 2, 1938 *"Felvidék,"* a heavily Hungarian speaking southern strip of land in Slovakia, was annexed to Hungary. As the new government viewed our family as Hungarian and Jewish, we were deported to Budapest. Komarno, my father's birthplace, was in that annexed area. In Hungary we were stranded without a place to live. After we arrived in Budapest, the Jewish community gave us an apartment; in exchange, my mother cleaned the synagogue and its offices. The Hungarians took my father to a Hungarian forced-labor camp for Jews, called *Munkaszolgálat.*[2]

Ernő, my oldest brother, died of pneumonia at home, in Budapest. Sanyi attended an orthodox school in Budapest, but when the officials at the school found out that our father worked on Saturdays, they threw him out. Neither of us went to school at all.

After the Germans occupied Hungary on March 19, 1944, the Hungarians forced us to move from our apartment to Teleky tér 3, a specially selected house for Jews, marked with a yellow Star of David above the entrance from the street. During the fall of 1944, we were forced to move again, to Akácfa utca 36, a house in the ghetto in Budapest. At first we were given soup once a day from the central

---

1.   **Encyclopedia of the Holocaust**, Macmillan, p. 1002, 1990

2.   *Munkaszolgálat:* Hungarian quasi-military labor service. Following the enactments of the *"Zsidó Törvények"* (laws restricting the rights of Jews in Hungary in 1938 and 1939), Jewish men between twenty and forty-eight were declared *"megbízhatatlan"* (unreliable), not trustworthy with arms, and drafted into labor service units within the Hungarian army, serving under non-Jewish regular and non-commissioned officers. These groups were assigned to dig ditches, cut down forests and, worst of all, seek and disable Soviet land mines. See **Encyclopedia of the Holocaust,** (ed.) I. Guttman; Macmillan 1990 pp. 1007-8.

kitchen. We were not allowed to leave the ghetto, but this did not stop us. A group of kids, including Sanyi and I, got together and gathered food stamps from various people within the ghetto. We sneaked out of the ghetto to buy food and supplies from the outside markets and shared half of this with the people who gave us the food stamps. After nightfall we broke into stores that had been abandoned by their gentile owners, who were forced to leave the ghetto. We looked for food and anything else we could use to survive. Outside activists, members of the underground resistance who wanted to save the Jews, gave us guns and hand grenades. We would go to certain addresses in the city and hide the ammunition in potato and flour sacks and return in the evening to the ghetto through a network of cellars.

Once, on the way back to the ghetto, I was carrying two baskets, one on each arm, and two huge Christian altar candles. The Jewish ghetto police and two Hungarian Fascists stopped me. They questioned me about the contents of the baskets and where I was taking them. While they were discussing how to handle me, I dropped the baskets and tried to run away. One of the Jewish police officers grabbed one of the candles and hit me on the shoulder. When he turned to talk to the others, I did manage to get away.

Another evening, there was a terrible incident. It was dark, about 6:30 in the evening, when my little brother Jenő and I were walking home after the curfew—against our mother's orders who wanted us to be home before dark. Two German soldiers with the Jewish police stopped and questioned us. I had no idea what could happen. My brother began to cry, and we tried to run away. One of the German soldiers came after us and grabbed my brother, who fell down. The soldier first kicked him and then stomped on his head and killed him. I ran home, and had to tell my mother what happened. She became very ill, but my mother and I returned to bring my little brother back home in a canvas tarp. The next day he was taken away in a handcart. No one protested; there were no repercussions. There were a lot of dead people in the streets, and each day they would come with handcarts to collect the dead.

I also witnessed Hungarians killing Jewish people on the streets of Budapest. The Danube River divides Buda from Pest, along the embankment of the river the Jews were lined up, often three people with their hands tied to one another, and the middle one was shot, causing all three to fall into the icy river. Life in the ghetto continued to be a battle for survival.

In 1944 my father was taken to the Chundorf Concentration Camp in Austria, near the Swiss border. They performed medical experiments on inmates in that camp. Of 20,000 people, my father was one of only 1600 survivors. After liberation, he returned on foot to Budapest, skin and bones, weighing 75-80 pounds. We were very happy to see him alive, but he did not survive mentally. We never spoke about the Holocaust.

When liberation seemed obvious, the Germans placed explosives under the ghetto and planned to destroy it along with all the occupants, possibly as many as 70,000 people. This mass murder was prevented at the last minute when diplomats from neutral countries threatened the officials that after the war they would be charged not with war crimes, but with mass murder.

After our liberation by the Russians, who fought from cellar to cellar to take over the ghetto, my parents, Sanyi and I returned to Komarno, in the new Czechoslovakia. My brother and I tried to go to school. We were the only Jewish children in the city and in the school, and the non-Jewish children constantly abused us. After a couple of months, we refused to return to school.

A year later, in 1946, I was one of the kids chosen by the Zionists to immigrate to Israel. There was a man, named Guttman, who had travel documents issued before the war to leave Czechoslovakia and enter Palestine under British rule. The war prevented him from using the documents. Guttman survived, but his wife and children did not. However, the papers for getting into Palestine were still considered valid. Guttman took an 18-year old girl with him who was using the documents issued to his late wife, and for this exodus, I became his son, Ernó Guttman. We managed to reach Marseilles, where we had to wait a month before we could board the Heliopolis, a Greek ship that arrived with us in Haifa on October 20, 1946. I managed to find my aunt and her husband in Tel Aviv and they took me in for a while, but they could not support me, so they sent me to a *moshav* for children, a permanent camp with a school.

My parents remained in Komarno with my brother who was convalescing after losing both hands in an accident after the war. He touched some ammunition left by the Germans that exploded. I left in 1946 and did not see my family for three years. The Czechoslovak government let my mother and brother leave legally, but my father had to leave illegally. We finally all reached Israel in 1949.

Life in Israel was very hard. Everything was new, including the new language. Eventually, I served in the Israeli army as a parachutist. After my term of service, my older brother and I developed a printing business in 1957. In 1967 I bought out my brother's share so that he could go to art school. He divided his time between Israel and Germany and became an accomplished artist in spite of his handicap. From an early age, I wanted to be a photojournalist, to capture the moment on film, so starting in 1964, I studied photography in a school in Tel Aviv and subsequently worked in Europe.

In the early 1980s, I moved to New York and engaged in several businesses. In 1987, I moved to California and went into the vending business until 1999, when I retired. I moved to Florida in October 2000. I had been married twice.

My father died in 1964, he was 64 years old. My mother was 97 years old when she died in July 1999. My brother passed away in November 1999, a few months after my mother's death. He was 68. I am the only one left of my family and I am living in Miami now.

Twelve Months in the Life of a Small Boy

✦

Peter Tarjan

My assignment is to write "My Story" for this anthology of the memoirs of Child Survivors of the Holocaust who live in South Florida. It is about my family, before, during and after the events that changed my personal life, from what I remember as a very happy early childhood—to something totally different. This transformation from bliss to gloom took only twelve months from the middle of March 1944 to the following March. The setting was Budapest.

Most of what I will report here is based on my memories, but I will lean on some tales, legends, facts and fantasies told by my aunts and uncles over the years. In the late 1980s, my aunt Ágnes gave me an envelope marked *"Utolsó Levelek"* (Last Letters) that contained a few postcards and fragments of letters written by my parents and a few other relatives and friends who all perished in the Holocaust.—Ágnes died at the age of 85 in 1992. Her friend emptied her apartment and a few months later she handed me a beat-up suitcase with photographs, documents, souvenirs, and most important among those, a bundle of letters and postcards written mostly by "Mama," my grandmother, and a few by "Papa," my grandfather, starting around 1941. Someone mailed the last postcard after several thousands of the local Jewish people, including Mama, Papa and most of our relatives, were put in cattle cars in Pécs and taken to Auschwitz. These letters and postcards tend to validate what I wrote for two previous anthologies.[1] [2]

---

1. *Young People Speak—Surviving the Holocaust in Hungary*, (ed.) A. Handler and S.V. Meschel; Franklin Watts, 1993, p. 115.
2. *Red Star, Blue Star-The Lives and Times of Jewish Students in Communist Hungary (1948-1956)* (ed.) A. Handler and S.V. Meschel; East Eur. Monogr., Boulder, dist. Columbia Univ. Press, 1997, p. 203.

Most people can tell you precisely where they are from—I am not so sure of my answer, I hesitate. Although I was born in Budapest, most of my family ties link me to a smaller town, Pécs, 180 km south and slightly west of Budapest, on the southern slope of a small mountain, the Mecsek.

Bözsi, my mother, and her older sister, Ágnes, were both born and raised in Pécs. Tibor, my father, also grew up there from the time he was six. Tibor was two years older than Ágnes; they knew each other as teenagers, but Tibor had not even noticed Bözsi, a little girl, six years younger than him, until after they had both moved from Pécs to the big city, Budapest, around 1930. My mother went there to study music. Ágnes aspired to be an actress. Tibor was assigned to a job there. Panni Kertész, who ultimately saved my life, became my mother's closest friend then, while they were both preparing to become piano teachers. We celebrated Panni's 90th birthday in London in October 2000 and phone her about twice a month. She'll soon be 93.

Pécs was the hub for both my parents' families. My maternal grandparents, "Mama and Papa" were living there in a modern apartment, after they sold their house and Papa retired from his trade, tailoring. At 75, Papa was still working in Uncle Ede's office, Mama's bachelor uncle. Mama took care of their home that included her father, my "Dédike," until he died in 1939. I was three at the time, but do remember him as very old and frail, with lots of white hair and a big white mustache.

Dédike's wife, Bertha, died in 1933, three years before I was born. Bertha was Uncle Ede's sister. Ede was everyone's favorite uncle, but a man of very strange habits. He took a walk with his dog on the Mecsek every day while he was healthy. He was a wealthy bachelor, but lived frugally. Uncle Ede was the luckiest among my relatives in Pécs, as he died in 1943, just before all hell broke loose for the rest of the family in March 1944. Many of Mama's letters were written on Uncle Ede's business stationary that indicated his financial interests in coal mining and steam shipping on the Danube.

My father's two sisters were also living in Pécs. Aranka, the oldest of four children, never married and earned her living in the leather craft, making purses, handbags, wallets, and so on.—Böske was the third of my grandparents' children.—Uncle Kornel, 11 years senior to my father, had been living in Zagreb since about 1922 with his wife and two children, Medy and Jancsi, who were both born there.

When Fáni, my paternal grandmother, died in 1910, Aranka was already 22. She raised her two youngest siblings, Böske, twelve, and my six-year old father. They moved to Pécs, where their father died in 1924. Böske, who was a pretty girl, had worked as a typist from the time she finished middle school at 14. She married a much older man, Miska, an attorney and enthusiastic soccer aficionado. They were childless, but they both loved children. They lived very comfortably and they seemed to be very happy together until the world crashed around them. During our frequent visits to Pécs, Böske and Miska often "borrowed" me for an afternoon. After lunch, Miska was required to rest in bed on doctor's orders. As a little boy I was also supposed to take a nap. But instead of napping, Miska and I playacted all sorts of fantastic adventures, Arctic voyages and tropical safaris, until Böske, our martinet, would end our horseplay.

We spent many vacations in Pécs where, being the youngest of the family and the only one of my generation, they all spoiled me. Aranka's shop was fascinating with all the complicated leather cutting and sewing machines. The smell of leather was familiar to me as my father also worked in the leather trade, but at the tanning side, while Aranka and her assistants were craftsmen.

My family in Budapest consisted of Ágnes and her husband, Miklós Takács, an unemployed architect, along with some maternal cousins. Around 1943 my father's half-brother, János, popped up out-of-nowhere. János had grown up with his mother, completely isolated from his four siblings. A year later he became another victim of the Holocaust at 33. As Ágnes and Miklós were also childless, they often borrowed me for a Sunday or a holiday. These events were great fun! We always lunched in a restaurant, often in the hills of Buda, and played a continuing fantasy game. They addressed me as Mr. Schwartz and I called them Mr. and Mrs. Somogyi. We pretended that we were all adults and conversed about the events of the world to the extent that a little boy was able to participate. Miklós would point to me while saying to the waiter: "Please, bring another raspberry soda for Mr. Schwarz!" The poor waiters never quite knew what to make of this weird bunch who addressed a little kid as "Mr. Schwarz."

Kornel was born in 1893 in Szekszárd. Grandfather had enough money in 1910 to send Kornel to study mechanical engineering in Berlin at the Technische Hochschule. He graduated just in time to be called up for military service for the Kaiser in World War I and serve on the Italian front. He was badly wounded and after his discharge, Kornel returned to Pécs. At the end of the war Pécs was under Serb occupation. The Serbs needed an engineer to supervise the city's public works and Kornel *Friedman* was the man for the job.—While Kornel was overseeing the public services of the town, Admiral Horthy was taking revenge against the liberals and leftists, especially the Communists, for the 1918-19 Commune, the communist regime that followed World War I in Hungary. Thousands were jailed, executed or escaped, mostly to Vienna. When the Serb occupation of Pécs ended around 1920 and Horthy's troops took over the government, Kornel's life was in danger for his Serb connection. Kornel left for Vienna and took Tibor, his teenage brother with him, for fear that the "White Terror," as Horthy's henchmen were called during my teens, would string both of them up on a lamppost for Kornel's "sins."

Vienna was not a good place to find work in that post-war period. Tibor attended high school while Kornel was looking for work. After nearly a year, Kornel met a Bosnian gentleman in a café, who owned a mill that was rendered inoperative during the war and needed someone to rebuild it and start it up again. My uncle grabbed the opportunity and stayed in Yugoslavia for more than two decades. During the Italian occupation in the early 1940s, Uncle Kornel and his family were interned. When the Germans took over, they escaped and joined Tito's partisans for two years until they were shipped across the Adriatic Sea to the already liberated southern Italy. They worked their way up via Rome to Torino and immigrated to the US in 1950.

To this day, Pécs is close to my heart for reasons of my happy early childhood there and for my attachment to the Mecsek, where I spent many peaceful days, often alone in its forests, which had much to offer with each season. In summary, my parents were quasi-immigrants to Budapest whose roots were very deep in Pécs. The place where I feel closest to my long lost family is there, in the synagogue—although I am not the slightest bit religious—and in the cemetery, where the remnants of the Jewish community, a few hundred survivors among 4000, commemorated the victims by erecting a wailing wall in 1946. Next to the wall is a grave where some of the survivors buried a block of soap made from tissues of the victims of the gas chambers in Auschwitz.

My father wanted to study law but the *Numerus Clausus*, the first modern anti-Semitic law in Europe, slowed him down. This law limited the percentage of Jewish students at the universities. My father became an apprentice tanner and enrolled in a correspondence law program to earn his J.D. A few years later, as he knew the company's business from the wet tanning floor to the corporate quarters, he was appointed to manage the company's branch office in Budapest. My parents rented a small, but comfortable apartment in the Jewish section of town. I was sent to the local Jewish elementary school in 1942. It was run by the state, but all the pupils, boys and girls from first to eighth grade were Jewish. My best friend was Vera, who was also an only child. Her family lived on the same floor as mine, merely two doors away. Vera was a year older than me. My heart almost broke when she went off to first grade and I had to stay home for another year.

She told me wonderful tales about school. When my time came to start first grade, it was a terrible disappointment. School turned out to be very boring.

My father did take me to the huge Dohány Street Synagogue, one of the largest in Europe. Hungarian Jews segregated themselves into two denominations: orthodox and *neologue*. The orthodox were, of course, much more observant. Their Rumbach Synagogue, only a few blocks from the Dohány Synagogue, drew lots of men with *payuts* or sidelocks, wearing big, round, black hats and black kaftans. The older, married women wore stiff wigs under their hats, or kerchiefs to cover their hair. The men wore *tzitzits* (fringes), but some of the orthodox were harder to recognize by their clothes than others. Many of the men wore beards, but not all. Some cleared their facial hair with a burning chemical salve that often caused severe rashes.

"Our" synagogue was much less traditional, although in America it would be similar to the orthodox and conservative branches. Men were seated on the ground floor and the women in the galleries, to allow the men to concentrate on their religious devotion and not be distracted by the sight of women. Even in recent years, when few people attend services and the galleries are closed, the men sit on one side and the women on the other at the ground level.

The rabbi and the cantor were forbidding figures in our temple in their priestly black robes and double-domed black hats. The sermons were long and very boring, but the organ music was beautiful as well as the choir on Friday nights. The one big event that stands out in my mind was Simchat Torah, in 1941 or '42. The synagogue was brightly lit and everyone was in a joyous mood, carrying paper flags and singing as we all marched around the huge synagogue to celebrate the end of the Torah cycle. I would think it was 1941, because Hungary was not yet involved in the war during the autumn of that year. By 1942 many of the Jewish men were drafted into military labor, sent east to the Ukraine to dig ditches, chop down trees and search for land mines with their bare hands. Some death notices had started to arrive in our neighborhood in 1942. There was little to rejoice about in 1942.

We lived in a largely self-imposed Jewish, but minimally religious environment. Most of the tenants in our seven-story apartment building were Jewish. My father's colleagues at the office were all Jewish, all my friends and classmates were Jewish as well as almost all my mother's piano and singing students. Anti-Semitism was in the air. Racial laws were enacted by the legislature to limit the employment of Jews in the public sector, keep Jewish students out of the public high schools, forbidding the entry of Jews into higher education, and so on. But our lives were still relatively stable, peaceful and comfortable.

My parents employed a live-in maid, Dódika, a Christian woman, who lived in our tiny maid's room. When she married a man in civil service—he wore a blue uniform—they lived together in that small room until they saved enough to move and quit her job with my parents. When Jewish property was confiscated by law, my parents arranged with Dódika to "safe-keep" some items of value for us. To her credit, she did return some of those items to Ágnes after the war. Bartering those items helped Ágnes and me from complete starvation after our liberation.

As our friends were all in the same slowly sinking ship as my family, they swapped jokes to cheer up one another. These jokes invariably dealt with the plight of the Jews and the war. Some began as Kohn and Grün were chatting…

Grün was returning home from abroad in the days when coffee was already a "controlled" commodity—meaning: hard to get at all, except on the black market. A customs officer stopped him as he was carrying a heavy burlap sack on his shoulder.

"What's in the sack?"—asked the officer.

"Bird food, sir!"—replies Grün.

"Are you sure?"—inquired the officer again.

"Absolutely, sir, it's for my parrot."

"Let me see! Open the bag!"—commanded the customs man.—Sure enough, it looked and smelled like green coffee beans. The customs officer thundered:

"You lied to me, it's not bird food!" and then Grün responded:

"Likes it or not, the bird gets nothing else!"

Others were about Móricka (little Morris), a six-year old Jewish boy, going on 40. One went like this: Móricka is walking with his mom hand-in-hand. A horse and cart are parked by the curb and Móricka begins to drift toward the horse. His mom's hold tightens and she says:

"Móricka, don't go near the horse! It might kick you!"—Móricka responds:

"Really? Does he know, too, that I am Jewish?"

A third class of jokes was about two degenerate Hungarian noblemen, Arisztid and Tasziló, satirizing the idiots who were running the country. Others started with Hitler, Stalin, Churchill and Roosevelt entering the Pearly Gate, etc…—Each of these stories gave a brief moment of escape from the everyday reality.

Another typical story about Kohn and Grün. meeting in a café:

"I want to say good bye. I am leaving."—says Kohn.

"Are you visiting your mother again in Soroksár (a village not far from Budapest) to get a fat goose?"—asks Grün.

"No, I am moving to New Zealand for good!"—says Kohn.

"To New Zealand...so far?"

"So far from what?...The question is whether it is far enough!"

Meanwhile, my parents were still able to spend two weeks at Lake Balaton in a rented cottage, where we swam, rowed in rental boats, or pedaled about on rented bikes along the lake. A few weeks in Pécs with my mother usually preceded or followed our summer vacations even after the war began.

For certain concessions from the Hungarian government, Hitler redrew the borders of the neighboring countries. Hungary, his loyal ally, received many of its territories lost in the Trianon Peace Treaty following World War I. Nationalism rose to a feverish pitch, the "patriots" began to dream of returning to the borders of Great-Hungary. The popular slogan was: *"Csonka Magyarország: nem ország!—Egész Magyarország: menyország!"* (Truncated Hungary: not a country! All of (old) Hungary: heaven!) Hungary was to be a nation of Christians. The Jews were "a question"—read: a problem that had many solutions, none of those the slightest bit attractive from a Jewish viewpoint.

In this atmosphere, my father received an offer to move to Brazil permanently, to work at the leather factory's new plant there. I don't know the financial aspects of the offer, but it was an opportunity to get out of Europe and escape the rising tide of fascism. My parents contemplated the possibility and then turned it down for two reasons: they could not imagine that the terrible rumors about Germany, the former Czechoslovakia and Nazi-occupied Poland could really be true, and even if those were true, the same horror could not be reproduced on Hungarian soil—they thought.

The second reason was our extended family...how could they move half way around the globe and leave our family and all our friends behind?—My father turned it down; it was a fatal mistake.

Refugees were steadily arriving in Budapest; first from Poland and Austria, then from Slovakia and Transylvania. Thin, bearded men in black kaftans and hats went from door to door in our Jewish neighborhood, asking for handouts in Yiddish. Few listened to their stories and almost no one believed them. There were Jewish refugees from Austria as well. My mother met a young woman, perhaps in 1942 or 1943. As both my parents spoke German fluently, they understood what this young woman had been through and how unstable her situation was in Budapest. My mother hired her to teach me German. She would wait for me in front of my school and we walked hand-in-hand to our apartment where we'd sit together as she would attempt to teach me German. How I hated those lessons…

The school year ended early for us in 1944, following the occupation of Hungary by the German Army. I have no idea what had happened to that very sad, frightened and lonely young woman.

There were also Hungarian speaking Jewish refugees from Bratislava, who told their tales that most Jews in Budapest would not believe either. A distant relative from Bratislava "predicted" with great precision the orders to be posted to restrict the lives of Jews after the Germans occupied Hungary on March 19, 1944.

My father was called up for *"munkaszolgálat"*—labor service in the military—in 1941. My mother and I took the train to visit him on a Sunday. It was a gray autumn day, but without rain. We spent the visitation period with my father entirely outdoors. Perhaps it was safer to speak about important and private matters this way. He wore the clothes he used to wear for our outings in the hills of Buda: heavy, ankle high, laced boots, a heavy canvas windbreaker over a rough sweater. On his left arm he wore a red-white-green armband and this costume was rounded out with a Hungarian military cap made of coarse, mustard color wool.

The tanning factory was a supplier of war-materiel. The military needed all the tanned leather it could get for making boots, belts, ammunition bags and so on. The factory claimed that my father's services were essential to win the war. The military released him and let him return home after a few weeks of marching, saluting and digging ditches "just for fun."—When my father came home, life continued pretty much as before.

In 1942 something happened between my parents. I'll never know the full story, but it seems that in the midst of all that trouble, my father had an affair with a woman. He moved out of the apartment and I only remember two things about this: our meetings at the leather trade's café, where he met his colleagues from the trade every afternoon. He used to order ice-coffee or sweet chestnut puree for me. There was an air of tension in that café. My father usually took a booth by the window. As people were coming and going, they often stopped by to exchange a few words with my father, a joke, some trade, but mostly domestic and world news. The other memories are from a ski trip to the Tatra Mountains. It was great fun! We skied during the day and ate well in the hotel's dining room, just the two of us.

I don't think my father ever had any close friends among his colleagues. In fact, I only remember one friend, Pista Kertész, one of Panni's two brothers.

They rowed a skiff on the Danube regularly; perhaps they owned it jointly. I do have a small snapshot of Pista and my father in the skiff.—My father was physically active. In good weather, on Sundays we would head for the hills of Buda by various streetcars. Ten to fifteen years later, as an engineering student in Budapest, I retraced many of those routes on weekends with my friend Michael Simon whose parents also came from Pécs.—We never spoke about our early memories of those hills or anything from the past, but we both loved those trails and vistas.—In the winter my father often took me skiing at Normafa. This was a great big open field with little sunshine. The snow would always remain there a bit longer than in other areas. There were no ski lifts in those days. We carried the skis to the top and skied down, then carried them up again and schussed down, all day.—Those outings were very therapeutic for everyone. All the adults and children seemed to have similar views, problems and hopes. Unlike in "civilian" life, they could freely say anything and everything in front of each other. They were all secular Jews, trying to make a living and raise children in a hostile environment. Their children were all born during "peace time," from the late 1920s to 1936. Few Jewish children were born after that year in Budapest, four years after Hitler came to power. According to Ágnes, my mother became pregnant once more, but she chose to have an abortion. It was not a good time to bring another child into this world.

Again, according to Ágnes, during their separation, my mother dropped me off at her sister's apartment and shop, where my father would pick me up for our outings. After our outing, he would take me back to my mother. One evening, as he was leaving, he asked if there was anything I would like. My answer was—as Ágnes reported decades later—to have my father stay, not leave. Evidently he stayed and never left my mother and me again except when he was forced by the authorities.

There were two myths among the Hungarian Jews who aspired to be assimilated: baptism and Hungarian sounding names. As far as I know my parents never gave any thought to the former, but my grandfather "corrected" the family name around 1910.

Kornel had left his parents' home by the time my grandfather, Mór Friedman, changed the family's name to Tarján, a name that sounded Hungarian and irresistible to his younger daughter. Kornel was not around and he continued as a Friedman.

Yugoslavia was occupied by the Italians, the favorite among Germany's European allies. While the Italians had treated their Jews well and Jewish communities thrived in Italy from the time after the Expulsion from Spain in 1492, under pressure from the Germans, the Italian occupiers did round up the Jews in Croatia and placed them in a camp on an island in the Adriatic Sea, where Horthy's navy once ruled. From that point on, I don't think that Kornel's three siblings had any contact with their brother. Twenty-five years later, after I met my "Yugoslav" family in the USA, Kornel and Jolán did ask me what I knew about their pleas to his siblings for financial help. I knew nothing and I assumed that those pleas never reached them. Actually, I remember asking Böske some 12-15 years later why they did not send help? I think her response was that whoever contacted her and Miska, seemed to be a shady character and they didn't believe what he told them. Although I was only six at that time, I feel a sense of shame for this to this very day.

Ilonka Berliner was a poor Jewish girl from a small village near Pécs. Her father was a very poor man. Ilonka finished six grades in her village and there was no more to be learned in that school. After a few years of cleaning and cooking under her mother's watchful eyes, Ilonka left home and came to Pécs to find work and perhaps a husband. She was probably sixteen when she arrived there around 1924. Ilonka had no other skills than cooking and cleaning, which she learned from her mother. She found work as a maid and cook for Miska and Böske. It was not a hard job as they had a spacious apartment close to the center of town; they had no children, no pets and no elder relatives. An older woman came once a month to scrub all the towels, sheets and wash their clothes in the days before washing machines. Ilonka cooked and cleaned. The washwoman also showed up for the big spring and fall cleanings of the apartment. On her nights off, Ilonka attended the local dance schools to meet young men. It seems that Pécs was an up-and-coming town for Jews; the young Jewish lads were either studying a profession or hoping to marry a girl with a dowry. Even better: marry into a business. Judging by her photographs, Ilonka was a pretty, well-dressed, well-groomed and lively young lady, but there were few if any Jewish suitors for this maiden. She finally married a sweet and very quiet tanner, my "Uncle Jóska." Ilonka, having lived with Böske and Miska, developed some sophisticated tastes, she liked novels, and music and she frequently went to the local theater where they performed all the schmaltzy operettas of Lehár, Kálmán and Johann Strauss. Jóska was a very simple man who was apprenticed at the age of twelve, after six grades, and became a tanner at the same factory where my father worked. Jóska was a small man, just a bit over five feet tall, but very strong from all the work he had done as a child. Jóska Tóth was born and raised as a Roman Catholic, but he didn't care much about the saints and the priests. It made no sense for a Christian man to adopt his bride's Jewish religion, so Ilonka agreed to convert. This created quite a drift between Ilonka and her family, but Ilonka became a true believer, she accepted Jesus and Mary, attended church, confessed and took communion. Later, she prayed every Sunday for Jóska's return from the war. In the back of the building, where Miska and Böske were renting their apartment, Ilonka and Jóska also rented a one-room apartment and settled in. Jóska lost his job during the depression and became a mailman. This was convenient, as the house was around the corner from the main post office in Pécs. Jóska could roll out of bed and be at work in five minutes. Ilonka continued to work for Böske and Miska. After all those years together, Böske and Ilonka, who were ten years apart, knew each other's secrets. Ilonka knew my mother's family as well and she adopted Aranka as her wise, older sister in lieu of her own, who resented her conversion.

After Hungary entered the war at the end of 1941, Jóska, who was already 36, was drafted. Due to his small stature, he was assigned to be an "officer's man." They were sent to the Eastern Front to fight the Russians. In 1943 or early 1944, some officers summoned Jóska and they asked him whether he wished to divorce his Jewish wife. If he agreed, it would be a simple matter. We'll never know exactly what transpired in that office as Jóska was a man of very few words, but he declined the offer. This act saved Ilonka's life as the authorities treated her as the wife of a Christian soldier, instead of a converted Jew. Jóska's unit was captured and sent to a POW camp somewhere in the frozen north of the Soviet Union. Poor Ilonka was convinced that her prayers to the Virgin and the saints would bring Jóska back alive. He did return in 1946, although with a serious disability, his left hand was smashed in an accident. The Russians put him on a train. By the time he arrived home, his hand was gangrenous and partially paralyzed, but surgery saved some function. By then Böske had returned from Auschwitz alone and was living with Ilonka, like two sisters.

After March 19, 1944 the noose tightened around the collective neck of the Jewish community. As my parents and grandparents, Böske and Miska also gave some of their linen, silver and other valuables to Ilonka and other gentile friends and acquaintances, including Aunt Teri, the washwoman. To their honor and credit, nothing was denied or claimed to be lost after the war, unlike in so many other stories.

March 19, 1944 was the beginning of the year that changed our lives. From Saturday night to Sunday morning the German army occupied Hungary. Admiral Horthy was invited to Berlin and during his absence the takeover occurred. The Germans had already lost the battle at Stalingrad; their troops were retreating. They lost in North Africa. Southern Italy was under Allied control. Although the Normandy Invasion by the Allies had not yet taken place, it was expected soon. Hitler was worried that the Hungarians could not be trusted as his allies. If left to his own devices, Horthy and his government would try to save their skin and declare neutrality, or worse, switch sides.

On that Sunday morning my father turned on the radio and heard German conversations in code. As it seemed safer for a boy to be on the streets, he sent me out to buy a couple of newspapers. I remember clearly that our usually busy street at the rim of the Jewish section was virtually empty. The stores were always closed on Sunday mornings. I walked several blocks to find a newsstand and returned with two papers with big headlines. That day was quietly spent at home. There were some guarded phone calls. No one knew what was awaiting us, but everyone felt a terrible fear. I think they all realized that those horrible stories told by those Jewish refugees about their experiences in Poland, the Ukraine, Slovakia and elsewhere—too awful to believe—were about to be experienced by us. We were going to be the new cast in a horror show with a carefully worked out script.

The noose tightened around each Jewish community in Hungary. The Jews and converted Jews, unless they were married to Aryans, were ordered into ghettos within weeks. Eichmann was an efficient executioner and an experienced administrator. The Hungarian gendarmes (*Csendőr* or rural police) as well as the majority of the local governments were willing, even enthusiastic errand boys for the execution of Eichmann's plan.

The stack of letters from my grandparents to their daughters survived. The letters cover several years. The early ones deal mostly with Mama's packages of cookies, preserves and minor family matters. My mother and Ágnes always shared everything as they saw each other several times a week.—Starting in April 1944, Mama's letters began to reflect her great fear, her confusion and my grandfather's hardheadedness. These letters spanned the next two months, until the beginning of July when she wrote the last postcard from the ghetto in Pécs, a heart-wrenching good-bye to her children. She was 56 and Papa was 75 when they were sent in a cattle-car to their death in Auschwitz.

There was no more news from Mama and Papa after that postcard. I wonder what my mother and her sister were thinking when they received that postcard and a similar one from their cousin, Margit and her daughter Licike. Officially, the Jews from Hungary were relocated by train to German occupied territories to live and work in camps, except those in Budapest. The older people will care for the children, while the young and able-bodied would work to support the war effort. I don't know whether my parents believed any of this or not. Perhaps they didn't even have time to think about whether the official story was true as they became preoccupied with their own troubles.

While my grandparents' friends tried to help, the behavior of many people in Pécs—as I learned years later—was awful. While the Jews were taken to the ghetto near the railway station, many people watched them with glee along the long avenue leading toward the station. There were even some priests who shouted their hatred toward those helpless people. On the other hand, some went to church and prayed for the Jews, some others hid their belongings and some went to the ghetto to pass food and other items to their Jewish friends over the fence and took letters from them to mail, like my Mama's last postcard.

When the war was over, the collective memory of the community was lost. Virtually no one was punished. Some former career officers were booted from the new army and the police and the gendarmes were disbanded. This collective loss of memory seems permanent. In early July 1984, I arrived in Budapest for the weekend during a business trip to Europe. As soon as I arrived, Ágnes told me to take the train to Pécs for the fortieth anniversary of the deportations to Auschwitz. As usual, I stayed with Böske who lived alone after Ilonka and Jóska, her younger partners for more than three decades, had died. On Sunday afternoon we went to the old synagogue. The men and women were still segregated in this synagogue, but I was able to greet many of Böske's old friends, most of them survivors of the concentration camps. Then I sat with the men for the somber service. Buses took the mourners to the Jewish cemetery for the public part of the memorial. Many rows of chairs were set up under the shade trees in front of the Wailing Wall, erected in 1946. Böske and I sat together. Official representatives of the local government, the Communist party, the police, the army, the trade unions and all the churches delivered their speeches and placed their wreaths at the Wailing Wall. My unspoken question to myself was:

"Who needs this? Where were they in '44?"

But as I tried to listen to their speeches I realized that these people are able to show pity, but no remorse whatsoever. The priests and ministers quoted the Bible and appealed to the Almighty for the souls of the victims. The public officials played on two themes. First: those were terrible times; everyone suffered a great deal. The second message was more repulsive: they told their version of history. The message was always the same. There was this dreadful, evil man in Germany whose name should not even be uttered—and they did not say it—who was single-handedly responsible for all the pain, suffering and death of the Jews.—I turned to Böske and quietly asked why the Jews permitted this to go on in their own cemetery? Who needs this circus, this public display of piety and refusal for any role or responsibility; not a word of apology?—Her answer was simple: "We live here and we have to live with them."

I felt indescribably happy that I did not live there, that I lived in the USA, far away from these former Fascists-turned-Communists.—A year later I was back for Böske's funeral. A few years later Communism gradually collapsed along with the Soviet Union. A writer named Csurka emerged with similar ideas to those, which fueled the engine that brought Fascism to power in Hungary. He is still in public life but his party had suffered some setbacks. Csurka's demagoguery was not enough to let him climb to the top, but enough to make me never want to set foot there. To be truthful—I am planning one more trip in 2004, for the 60th anniversary of the deportations. I am afraid that very few if any of the deportees will still be alive to join the mourners. The youngest survivors in Pécs were my friends, the Somogyi twins, who will turn 71 that year. They were Mengele's guinea pigs at the age of 10 and survived because of the fascination with multiple births of that doctor from hell. The twins also live in the United States.

Now I have to turn to my own story. As in much of Europe, posters for sports, entertainment and public affairs are posted on the walls, fences and advertising columns on the streets. During March and April 1944, posters appeared almost every day with new restrictions for the lives of Jews: telephones were disconnected, radios were confiscated, "deadly" sporting equipment, such as my father's weights and springs for working out, were to be handed in; cars, motorcycles, bicycles had been taken earlier for the military. Jobs were lost, Jews were not allowed to employ Christians, Jewish owned stores were closed, the Jewish schools were closed, the yellow star of specific dimensions and color was to be affixed to our clothes to be worn indoors and outdoors, and so on.

Our building was declared to be a "Star House." The Christian tenants could either stay or move into the vacant apartments elsewhere of former Jewish tenants. A large yellow Star of David was painted above the front gate. The number of occupants in each apartment was increased easily by five or even tenfold. In addition to Ágnes and some friends moving into our apartment, a completely strange family took over our second room. As I think about that time, the interesting part was the way the children responded to all this tumult. There were more kids to play with, new games to invent. The adults seemed happy when the noisy children left those crowded apartments to play along the gangway and on the stairs. We played cowboys, Indians and often reenacted the horror stories that we all heard at our meals discussed by the grownups. Fascination was mixed with terrible fear whenever one of the kids announced that his or her mother received a military postcard that the kid's father was either killed or not accounted for.

The summer seemed to pass rapidly. My father was in forced labor around Budapest and frequently managed to come home for a day or two. On several occasions, my mother received orders to report for forced labor. One night, just before dawn, she awakened me as I was sleeping under her piano. She kissed me goodbye and promised to return soon from the infamous Brick Factory where she was to report. That evening she was back. This might have happened more than once. I don't know whether it was her ingenuity, bribes or good luck that she was able to return, but she managed.

October 15, 1944 was a beautiful, warm autumn day. The trees had turned gold and red. My father was on leave with us. There was some commotion and we all rushed out on the long gangway on our floor to join our neighbors who were all listening to a radio placed by one of our remaining gentile neighbors in a window. It was the voice of Admiral Horthy—whom the Germans had kept in office during the occupation. He announced Hungary's neutrality, the end of the war! It would be hard to describe the joy and the sudden burst of optimism among our neighbors. Miraculously, all those present felt that they survived the war.—Little did we know...The Nazis kidnapped Horthy's son and he was threatened with his son's execution unless he yielded power to the "real" Hungarian Nazi party, the *Nyilas* Party (the "Arrowcross")—and he did. Within hours, young Arrowcross hoodlums took over the streets and the final terror began to unfold under Adolf Eichmann's direction. My father returned to his unit. My parents acquired three different Swiss *"schutzpasse"* (protective letters). They all looked a little different, they were probably all forgeries. These papers stated that the bearer was under the protection of the neutral Swiss government and should be treated as any citizen of a neutral country. Similar papers were issued by the Swedish consulate under the direction of Raoul Wallenberg, the Vatican, Portugal and Spain, as well as the European Consulate of tiny El Salvador in Geneva, whose First Secretary was George Mandel-Mantello, a brave and extremely clever and dedicated Hungarian Jew. Karl Lutz headed the Swiss mission and Angelo Rotta was the Papal *Nuntio* in charge of diplomatic affairs. Aside from the legendary Wallenberg, Giorgio Perlasca's name also became a legend. Perlasca, a former Italian Fascist, had fought on Franco's side during the Spanish Civil War in the mid-thirties. He was honored by Spain. After that adventure, Signor Perlasca became a meat salesman with an assignment in Hungary. He broke with the Italian Fascists. His name was on the Gestapo's list in March 1944 and Perlasca went on the lam. He was arrested and then with the help of the Spanish consul, he received, predated, honorary citizenship of Spain. He found a haven at the Spanish consulate. When the Spanish diplomatic mission was recalled in November 1944, Perlasca accepted the responsibility for the protection of all those Jews with Spanish protective papers. Thanks to Perlasca's determination and cunning, the majority of those people did survive.

With the fake guarding of a hired soldier, my mother and I, along with her friend and neighbor, Jolán Deutsch and her two-year old daughter, Trudi, trekked across town to the International Ghetto, a creation of Wallenberg and the other foreign diplomats. We found shelter in a modern building at Szent István Park 25, right by the Danube. At one count there were 72 people in a three-room apartment with a single bathroom. The headcount fluctuated as people moved in and out either voluntarily or by force. Everyone lived from day to day. Rumors were flying about the atrocities committed by the Arrowcross both inside and outside the Ghetto. Some managed to obtain false papers and disappear.

Everyone had some plan or multi-layered plans for survival. The Red Army was within a few hours drive; much of the eastern part of the country was already liberated. But this did not stop, but rather, it encouraged the Nazis and the Arrowcross to carry out their horrible plans.

At the end of November a gang of young Arrowcrossmen entered our building and ordered all women whose children were over two years old, to report, with their packs, in the backyard within a few minutes. Our quarters were on the sixth floor above the ground level. My mother made some quick arrangements for me with Jolán and left to join the others. I don't remember what she said to me before she left. My last memory of my mother is waving to her from the window of our room as she was waiting with her pack on her back among the other women in the small courtyard. She was among the 30 or 40 thousand people who were marched toward Austria when there were no longer any cattle-cars available for their deportation. This was Eichmann's solution to this technical problem.

Jolán knew a gentile military tailor who appeared at our Swiss-protected house and took me off her hands. Presumably my mother had left some money with Jolán to pay for this. The tailor tried to place me in one of the many orphanages set up for Jewish children. Not one would take me. At night he ordered me to hide in the loft of his shop in the dark and not make the slightest peep or else! I had never before or since experienced such fear as while I was left alone in that creepy place in total darkness. By this time all the windows had to be covered with black cardboard to prevent any light from leaking out and calling the attention of the Allied bombers to the place. It was pitch dark in there.

The tailor spent two or three days taking me around town. We even visited the Ghetto where Ágnes was cooped up after her return from the infamous Eichmann March. She had escaped with another woman and ran into a farmhouse where they swapped their sporty clothes for that of countrywomen. They were captured a few hours later and put into another column of marchers. As they passed the same farmhouse, the guard let them go in and swap their clothes and boots back. The farmer was willing, and they marched on toward their terrible destiny in Austria. The caravan stopped for the night at the border. That evening a private car of the Brazilian consulate arrived with a list of names. Thanks to her childhood friend who worked for that consulate, Ágnes was on the list. They drove her and a few others back to Budapest and dropped her off at the Ghetto. I'll never know how that tailor learned about Ágnes's whereabouts, but we found her in a windowless, crowded cellar. She looked very, very old, although she was only 38 then. She told the tailor to take me anywhere; it didn't matter where. Any place would be better than the ghetto where there was no food, no heat, people were dying from various infectious diseases and rumors were widely spread about the ghetto being mined to be blown up before the Russians would take it.

On we went...another night in that black hole and perhaps another. I only remember the terror I felt in the dark.

At last, he was able to deposit me at the orphanage of the Swedish Red Cross near the Western Railway Station. A few ordinary apartments had been converted into a children's hostel. There were about 10 boys in my room ranging from a baby to some teenagers. The teenagers entertained themselves by scaring the young ones with horror stories of what was going on in the city.

It is a mystery to this day how Panni learned that I was in that orphanage. She does not remember. But she came to visit me and told me that she and her mother were cooped up in a Swiss protected house as her older brother had been living in Zurich as a musician for more than a decade. There were 20 people in her room, all her relatives, including a cousin with dysentery and a retarded teenager. She seemed impressed with the Swedish children's shelter, but gave me her address, Tátra Street 4, and told me to come there if bad things were happening at the shelter.

A day or two later the shelter's director asked each child into his office one by one. This Mr. Fogarasi told me that the orphanage was going to be evacuated and if I had any place to go, I should leave after dark. I packed my little black suitcase and went downstairs where the superintendent was in charge. The front door to the building was connected via a long hall, a tunnel, to the courtyard. A few kids were waiting at the tunnel's courtyard end for the superintendent's signal. When my turn came, he opened the front door and let me out. As I remember, I did not know which way to go to Panni's place. It was a busy area in the city a few days before Christmas. I was amazed that many of the stores were brightly lit and a lot of people were going about their business.

A woman stopped me and began to question me. I had been instructed for months to be discrete with strangers, but at last she won. I told her where I was going. She took my hand and we walked to Panni's building. It was not very far, perhaps a 15-minute walk. When we arrived, the gate was locked. She rang the bell and the superintendent came to the gate. We asked for Panni. He made us wait until Panni arrived. He did not want anyone in the building without papers. Finally, Panni convinced him to let me stay for just one night. Some thirty years later Panni remembered that she had asked the woman what she was going to do in case she could not leave me there. She told Panni that she was going to take me home. I will never know who that woman was, but she was one of many whom I can thank for being able to write this story now.

Panni's family lived in a room that was more crowded than any of my previous stations. It was in the abandoned apartment of a famous children's writer whose name was Grätzer. They found me a place to sleep on top of a small desk under a bookshelf, where Grätzer's books were lined up.

As far as I remember, I never left that apartment even for a minute for the next few weeks until the Russians liberated us. During the air raids everyone rushed to the cellar except Panni, one of her uncles and me. I am only guessing, but I think the "super" was told that I had left and I was not to be seen by him. Uncle Béla and Panni stayed with me during the bombing raids with the excuse that they could not stand the smell of the crowded cellar.

Food was scarce. Our diet consisted of pea soup. Somehow, they had a big sack of dry peas. Each day we soaked some in a huge pot of cold water and when the shells became swollen, we squeezed the split peas out of their shells as we sat around the pot. They thought the shells were indigestible or even harmful. We dried the shells and added those to the fire in the tiny stove where the peas were cooked without salt or anything. Just boiled peas, nothing else for several weeks.—After the war, when there was enough food, I could not eat peas for many years.

There were two rather diverse forms of entertainment. First, I worked my way through Mr. Grätzer's wonderful books about "Sicc," a weird but very smart cat. Meanwhile, our street turned into a battlefield. Our building was only the second from a main thoroughfare, Szent István Boulevard. The main fighting was on that boulevard, but the terrace across from our broken window was used as a machine-gunner's nest. At first, the Germans used it and then it was taken over by the Russians. I remember watching the action on that balcony from my "front-row-center seat." A gunner was shot. His fellow soldiers dragged the wounded soldier into the apartment and another took over the machinegun. This drama was repeated numerous times without the soldiers ever paying any attention to us.

At last, the fighting ended in the neighborhood around the middle of that very, very cold January. The broken windows were patched with paper and there was just enough wood from Mr. Grätzer's furniture to cook the peas. We wore all our clothes when the first Russian soldier came to search the building for enemy soldiers, room-by-room. One of our fellow residents, an older Jew from another room, was a prisoner of war in World War I. He did remember some Russian and he went to greet our liberator with an enthusiastic *"Zdrastvuyte! Zdrastvuyte druzhba!"* (Welcome! Welcome, friend!) The Russian soldier took the man's pocket watch, pushed him out of the way and proceeded to search the three rooms one by one. At gunpoint, he confiscated all the wrist and pocket watches of the residents. Everyone cooperated except the retarded teenager who wore his pocket watch on a chain. The soldier demanded it and the boy became hysterical. They began to wrestle over that watch while the boy's parents tried to restrain him. Their concern was their son's safety, not his pocket watch. The soldier got his way and took the watch. The boy sobbed for hours and hours for his watch. The Russian looked around and found another treasure. A photograph of the Grätzer kids had been transferred to a plastic or glass block with a light bulb in the box. A treasure in the eyes of our liberator! He tried to light it up, but we had not had electricity for several weeks already. He took all the loot and left. We were all stunned. I guess that everyone expected our liberation to be a joyous and dignified event. It was anything but that. A day or two later the fighting did quiet down in the neighborhood. Some of the men went out to find food. There were dead horses lying everywhere on the street. As the winter had been extremely severe, the horses were frozen solid. With saws and axes, chunks of horsemeat were carved out and cooked whatever way possible. In a few days, a bakery began to operate in the neighborhood. One of Panni's cousins returned with a quarter of a loaf of gooey corn bread. It was half-baked and stuck to our teeth, but it was our first bread after a long time. I had almost forgotten the taste of bread by then.

The ghetto was saved at the very last minute by Wallenberg, Perlasca and others from getting blown up. They threatened the commander that he would have to stand trial after the war not as a soldier, but as a mass murderer, if he allowed the ghetto to be blown up. Ágnes was saved with tens of thousands of residents of the ghetto. She returned to my parents' building to find the apartment empty. Jolán's mother was already back in her tiny one-bedroom apartment and it was well heated with chopped up furniture and other debris from the bomb damaged buildings. "Aunt Róza" took her in along with her own children who began to return from their various hiding places. Jolán and Trudi had survived in hiding. Jolán's blond hair and blue eyes let her pass for a refugee with false papers, but Trudi's beautiful dark hair and black eyes almost gave them away. Of all places, they found shelter in one of the Arrowcross offices. A man suspected that Trudi, not quite three, was a Jewish child. The man asked her:

—"Did your mommy ever have a star?"—referring to the Star of David mark.

—"Yes,"—answered Trudy—"my mommy always calls me her little star!"

Ágnes heard that someone had seen me somewhere. She came to search for me and found me with Panni. We both moved in with Aunt Róza. It was a miracle how all those people managed to sleep in that tiny place.

Ágnes made contact with her ex-husband, Miklós, who had worked in the antiFascist underground. He had rented a dozen or so apartments after he dyed his prematurely white mane red and grew a matching red mustache. Dozens of people were hiding in those apartments. One of those apartments was in a suburb where Miklós was staying with his wife and his latest in-laws. They had enough room and firewood to take us in. The building was partly occupied by the regional headquarters of the Red Army. The area was severely bombed, but that modern building was relatively intact. The Russians seemed to be extremely primitive. They used the marble stairway instead of the bathroom, as there was no running water. Despite the cold, the stench was awful.

Around the middle of February I ran a very high fever. They bundled me up, hoping that it was nothing serious. A drunk Russian soldier forced his way into our place demanding watches and other things. Miklós and the others knew that the Russians were very afraid of contagious diseases. It was rumored that the Red Army shot soldiers with such afflictions to stop the spread of the disease. While the soldier was gesturing wildly with his revolver, they called his attention to me. It worked! He did believe that I had a contagious disease and left in a hurry.

He turned out to be right. The fever did not go away and Ágnes took me to one of the local hospitals that began to operate. The hospital had nothing more than a place to warehouse sick children. The windows were broken; there was neither food, nor medicine for anyone. Two children were placed head-to-toe in each large crib. Every morning a nurse came to check who was alive and who was not. They always found a few dead children. Their bodies were removed and another sick child soon filled the vacant half of the bed. My high fever kept me in a fog most of the time, but I do remember those morning visits. The diagnosis was uniformly typhoid fever that spread through head lice. The only therapeutic measure was to shave every child's hair. As an undernourished skeleton with a shaved head I must have looked like the half corpses the American liberators photographed in the German concentration camps. I survived that hospital only because of the efforts of Ágnes. She recovered a hidden gold bracelet from a friend and day-by-day bartered a link of that bracelet for some flour and a couple of eggs. She baked some sort of a pancake at Aunt Róza's, where she had returned to stay and every day she walked to the hospital to deliver my share of the pancake.

On March 11, 1945 word reached Ágnes that Uncle Pista Harnik, a friend and former colleague of my father, had arrived on a Russian driven truck from Pécs and was returning there the next day. Uncle Pista was liberated from a Jewish forced labor battalion in eastern Hungary in October 1944 and returned to Pécs with others, all hoping to find their families there. All those men lived in a big house awaiting some miracle to be reunited with their wives and children. Uncle Pista was working at the tanning factory, producing for the Red Army. The Russian driver agreed to let him take three boys to Pécs. As I was the sickest, I sat up in the cabin with the driver and Uncle Pista. He found his wife's nephews, the Somogyi twins, in Budapest after they had returned from the concentration camp. They were 11-years old and well enough to ride in the back of the truck. Due to my high fever I don't remember the details of the long ride, but do remember the tears and hope in the eyes of the men in that big house when they first saw the three of us arriving in Pécs. Their hopes were false. The Somogyi boys were the only children to return alive from that hell.

The next morning someone took me to the local children's hospital that seemed like heaven on earth. They had windowpanes, clean, white sheets, heat, warm running water and tender loving care for their patients. Word got around that the Steiners' 8-year old grandson was alive and back in Pécs. My grandparents' friends came to see me and brought cookies and preserves, more than anyone could eat. A nice lady volunteered to donate blood and we were lying side by side as her blood was flowing through a rubber tube into my vein. For years she always reminded me that we were of the same blood.

I arrived in Pécs on my father's 41st birthday, on March 12, 1945, a week short of a year when the Germans occupied Hungary and our troubles began. The loving care and the good food helped me recover from the typhoid fever in a few weeks. By then Ágnes also had managed to get a lift to Pécs. She found an apartment and began to try to recover my grandparents' belongings with some success. The "Joint" also helped the survivors with clothes, medicine, food and even cash.

Jóska Fleischer, an old friend of Ágnes and her cousin, Margit, showed up in Pécs with a huge brick of butter in the back of his horse-drawn buggy. That Jewish man came from Bonyhád, a small town where Margit and her family were living before their deportation. Jóska was also living in a commune of Jewish men, hoping for the return of their families. Meanwhile, they formed a farming cooperative. Food in Bonyhád was even more plentiful. He convinced Ágnes to move to Bonyhád and reclaim her cousin's book and paper goods store along with a printing shop. By then, I had been back in third grade for a whole day. We rode on the little buggy to our new station in Bonyhád, where we moved into our cousins' former home and reopened the store to the delight of the local high school students and their teachers. There had not been a bookstore since the Fascist printer, who took over the store and shop, was sent to jail after the village was liberated.

A few weeks later we heard the news that Böske had returned from the concentration camps to Pécs and was living with Ilonka. I was put on a bus to visit her. Böske was a huge woman when I last saw her. She was thin and quite pretty with her short hair that just began to grow back after the Germans had shaved her head.

A very busy year passed by. I finished fourth grade while helping Ágnes in the store. Jolán and Trudi made their way to Bonyhád in search of food and comfort. We all lived under one roof until Jóska's brother asked Jolán to marry him. She was a young widow with a lovely child. Uncle Laci became a farmer after his time in a Jewish labor battalion.—Ágnes became antsy and decided to move back to Budapest in search of a job. She left me with Jolán and Laci until she would find a place for both of us to live in Budapest. I was 10 and in fifth grade. Not a day passed without wondering whether my parents would return. Ágnes kept encouraging me to believe that my father would certainly return, as he was strong, young and determined.

Two years after my first arrival at the children's hospital in Pécs, I developed some very severe pain in my belly and vomited all night. Jolán's doctor asked me about what I had eaten and concluded that a hot bun caused the trouble. I could hardly move and kept on throwing up for two days. At last, Jolán put me on a bus and sent me to Pécs, to the nearest hospital. The distance of 40 km took 5-6 hours on a rickety old bus that stopped at every other tree. Jolán also telephoned Böske, who was waiting for me at the bus station. She put me in a taxi that drove us to the children's hospital. In a glance the surgeon diagnosed appendicitis and they rolled me into the operating room. My appendix had perforated by then and they had to leave a long glass tube in my abdomen to drain the puss for weeks. My hospital stay was complicated by a case of hepatitis from the reused needles or other instruments. After two months, I returned to finish fifth grade. As soon as school was over, I was sent back to live with Böske, Ilonka and Jóska until Ágnes would find a place for us. She never did.

I joined the Jewish Boyscouts in 1947 and became a friend of the Somogyi boys and a few transplanted Jewish kids in town. The Communist government banned the scouts and we were reorganized into a Zionist group, a part of Hashomer Hatzair. It was a very happy time, although school was a nightmare. Böske sent me to a Roman Catholic school, run by monks. The school was teeming with little anti-Semites. During the spring of 1948 most of my Jewish friends disappeared one by one. They were making aliyah with Zionist groups. One day it was my turn to leave. Overjoyed, I ran home to announce the news that I could leave with a group of children in a day or two. Böske's response was that I could only leave over her dead body…—I was stuck between official Communism and unofficial anti-Semitism for the next eight years. In high school, I earned good grades and managed to enter the Technical University as a student of electrical engineering. That was my way of getting away from Pécs that had lost most of its charm for me. I took part in the 1956 Uprising against the Communists and after its defeat by the Russians, I escaped to Austria, mostly on foot. After a few weeks in refugee camps I was assigned to a Navy ship for my journey to the United States. It was a stormy trip in late December. A few days after landing in the USA, with help from HIAS, I was on the phone with my Uncle Kornel, who was living in Belmont, near Boston. He flew down to Newark and signed me out of the refugee camp at Camp Kilmer. We flew back to Boston on a Saturday night. The next day we had a big reunion at his daughter's, Medy's house, where I met, in effect for the first time, Uncle Kornel's wife, daughter and grandchildren: Ronnie and Gary, two cute little boys, while their third grandchild was still "in the oven." Melinda was born four months later. Thanks to my uncle's friends, by the following Tuesday I had a job offer and began to work at MIT as a metallurgical X-ray technician. I had no clue what my job was.

Uncle Kornel's son, Jancsi, born Ivan, who became Van in the US, was studying mechanical engineering on the G.I. Bill at Purdue University in West Lafayette, Indiana, having served for 33 months in Korea. He invited me for a visit to Purdue. With my first paycheck I bought a plane ticket and went to get acquainted. Thanks to Van's organizational genius, two days later I was awarded a scholarship, and gave up my job in Boston. Jancsi became my mentor and the brother I never had. Living in a small Midwestern college town was a new and very different experience. Purdue offered me a golden opportunity to complete my Bachelor's degree in two years. Many individuals and the local Jewish organizations were very kind to me. Two years later I returned to MIT as a graduate student.

In the middle of March 1959, the phone rang in our cramped office for graduate students. Medy called to tell me that Jancsi was killed during the wee hours in a car accident. The loss was devastating for all of us. Jancsi was full of love for everything in life: women, friends, cars, mechanisms, music, pasta, photography, a long list. After having lost my family under uncertain circumstances, this loss, so sudden and so definite, was devastating.

To sum up the next forty years: I finished my Master's degree and went to work in Syracuse. The work was dull, so I changed directions and went back to study biomedical engineering at Syracuse University. I found a friend in Syracuse whose girlfriend, Marcia, was studying at Brandeis. Marty and I drove back and forth in my ancient car to visit our girlfriends every few weeks. Marcia's roommate, Susanna, was from New York. After Marcia and Marty married and set up house in Syracuse, Susanna often drove up to visit them. I was the fourth in our outings. Susanna and I were married on December 26, 1964. We moved here and there together, traveled a lot and along the way we were blessed with two little guys. Joshua was born in 1968 and Aaron arrived three years later.

We raised the boys in Miami where I worked for a medical device firm for 19 years. Since 1987 I have been on the engineering faculty of the University of Miami.

Susanna's father was Jerome Moross, a well-known composer of film, theater and concert music. Her mother, Hazel, who was the sweetest person, and Jerry died of cancer and heart disease in rapid succession in 1983. Susanna, has dedicated herself to promote and reconstruct her father's music. A few years ago another composer remarked to her: "Every composer needs a daughter like you!"

Uncle Kornel died from liver cancer in Boston in 1978; he was 85. Böske followed her brother in Pécs in 1985. Her heart gave out at the age of 86. Ágnes died in Budapest from kidney failure in 1992, she was 85. I visited all three of them regularly. Susanna and I also visited Hungary with the boys in 1988, and Ágnes, who was much more mobile and fit for travel than Böske, visited us twice in America and once in London. These survivors all tried to be substitute grandparents to our children. May they rest in peace with all our martyrs of the Holocaust!

Epilogue

Aside from celebrating the coming of age of our group, Child Survivors of the Holocaust in South Florida, we intended to accomplish several objectives with the publication of this anthology.

First, the twenty-six contributors wanted to leave as permanent a record of their personal histories for their families and friends as the printed word can provide. *Verba volent, scripta manent*—as the Romans used to say. This has been accomplished!

Second, we wanted to provide the reader with a special vantage point to understand the Holocaust, if that is possible: a viewpoint from below the sight-line of adults, the way children under the age of thirteen saw the world collapse around them and responded not only to their own persecution, but reflecting the reactions of their parents and older family members to the indignities, deprivations, pain and suffering. Many stories of child survivors have been recorded within the framework of oral history projects, where an interviewer, often a psychologist or psychiatrist, guided and elicited responses from the subject. The stories in this collection have flown freely, without any steering or manipulation. This may increase their impact and credibility. Perhaps the self-imposed discipline of writing about oneself has reduced the intensity of our emotional responses that interviews often bring out. This is a form of self-defense, but at the same time it focuses on such events that the writer considers most important to report. We hope that this second goal has also been accomplished.

Third, we have been told over the years that "You were too young to remember..." and were dismissed as irrelevant witnesses to the horrors. This book should serve as proof that children not only remember, but also carry the scars of their childhood experiences forever.

Fourth, each of us wanted to pay tribute to our relatives who perished in the Holocaust. Probably each of us feels that we achieved that goal to the extent possible by publishing these stories. We shall not forget those martyrs and we do want others to preserve the memory of the tragedy of the Nazi Holocaust that took the lives of six million or more, about a quarter of those children. We must remind the world of those horrors that we experienced to ascertain that it should never happen again.

We, who escaped the final solution, will never forget and will work hard to assure that our children and their children will know our tragic history. Never again!

0-595-30925-9

CPSIA information can be obtained
at www.ICGtesting.com
Printed in the USA
LVOW12s0742200516

489118LV00001B/1/P